P9-DJL-724

Lucy Kerbel

Lucy Kerbel is the Director of Tonic Theatre and an award-winning theatre director. Having begun her career as Resident Director at the National Theatre Studio and English Touring Theatre, Lucy went on to direct a range of classics, new writing and productions for younger audiences.

It was while directing around the UK that Lucy became interested in the question of gender equality in theatre. She recognised that the industry would need better support if it were to achieve greater balance in its workforces and repertoires, and so in 2011, with the support of the National Theatre and Royal Opera House's Step Change scheme, Lucy founded Tonic Theatre to go some way towards achieving this.

In addition to directing and her work with Tonic, Lucy does consultancy, lecturing, and works extensively in theatre education. *100 Great Plays for Women* is her first book.

Lucy Kerbel

Foreword by Kate Mosse

NICK HERN BOOKS
London
www.nickhernbooks.co.uk

100 Great Plays for Women
first published in Great Britain in 2013
by Nick Hern Books Limited,
The Glasshouse, 49a Goldhawk Road, London W12 8QP

Reprinted with revisions in 2013

Cover image by iStockphoto/77studio
Designed and typeset by Nick Hern Books, London
Printed and bound in Great Britain by
Ashford Colour Press, Gosport, Hampshire

A CIP catalogue record for this book
is available from the British Library

ISBN 978 1 84842 185 1

Contents

CONTENTS

CONTENTS

Foreword
Kate Mosse

When I was six, my parents took me to see a production of Labiche's *The Italian Straw Hat* at Chichester Festival Theatre. It was 1967 and people dressed up to go to the theatre then. A blue party dress and black patent shoes, small hands in large, walking up from the foyer into the auditorium. A shiver when the lights went down and a dazzling realisation that, in this place – in the theatre – anything was possible. That it was a magical world, both commonplace and utterly transformed.

Even now, I have that shiver of anticipation when the house lights dim and still feel there are few places in the world more exhilarating, transformative, significant than a theatre. It's somewhere we are entertained, of course, but also where we are challenged, moved. A place of revolution and substance, where emotions and ideas that matter – faith, loss, remorse, pity, fear, hate, doubt, hope, love – are laid bare. A place where orthodoxies and inequalities are confronted. A place where the best and the worst of ourselves – our Society – is reflected back at us.

But what is being reflected? Should art reflect reality or strive to change things or both? Was every corner of Society there, every shape and size, or just a small part of it? For Lucy Kerbel, a director – and founder of Tonic Theatre – it was puzzling and why she decided to write this book. 'I could be pretty sure that nine times out of ten,' she writes, 'the women on stage would be outnumbered by the men... the ratio of male to female roles didn't seem to alter regardless of whether I was watching Shakespeare or new writing.'

Supported by the National Theatre Studio, Kerbel realised although the theatre industry was increasingly focusing on the question of gender imbalance – and deciding what could be done about it – many writers, directors and actors – such as Janet Suzman in her 2012 book *Not Hamlet,* or novelist Stella Duffy – were frustrated by the situation: 'When we do not see ourselves on stage,' Duffy wrote in a blog earlier this year, 'we are reminded, yet again, that the people running our world (count the women on the Front Benches if you are at all unsure) do not notice when we are not there. That they think men (and yes, white, middle-class, middle-aged, able-bodied men at that) are all we need to see.'

I can't imagine there's a single artistic director who consciously thinks that. But, at the same time, when programming plays one admires – or work destined to carry the burden of the box office – Kerbel, as she explains in her Introduction, realised how easy it was for directors simply to fail to notice how the repertoire favoured men with more stage time, more varied roles, more lines. Or to notice, but decide it wasn't a priority. As Elizabeth Freestone of Pentabus observed in 2012: 'The theatre world remains strangely passive in the face of overwhelming evidence of its failure to address the gender imbalance both on and off stage. Programming, commissioning and casting decisions are routinely made without any consideration of gender.'*

One of the ways inspirational directors and artistic directors do address the imbalance (particularly within the classic core canon) is through gender-blind casting and it's becoming more and more popular. From Fiona Shaw's Richard II in 1995 and Kathryn Hunter's Lear two years later to Phyllida Lloyd's dazzling all-female *Julius Caesar* at the Donmar Warehouse in 2012, this is a sign of the determination both to confront the issue head on and accelerate change. To enrich the experience of women and men on and off the stage, to refresh and extend the work. For 2014, the Manchester Royal Exchange has already announced a female Hamlet – more than a hundred years after Sarah Bernhardt first played the Danish Prince in 1899. Gender- (and colour-) blind casting is a significant creative decision too, though, not merely about the numbers. There are exciting artistic benefits. When imaginative, radical casting decisions are taken, a text often changes, reveals its true self, shifts, slides, transforms. It can throw the spotlight back onto the words, to the intention of the writer, or reveals a previously hidden beauty or purpose.

Even so, Kerbel realised the idea that gender-blind casting is necessary – in part, at least, because of a lack of good, performable, plays for women – informed the discussion. 'But,' she wondered, 'had anyone actually checked?'

* Charlotte Higgins' excellent analysis of key research – notably, work carried out by Elizabeth Freestone of Pentabus, also out of the NT Studio – was published in the *Guardian*, December 2012. See also work by Professor Maggie Gale of the University of Manchester, July 2013.

She set off with notebook and pen to see what was out there. The result? This gem of a book – a selection of 100 great plays with majority female casts, as well as ten monologues for solo performers. Here are stories of war and faith, politics, science, history, our attempts to conjoin our emotions with those of women and men living centuries ago, and plays that show us how we live now. The earliest plays date back to the fifth and fourth centuries BCE, the most recent where the ink is barely dry. Some could be termed as feminist – insofar as their purpose is political, as well as cultural – where others are meditations on women's and men's lives. It doesn't matter whether the author is female or male, only that a broad and full range of female experience is represented. In other words, that the drama reflects life in all its colours and hues and shapes.

Leading artistic directors – not least of all Vicky Featherstone at the Royal Court and Josie Rourke at the Donmar Warehouse, amongst others – have already had an enormous impact and, through choice of work and casting, transformed the look of some of our stages. But here Lucy Kerbel has done hard-working directors and artistic directors, of spaces large and small, a great service. By gathering together so many vibrant and varied pieces of theatre, she's provided evidence to refute the time-worn excuse that there aren't any great plays for women. It's up to everyone, now, to seek out these plays, to read them or programme them. So when the lights go down in the auditorium, we can choose not to notice a disproportionate lack of women. Or we can notice and decide it doesn't matter. But, thanks to this book, we can't any longer pretend that there aren't at least one hundred great plays for women.

Kate Mosse is the author of six novels, a collection of short stories, three plays and four works of non-fiction, including The House: Behind the Scenes at the Royal Opera House *and* Chichester Festival Theatre at Fifty. *She is currently working on a major history play.*

Introduction

'There just aren't any good plays for women...'

is a phrase I got used to hearing. I heard it a lot from my colleagues in theatre when I began to ask, quietly and a little nervously at first – why don't we see more women on stage? I'd had a growing realisation that when I watched a play (which, given my job as a theatre director, was at least once a week, generally more), I could be pretty sure that nine times out of ten, the women on stage would be outnumbered by the men. I noticed that this was the case in older plays, plays written in periods in history when women's lives weren't considered interesting or complex enough to hold the attention of an audience; but I also noticed it in new plays, plays written now, in a time when women apparently play a more equal role in our society. The ratio of male to female roles didn't seem to alter regardless of whether I was watching Shakespeare or new writing.

I noticed that when women did make it on stage, they tended to be of a narrower age bracket and physical 'type' than their male counterparts. And crucially, that when they were on stage, they were less likely to be at the heart of the action. Instead, they seemed often to be at the periphery of what was going on; they played the mothers, wives, love interests and daughters of protagonists, but were rarely protagonists themselves. Yes, there were the exceptions – the Electras, Mother Courages and Saint Joans. But generally the women in these plays were on their own on stage, surrounded by a sea of men. Regularly too, what seemed to be defining them was their very 'femaleness' – their predicament as lone women struggling through a man's world. It was almost as if being a *woman*, rather than being a *human*, was the beginning and end of their stories.

When I thought about it, I found the apparent lack of women on stage curious. Women buy the majority of theatre tickets, make up half of the acting profession, represent the healthiest proportion of just about any amateur dramatic society, youth theatre or school drama club, and are more than half the population. So why, comparatively, are so few of them visible on our stages? Surely women's existences couldn't be totally devoid of interest to audiences or those people putting on plays? Again and again, the only explanation I was offered with a resigned shrug was:

'There just aren't any good plays for women.'

It wasn't that this phrase was said in an aggressive or dismissive manner. Usually it was said with a sense of regret, sometimes with a note of frustration that belied the speaker's annoyance at the apparent dearth of decent female-focused material. Often it was delivered like a universal truth: no, with the exception of Caryl Churchill's *Top Girls*, no one in the history of playwriting had managed to deliver a single decent play that had more parts for women than men.

But had anyone actually checked? Were we just assuming a gaping hole? Were there really not any brilliant plays written for women beyond *Top Girls*? My scepticism deepened during a working visit to Sweden in 2009. While being shown around the home of Riksteatern, Sweden's national touring theatre, by one of its Creative Producers, I enquired how many men and how many women were employed annually as actors in its repertory company. 'Half and half' was the reply. 'But what do you do with the women when there aren't any roles for them?' I asked. My tour guide was somewhat perplexed: 'Why wouldn't there be any roles for them?' she replied. She went on to explain that in Sweden, many of the theatres have collectively agreed to endeavour to employ a roughly equal number of men and women across all parts of their organisation, *including* on stage. This means that the Swedes have become very good at digging out neglected but brilliant plays with casts of women, and have an incentive to encourage their living playwrights to focus as much on writing for women as writing for men. So as far as theatre goes in Sweden at least, 'There just aren't any good plays for women' isn't really a statement that holds water.

I decided to put it to the test upon my return to the UK. With the support of the National Theatre Studio, I undertook a period of research to see if I could find a range of really strong plays – perhaps twenty – with predominantly or entirely female casts in which women play at least an equal if not dominant role in driving the action on stage. I was determined that the plays should be of the highest quality. The phrase I'd heard again and again was 'There just aren't any *good* plays for women', not 'There just aren't *any* plays for women'; so I resolved to focus on plays that I felt theatres should and could proudly stage for their audiences today, plays that have stood the test of time and are likely to go on doing so into the future.

I read any play with a female-heavy cast that I could get my hands on, spending hours combing the shelves of bookshops and libraries, trawling the internet and sorting through boxes of neglected plays in the storage rooms of theatres and drama schools. I rejected many of the plays I came across – there are a lot of mediocre plays written for mainly female casts. But then, there are a lot of mediocre plays written full stop. The good news was that it didn't take me long to realise that twenty plays was not remotely ambitious enough. The goalposts quickly moved, and I decided to aim for a much greater number. As the pile of quality playtexts on my desk grew higher and higher, the evidence against 'There just aren't any good plays for women' grew stronger and stronger.

The range of outstanding plays for women I found was as wide as it was vast. They stretch from the well-known to the obscure: from plays we know and love but never quite realise are predominantly female, through to those that have all but disappeared from public view. The 100 I have chosen to write about here really are the tip of the iceberg; personal favourites that I hope will whet the reader's appetite to seek out more. It's not an exhaustive list, and there are strong biases within it; it's decidedly Western (with a particularly heavy focus on British and American writers), and – reflecting the increasingly full role women have played in our society over the last hundred or so years – features far more plays written in the twentieth century than any other period.

This book is a reflection of my personal taste and the material that has been available to me. It doesn't claim to be a definitive study of all plays ever written for women (and given that I've only sought out plays written in English or translated into English, it certainly can't be), but rather it is a starting point, in which I share my passion for a selection of plays that I feel for one reason or another are of particular merit. There will be plays that some readers will feel surprised, even disappointed, that I have missed out. But this is a purposefully subjective list of 100 plays. Someone else compiling this book would undoubtedly have made different choices to mine, and what is so exciting is that there *are* choices to be made. Rather than scraping the barrel to find great plays for female-heavy casts, I have been overwhelmed by the quantity of material that exists – far more than I could ever work my way through, or could contain within these pages.

What You Will Find in this Book

The book contains 100 separate entries on the featured 100 plays. Each entry begins with something that looks like this:

1 **Three Tall Women**
by Edward Albee (*b.* 1928, USA)

First performed: Vineyard Theatre, New York City, 1994

Cast breakdown: 3f, 1m

Publisher: Dramatists Play Service, 2002

This details each play's title, playwright (with the year and country of their birth), the location and year of its first performance (with additional information given when the year of the play's completion differed significantly to that of its first performance), cast breakdown and publisher.

Following these details you will find a paragraph on what each play is about – not quite a synopsis because I didn't want to spoil the plot – but enough of an insight to give a sense of the story and world of the play. Following this, there is an introduction to the play, outlining what it is that makes it brilliant, and worth considering for production today.

At the back of the book there is an appendix of ten great one-woman plays. It seemed important to include plays for solo performers in this book, but they didn't quite feel at home in the main list of 100. So they've been given their own, shorter section.

Criteria for Selecting Plays

I imposed two criteria when searching for plays. Firstly, I decided I would only focus on those that are female-heavy – those with an *entirely or predominantly female cast*. Secondly, for the sake of usefulness to the reader, I decided to feature only *plays that have been published*; there seemed little point in including plays which would be nearly impossible for readers to access.

Plays with entirely or predominantly female casts

Some of the plays in this book have all-female casts and some have mixed (male/female) casts. In those that do have mixed casts, the majority of roles are always for women (the only exceptions being *Happy Days* and *The Jewish Wife*, which each use one female and one male performer, but given how heavily they revolve around their female characters, they felt worth including). I wanted to find plays in which women are the norm, rather than the exception, and which contain a range of wonderful roles for female performers, the sort of roles actresses really *want* to play, rather than those that simply pay the bills.

Given the criteria that all the plays should have majority female casts, certain works often deemed 'greats' for women – such as Oliver Goldsmith's *She Stoops to Conquer*, David Hare's *Plenty*, Shelagh Delaney's *A Taste of Honey* and Simon Stephens's *Port*, for instance – are absent. They're great plays undoubtedly, but they don't belong in this collection. You'll notice an absence of certain writers in this book – William Shakespeare, Aphra Behn and Anton Chekhov among them – who, despite having written some outstanding roles for women, never penned any female-heavy plays – or at least none we know of. Similarly, plays that comment on the role of women have been discounted if they do not have predominantly female casts, however successfully or powerfully they do so. Daphne du Maurier's *The Years Between* and, more recently, Lucinda Coxon's *Happy Now?* are examples of excellent and important plays on the changing role of women in society that I have chosen to exclude because the focus of this book is very much on the number and quality of roles *for* women, not the fact that they are *about* women.

Included in the collection are three plays which can be performed by casts of any size or gender – Martin Crimp's *Attempts on Her Life*, Sarah Kane's *4.48 Psychosis* and Märta Tikkanen's dramatic poem *The Love Story of the Century*. Although countless plays follow this format, the particular focus on female voices in these three made them feel like useful additions.

Plays that have been published

To maximise the usefulness of this book, it seemed vital that all the plays listed in it are in public circulation. The idea behind this book is that if any of the plays stimulates the interest of the reader, they should be able to buy a copy, new or second-hand, order one at a local library or, at the very least, read a copy in the British Library reading rooms. This decision necessarily discounts plays that have not been published, regardless of how successful they may have been in production. If you are not able to access the texts, it felt of little use to include them here. While it will require a greater level of dedication on the part of the reader to lay their hands on copies of some of these plays than others (essentially those out of print or on limited print runs), second-hand online booksellers, publishers and the playwrights' agents or estates should be helpful in locating copies of some of the more difficult-to-find titles.

The decision to include only those plays that have been published does of course come with its own problems. One need only look at the example of Githa Sowerby's remarkable *The Stepmother* (the manuscript of which languished in a cardboard box in the basement of Samuel French's bookshop for over eighty years before fortuitously being discovered and finally published) to see how easily plays existing only in manuscript form can be lost. It's worth bearing in mind too that plays written by women or about women would realistically have been less likely candidates for publication or even public performance in the past.

To help the reader I've detailed a publisher and year of publication for each of the plays. These are not necessarily the first or indeed only editions of the plays available, rather they are the versions that seemed most widely and easily accessible at the time of writing this book. For those plays that have been translated into English, rather than written in English originally, I have recommended a particular version. Given how widely different translations of the same play can vary, though, readers may like to compare several versions and find one that best suits their tastes.

Another rule I imposed on myself was to feature each writer just once. It would be relatively easy to construct a list of nearly 100 great plays for women from the works of April De Angelis, Caryl Churchill, Sarah Daniels and Bryony Lavery alone! So for the sake of variety, I decided that each writer should be represented in this collection just once. Readers should bear in mind that many of the writers within the 100 have written several outstanding female-heavy plays, and a quick look at a website such as doollee.com will help reveal these.

Variety

Beyond these specific criteria, I sought to characterise the compilation of 100 plays with a spirit of variety and aimed to cover as broad a range of genre, style, scale and subject matter as possible. There are bold epics in this collection, and there are delicate chamber pieces; there are plays big enough to fill our most sizeable stages and pieces for tiny studio spaces; there is searing polemic and light entertainment. Some of the plays in this volume have played to packed houses in the West End or on Broadway; others have been seen by just a few hundred people in a room above a pub. All are worthy of wider attention and will offer a wonderful theatrical experience to audiences and performers alike.

Above all, it felt important to me that the plays I selected challenged assumptions of what plays for female casts can be about. Yes, there are a number of domestic dramas within the collection, dealing with the traditionally female domains of family, marriage and motherhood. But there are also plays about war, politics, science, business, religion and countless other aspects of the human experience that impact as heavily on women as they do on men. It is this diversity of subject matter that I find so exciting.

Finally, it is important to emphasise that this book doesn't attempt to be an exhaustive authority on every play ever written for a female-heavy cast. Rather, it is purposefully selective, offering only examples of the very best writing for women. It's designed to get brilliant plays into the consciousness of directors, producers, teachers, drama schools; anyone, in fact, who makes decisions about what plays to present to audiences. My sincere hope is that people at all levels of theatre – amateur, student and professional – will perform these plays, and so many more like them, and award them the place in the repertoire they so richly deserve.

Let's kill off, once and for all, the myth that 'There just aren't any good plays for women'.

Acknowledgements

Thank you…

To the many colleagues, friends and industry professionals who took the time to meet with me and share their recommendations of great plays for women. The knowledge and passion of this vast collection of actors, directors, writers, literary managers, artistic directors, academics, teachers and theatre-lovers made this book not just possible, but a pleasure to research and write.

To Matt Applewhite and Nick Hern for saying 'yes' and then getting me through the next three years. My sincerest thanks to them, along with Robin Booth, Tamara von Werthern and everyone else at Nick Hern Books.

To the National Theatre Studio for its support on this project and for so much more – I am hugely indebted to it as an organisation. Also to the National Theatre's Literary Department for dealing with my constant shelf-raiding visits with such good grace, and especially to Sarah Clarke for keeping me endlessly supplied with scripts.

To English Touring Theatre for giving me somewhere to write and somewhere to feel at home. This extraordinary act of generosity was largely responsible for keeping me sane, and prevented the writing of this book from being the lonely experience it could have been.

To Kate Mosse for her instant enthusiasm about the project, for her warmth, encouragement and advice.

To everyone who put up with my grumbling and also to those who held my hand at various points along the way.

Above all, to Purni Morell who first said, 'You should write a book about this', and then gave me the means by which to begin. This book has been written because of her.

1

Three Tall Women
by Edward Albee (b. 1928, USA)

First performed: Vineyard Theatre, New York City, 1994

Cast breakdown: 3f, 1m

Publisher: Dramatists Play Service, 2002

Edward Albee's Pulitzer Prize-winning dissection of one woman's life follows ninety-one-year-old 'A' as she interacts with two younger versions of herself. 'B' is 'A' at fifty-two and 'C' is her at twenty-six. As 'A' approaches the point of death, she squabbles, colludes and commiserates with her younger selves, picking over the events of her life and the decisions she made along the way. Her brain afflicted by dementia and her body ravaged with age, she cuts an imposing figure even when propped up against pillows in her sickbed, immobile and largely helpless. A fastidiously detailed character study that is as poignant as it is powerful, *Three Tall Women* is an extraordinary theatrical imagining of the workings of a senile mind.

Albee's depiction of a woman suffering the later stages of senile dementia is as honest as it is technically accomplished. At turns endearing, grimly funny and desperately sad, this snapshot of old age is one that is weighty and endlessly engrossing. The play contains the mixture of quirkiness, quiet brutality and steely wit one expects from Edward Albee and, often considered one of his more personally reflective works (it was written shortly after the death of his adoptive mother), it cuts to the heart of human frailty, agency and identity.

Blowing all logic out of the water, Albee plays with character, time and place to create an alternative reality that is intriguing, unsettling and yet, somehow, oddly life-affirming. Epic in scale despite taking place entirely in A's bedroom-cum-sickroom, what initially seems to be a run-of-the-mill domestic encounter between three women gradually reveals itself to be what it is – a massive, sharply drawn and chilling portrait of the entire lifespan of one human being.

Albee creates three female characters the likes of which are rarely seen on stage. Fiercely intelligent, impressively sharp and yet far from likeable, all three appear to have been drawn with a combination of hostility and affection. These three tall women command the space, address the audience directly when it suits them, and are never short of a wise quip or injurious put-down towards their other selves. Alternatively drawn towards and repelled by one another, their three-way relationship is a charged and fluid one. Boundaries are constantly redrawn, allegiances re-established and statuses reconfigured as they gang up on one another, vie for supremacy, or fight desperately to establish their autonomy from the other two. Albee structures these volatile interactions with his characteristic level of detail and precision. Every comma, colon, dash, stress and pause in the script feels considered, every stage direction a story in its own right. The dialogue has a muscularity and rhythm that give this physically sedate play a marked tension and its vibrancy will continue to ring in the audience's ear, long after they have left the theatre.

To achieve its full effect in performance, *Three Tall Women* is a play that demands mental gymnastics of its cast and a detailed analytical approach from its director. In addition to the speed and frequency with which the women's relationships are constantly reshuffling, A's senility poses challenges. Her thought processes – which form the backbone of the play – are far from direct. She swerves between past and present, jumps from subject to subject and is at times wholly irrational in the direction taken by her thoughts and words. Setting the emotional tone of the piece, she switches from despair to glee, aggression to vulnerability, confusion to absolute self-possession, often in a split second. B and C, as alternative versions of A, must navigate their way along this unconventional path as closely as A herself and it is a play that demands an extraordinarily close level of listening among its actresses. Very much an ensemble piece which almost certainly won't work unless the three main performers are committed to working as a team, *Three Tall Women* poses emotional, intellectual and technical challenges to its cast. It is an enticing prospect for any actress who wants to stretch herself, and who loves playing funny, conflicted, driven and unpredictable characters.

First performed: Royal Court Theatre, London, 1958

Cast breakdown: 8f, 6m (doubling possible)

Publisher: Methuen, in *John Arden Plays: 1*, 1994

Members of the Travelling community, the Sawney family, have been forcibly rehoused. Finding themselves tenants of a shiny new council house and unable to 'abide inside', the Sawneys are less than impressed by the life imposed on them. Their displeasure though is nothing compared to that of their next-door neighbours, the Jacksons, whose neat, respectable and upwardly mobile existence is thrown into crisis with the arrival of the tumultuous Travellers. As the lives of the Jacksons and the Sawneys become increasingly entwined, both families' previously steadfast belief in their own superiority begins to unravel. Confronted with one another's alien existences, and questioning their own for the first time, they begin to resemble one another in surprising and darkly comic ways.

Plotted across seventeen episodic scenes with songs between each, *Live Like Pigs* is a boisterous, irreverent and wildly energetic piece of theatre. Much like the ever-changing temperament of the Sawney family, it's a play that swings between elation and despair, exuberant one moment and stormy the next. Performed by a big, ensemble cast, it has a storyline that twists and turns, darting between pathos and humour. Messy, gutsy and full of less than savoury characters prone to passionate outbursts, it's a play characteristic of the post-*Look Back in Anger* era and must have seemed worlds away from the polite, restrained dramas set in well-kept middle-class drawing rooms that had dominated English new writing just a few years before. The interior and exterior of the Sawney's new council house ('the dull sort – not one of the agreeable designs given prizes by County Planning Committees,' Arden clarifies in his stage directions) is depicted in all its disarray. Within a day or two of the family's arrival it's a tip; piles of bedding stand in for proper beds, the place is filthy and the rooms are filled to capacity with itinerant associates of the Sawneys. In their waking hours the family spills out onto the doorstep, into the garden and the street beyond, and at night-time are just as likely to be found sleeping in the kitchen or the hallway as in the bedrooms. This unruliness and the relaxed attitudes towards personal privacy engendered by it are what elicit a combination of horror and morbid fascination in their neighbours.

Arden considered *Live Like Pigs* to be 'not so much a social documentary as a study of differing ways of life brought sharply into conflict and both losing their own particular virtues under the stress of intolerance and misunderstanding'. Regardless of this, responses to the play's 1958 Royal Court premiere largely hinged on attempts to decipher what Arden's particular political 'message' might be. 'On the one hand I was accused by the Left of attacking the Welfare State: on the other, the play was *hailed* as a defence of anarchy and morality,' he commented. Both responses, Arden believed, missed the point; despite claiming to 'approve outright of neither the Sawneys nor of the Jacksons', he nonetheless argued, 'both groups uphold standards of conduct that are incompatible, but which are both valid in their correct context'. The drama of *Live Like Pigs* comes not from taking a didactic stance for or against either group's lifestyles, rather from depicting the destabilising but potentially enriching effect that differentness can have on a community.

Long before Jez Butterworth would bring the collision between a free-wheeling outsider and his conventional English neighbours to the Royal Court stage in his 2009 hit play *Jerusalem*, Arden was exploring this territory in *Live Like Pigs*. Both plays share a similar sense of irreverent humour, combine references to folklore with realism and give a provocative nod to bigger questions of what 'community' means in England. But while in Butterworth's play the involvement of women is limited, in *Live Like Pigs*, Arden gives the female characters an equal share of the action and the humour. The play features a delicious range of female roles, among them Big Rachel, a 'termagant' and the statuesque head of the Sawney household; Rosie her stepdaughter, forever in Rachel's shadow, weary yet passionate; Rosie's daughter Sally, 'a wicked little ten-year-old with Woolworths spectacles, and a great capacity for loud excitement'; the 'malicious fairy' Daffodil and her outlandish mother, Old Croaker. The Jackson women, although initially conventional in comparison, gradually emerge as the complex, vivid and vibrant women they really are beneath their buttoned-up respectability. As the Sawneys (literally) bring out the beast in their previously docile neighbours, so Arden unleashes a delightful blend of absurdity, rebelliousness and energy to the stage in the form of these fantastically refreshing female characters.

3 | She Ventures and He Wins
by 'Ariadne' (identity unknown)

First performed: New Theatre, London, 1695

Cast breakdown: 7f, 5m (doubling possible)

Publisher: Phoenix, in *Female Playwrights of the Restoration*, 1994

Charlotte is in search of a husband. In possession of a considerable fortune and a 'frolicsome' humour, she is determined that the man she marries will want her for who she is, not for her estate. Eyeing up the even-minded Lovewell as a promising candidate, she decides to put him to the test. Aided and abetted by her cousins Juliana and Bellasira, she implements a series of trials designed to measure the constancy of his love. As Lovewell passes each with flying colours, Charlotte's tests become ever more fantastical. Across town, Urania is having trouble with Squire Wouldbe. Despite already being married to the inestimable Dowdy, he seems determined to direct his wholly undesired attentions towards Urania. Spotting an opportunity for mischief, as well as a way to put him firmly in his place, Urania embarks on a campaign of trickery intended to dampen Wouldbe's ardour and send him safely back to his wife.

Those who enjoy the tropes of Restoration comedy will find them in abundance in *She Ventures and He Wins*. There's the usual cross-dressing, overheard conversations, mistaken identity, hiding in confined spaces and intercepted letters, plus a few songs thrown in for good measure. It's an admittedly gentle comedy with a more than ludicrous plot and a predictably happy, marriage-orientated ending. But it's also a play that is attractive largely because of the steering role the women take. Almost without exception, it is the women who drive the action, hatch the plots and propel the narrative, and they get the opportunity to be mischievous, meddling, mercenary and at times downright Machiavellian. The tests to which Charlotte subjects the bewildered Lovewell become more brilliantly contorted the more ardently he appears to love her, while the misery Urania inflicts on Wouldbe feels at times akin to the baiting of Malvolio in *Twelfth Night*. The male characters, whilst delightfully sharp, witty and colourful in their own right, function predominantly as the women's willing accomplices or their unwitting victims. It's little wonder that Ariadne refers to the play in its prologue as 'a women's treat'.

Nothing is known about 'Ariadne', other than that she declared herself to be 'a young lady'. While female playwrights were fewer than their male counterparts in the Restoration period, there was a notable number of them getting their work produced on London's main stages, and Ariadne was one of them. She was unusual in that she wrote under a pseudonym and while certain theories for her identity have been suggested, none have ever, or most probably ever will, be proven. What we do know is that *She Ventures and He Wins* first appeared in September 1695 at the New Theatre in Little Lincoln's Inn Fields in London. The female leads were played by theatrical stars of the day; Urania by the delightfully named Ann Brace-girdle, and Charlotte by Elizabeth Barry (who, according to the suspicions of some academics, may have been Ariadne herself). Our knowledge of the play's existence, and that of Ariadne, is largely thanks to the script having been published in 1696, the year after its initial production.

Across the five short acts, Ariadne has her delightfully funny cast zipping across London between assignations, 'accidental' meetings and not-so-innocent social calls. Constantly nearly tripping over one another as they dash around the city on foot or in hackney cabs and coaches, the two storylines criss-cross throughout the action before coming to a pleasing combined denouement in which Charlotte and friends enjoy an evening at the inn in which Urania works and are there able to witness the latter's execution of Wouldbe's ultimate humiliation. All of London's society is represented; Charlotte and her equally wealthy brother Sir Charles, 'younger brother of small fortune' Lovewell, tradeswoman Urania, and social-climber Dowdy – forever embarrassed by her pawnbroker mother's attire ('don't go in that pickle, mother; 'twill disgrace me now I am a gentlewoman' being just one of her many anguished pleas). The play is unrelentingly jolly, never takes itself too seriously and, although undeniably silly, gives a lovely glimmer of insight into life in late 1600s London. There's something delicious in knowing that what an audience in 1695 found funny can still make us laugh today, and Ariadne's fast-paced farce about the fun that scheming women have whilst navigating 'love's wide labyrinth' is undoubted to do just that.

4 The Assemblywomen
by Aristophanes (*b.* around 445 BCE, Athens)

First performed: Athens, 392 BCE

Cast breakdown: 10f plus a chorus of women, 5m (doubling possible)

Recommended version: by David Barrett

Publisher: Penguin, in *The Birds and Other Plays*, 2003

Praxagora and her female neighbours have been up to something. They've been covertly tanning themselves in the garden, have ditched their razors, grown impressive armpit hair and have been fashioning for themselves some rather fetching fake beards. This morning they've snuck out of bed before sunrise, put on their sleeping husbands' clothes and have surged, en masse, to the parliament building. They know that the first free men to get a seat in the parliament have the right to pass the laws for that day and, fed up by the shoddy governing of their menfolk, the women have decided it's their turn to take charge. As the curiously feminine-looking mass of pale-faced young 'men' fill the parliament building, a law is passed giving women control of the state. Praxagora is selected as Governess and she has some radical reforms to propose.

Ask most people what Aristophanes' greatest play is for women and more often than not, the immediate and unqualified response will be *Lysistrata*. *The Assemblywomen* (sometimes translated as *Women in Power* or alternately *Women in Parliament*) is an interesting if odd piece of work by Aristophanes and, given how widely discussed, read and performed *Lysistrata* is, it seems pertinent to turn the spotlight on to its often overlooked sister. The play has gained a reputation through the criticism of certain academics and editors (who perhaps didn't get the joke?) as being a puerile piece of inconsequentiality at best, and an absolute clanger at worst. Not so. *The Assemblywomen* is an extremely funny, delightfully silly piece of satire which, with its close-to-the-bone humour, manages to speak volumes about power, and the structures that enable it. Certainly the play functions around a pretty ludicrous premise and the idea of the female population successfully passing themselves off as men, albeit with the aid of some expertly constructed fake beards, is, of course, ridiculous. But the cross-dressing, gender-bending antics of Praxagora and her associates is what gives the play its carnivalesque energy and riotous tone. This being Aristophanes, there's plenty of toilet humour (indeed the scene in which Praxagora's husband suffers alternate bouts of diarrhoea and constipation will test even the most iron-stomached of audience members) and sexual innuendo is rife.

Aristophanes wrote the play at a time when Athens was in decline and the society he depicts on stage is one in which politics is effectively eating itself. Indeed, the state is malfunctioning to such an extent that there's only one thing left to do: commit the unthinkable and give the women a crack at running things. Taking power, Praxagora steps into a political landscape in which men only bother to turn up to parliament in order to get their attendance fee, where personal interests dictate policy and corruption is the norm. Within a few hours of seizing control she announces a Communist state, one in which there will be no personal property or wealth, but rather a mutually owned and equally shared common pool of resources. Meals will be eaten at long communal tables set up in the squares and plazas and no citizen will ever lack for the food, clothing, tools, or utensils that he or she needs. It's a utopian ideal and, of course, one that looks set swiftly to fall apart, Praxagora having trusted the goodwill and honesty of her fellow citizens somewhat further than they deserve. While the citizens are more than happy to enjoy the public dinners gratis, they're less keen to relinquish their property to the state, and it only seems a matter of time before the women's grand designs will grind to a halt.

Today *The Assemblywomen* is rarely performed and, when published, it tends to be as part of a 'Complete Plays of Aristophanes'-style compendium, rather than in its own right. With its musings on how the world may look if ruled by women, it's a play that deserves greater attention among modern audiences, experiencing as they are a greater concentration of female politicians than ever before. Aristophanes' depiction of an unravelling state searching for a new way to define itself will similarly prove portentous to any society undergoing a crisis of identity or confidence. Admittedly, finding a really good translation of *The Assemblywomen* is tricky. Perhaps it's up to some enterprising writer or translator to conceive that contemporary, charismatic and edgy version of *The Assemblywomen* to which a twenty-first-century audience can warmly relate.

5 | The Chalk Garden
by Enid Bagnold (b. 1889, UK)

First performed: Ethel Barrymore Theatre, New York, 1955

Cast breakdown: 7f, 2m (doubling possible)

Publisher: Samuel French, 2010

Miss Madrigal responds to an advertisement for a hired companion to a young lady. What she finds at the interview is Laurel, a startlingly precocious sixteen-year-old (with a penchant for setting things alight), her eccentric ex-society hostess grandmother Mrs St Maughan, and a rather odd domestic set-up in which Laurel's mother Olivia appears to have been wilfully edited out of the picture and the servants are in constant revolt. Despite her misgivings, Madrigal – an avid gardener – is persuaded to stay, largely through the promise that she can put her talents to use on the house's wayward and hitherto mismanaged chalk-soil garden. While Madrigal succeeds in instilling some sense of restraint in both Laurel and the garden, an appearance from an old friend of Mrs St Maughan's threatens to reveal Madrigal's shadowy past.

As the curtain rises on *The Chalk Garden*'s middle-class sitting-room set, an audience could be mistaken for anticipating a sedate, conventional evening of enjoyable but largely unchallenging 1950s light comedy. *The Chalk Garden* in fact delivers far more. It is a wonderfully quirky, almost subversive play in which a jubilant sense of abandon reigns. It features a cast of characters who, from the lady of the house down to the manservant, all know how they *ought* to behave, but appear to have decided long ago that far more fun can be had by throwing all decorum out of the window. It's a household that revels in its own dysfunctional approach to daily life and in which the relationships between its inhabitants are bizarre to say the least. Into this chaotic landscape, the straight-laced Miss Madrigal arrives and attempts to impose a semblance of order. Understanding that the constant near-hysteria in the house is far from conducive to the well-being of the already highly strung Laurel, Madrigal attempts to cultivate a more nourishing environment in which the child can grow. The house's garden, built on lime and chalk soil and entirely unresponsive to Mrs St Maughan's misguided efforts to make it thrive, is a barely concealed metaphor for her inept attempts to parent Laurel through a combination of indulgence and selfish obstinacy.

Despite its wit, the play serves up a stern critique of those people who manufacture crises as a way of justifying poor behaviour in themselves and their offspring. Mrs St Maughan repeatedly excuses Laurel's wild and wilful behaviour on the basis that some years ago she ran away and 'by some extraordinary carelessness was violated in Hyde Park'. This incident (later proved to be a figment of Laurel's fertile imagination) was seized upon by Mrs St Maughan as evidence of Olivia's inability to care for Laurel and one that necessitated her assuming custody. While Mrs St Maughan enjoys presenting herself as a martyr, dedicated to turning her 'old age into a nursery' for her granddaughter's sake, Olivia, who arrives during the action determined to reclaim Laurel for herself, is far more critical of her mother's motives. Madrigal too is unimpressed and, taking charge of the household with all the tenacity of Mary Poppins and none of the charm, proceeds to focus determinedly on dispersing the hysteria that Laurel and Mrs St Maughan so love to create.

The play provides some wonderfully comic and highly unusual female characters. Laurel in particular must have been an absolute breath of fresh air when she first appeared on the 1950s stage, being neither the typical ingénue nor a passively sexless young girl. Rather she is feisty, macabre and scintillatingly dark, a wise-cracking fire-starter who runs rings around the 'grown-ups' in the play and forms a highly entertaining double-act with Maitland, the somewhat camp manservant. Madrigal too is an intriguing proposition for an actress, enigmatical, emotionally contained and yet the undisputed engine of the piece. Mrs St Maughan, still tenacious, poised, and determined to preside with some degree of dignity over her madcap household – despite an increasing tendency to mislay her false teeth – is a wonderful prospect for an older actress. Even Olivia, the daughter who wilfully refused to be the sparkling debutante her mother so wanted her to be, is given two fantastic scenes. Unsurprisingly it's a play that has been frequently revived and attracted an impressive array of leading ladies. Over the years Peggy Ashcroft, Helena Bonham Carter, Edith Evans, Deborah Kerr, Hayley Mills, Margaret Tyzack and Penelope Wilton are among those who have made their mark on Bagnold's bold, unconventional and irrepressibly energetic comedy.

6 The Amen Corner
by James Baldwin (b. 1924, USA)

First performed: Howard University, Washington DC, 1955

Cast breakdown: 9f, 5m (doubling possible. Could also be performed with additional non-speaking male and female cast members)

Publisher: Penguin, 1991

Things aren't looking good for Sister Margaret. A pastor who rules the congregation of her Harlem church with an iron fist, Margaret is slowly becoming aware of growing dissent. A small but vocal faction is stirring up trouble, criticising Margaret's approach and asking questions about where exactly the money from the collection plate is going. If she didn't already have her work cut out keeping her fractious flock in line, the sudden reappearance of her estranged husband Luke sends matters from bad to worse. Not only is Luke living the devil's life, making his money by playing jazz, the old sinner drops the bombshell that it was Margaret who left him some ten years ago not, as she had always claimed, the other way round. With a teenage son going through a crisis of faith and attempts to topple her more likely every day, Margaret must fight to maintain her authority, both in the pulpit and at home.

The Amen Corner, written in 1953, was James Baldwin's first play. *Go Tell It On the Mountain*, his debut novel, based on his own experiences as a boy preacher, had taken him the best part of a decade to complete and *The Amen Corner* was written in the summer after the novel had found a publisher and was being prepared for release. Baldwin's decision to focus at this point on playwriting came not so much from an urge to conquer the theatre world, as from a desire to avoid falling into the trap of attempting to emulate his earlier success. This was as much for his own creative development, he subsequently commented, as to sidestep the expectations he suspected would be placed on him by the contemporary literary world. 'Now I was a writer,' he recalled, 'a *Negro* writer, and I was expected to write diminishing versions of *Go Tell It On the Mountain* forever.' At the same time, Baldwin was aware that *The Amen Corner*, with its female protagonist and focus on the political machinations of a black gospel church, was unlikely to meet the approval of the 1950s New York theatre scene and, indeed, it would not be until 1965 that the play received its first professional production. Although not writing to ingratiate himself to the theatre industry, Baldwin did, however, recognise the platform that theatre offered him to express his anger at the stultifying effects of state-sanctioned racial prejudice on individual lives. He drew on his own experience on a different type of stage – the pulpit – in his crafting of the play, later saying, 'What I wanted to do in the theatre was to recreate moments I remembered as a boy preacher, to involve the people, even against their own will, to shake them up, and, hopefully, to change them.' Indeed, his music and song-infused play would communicate vividly his feelings on what it was to be black in 1950s America.

'I remember you when you didn't hardly know if the Holy Ghost was something to drink or something to put on your hair,' Luke observes upon his arrival into Margaret's new life. He returns after a ten-year absence to find his wife's transformation is complete; Margaret is no longer the 'funny, fast-talking, fiery little thing' he married – she has found God, been saved, and entirely rewritten who she was. Now, a picture of piety and holding no truck with sin, Margaret keeps her congregation in check with tyrannical force. Fear, manipulation, public humiliation; nothing is outside the pastor's armoury in her quest to save souls and better serve the Lord. And yet, despite her formidable persona and zealous tendencies, Baldwin never manages to be quite so hard on Margaret as she is on her flock. In his portrait of the female pastor, he draws an intelligent and charismatic woman who, despite her faults, remains a profoundly impressive person, one whose intentions remain laudable, even when misguidedly applied. Her ruthlessness is mitigated by her deep desire to serve her God and her community, as well as her unshakeable, albeit poorly expressed, love for her son. Margaret, Baldwin suggests, is a highly capable woman who has been deeply damaged by the limitations placed on her by her society, one that denies her and her family the ability to advance, or the freedom to conduct themselves as they would choose. 'She is in the church because her society has left her no other place to go,' Baldwin comments in his introduction to the play. Margaret is a victim of her circumstances and, Baldwin suggests, it is only through her 'merciless piety' that she can express her feelings of rage towards a world that is doing terrible wrongs to her and her people.

A revival of the play, starring Marianne Jean-Baptiste as Margaret, played at the National Theatre in 2013.

Five Women Wearing the Same Dress
by Alan Ball (*b.* 1957, USA)

First performed: Manhattan Class Company, New York, 1993

Cast breakdown: 5f, 1m

Publisher: Dramatists Play Service, 1998

In a mansion in an 'old-money suburb' of Knoxville, Tennessee, a wedding reception is just getting started. While the bride works the crowd downstairs, her five bridesmaids, all of them decked out in the same hideous gown, seek refuge in an upstairs bedroom. There's Trisha and Georgeanne, school friends who have long since grown distant to the bride as well as one another; Meredith, the bride's leather-jacket-wearing younger sister, apparently intent on casting a dampener on the day; and pious, tee-total virgin cousin Frances. Finally there's Mindy, the groom's sister, who is understandably displeased that her girlfriend of nine years hasn't been invited. As the realisation hits the five bridesmaids that none of them actually likes the bride, a spirit of camaraderie is born. Revelations fly and the combination of a free bar and long-suppressed emotions lead to secrets and desires coming startlingly and hilariously to the fore.

Alan Ball is best known as the Oscar-winning writer of the movie *American Beauty* and creator of hit TV shows *Six Feet Under* and *True Blood*. While his plays receive less attention than his screen work, audiences coming to *Five Women Wearing the Same Dress* will recognise the darkly humorous handling of quiet suburban crises with which Ball's TV and film work has become synonymous. So, too, Ball's talent for writing refreshingly complex, intelligent, funny and often downright weird female characters is very much in evidence (even before such creations as *American Beauty*'s Jane Burnham and *Six Feet Under*'s Brenda Chenowith, Ball was honing his writing skills on female-led sitcoms such as *Grace Under Fire* and *Cybill*). Indeed, it's not inaccurate to describe *Five Women Wearing the Same Dress* as a jackpot for actresses. The five women, who range in age from early twenties to early thirties, are all fantastic comic roles, as funny as they are troubled, and have vast hidden depths, despite their initial appearance as the embodiment of various stereotypes. If anything, it is the women's quiet battles not to be pigeonholed, as well as the way in which Ball constantly messes with his audience's expectations, that gives the play its particular bite. Don't let the seemingly fluffy setting of a wedding reception fool you; *Five Women Wearing the Same Dress* is no gentle romcom.

A consistently funny, although occasionally brutal dissection of heterosexual marriage customs and romanticism, the play highlights the odd disconnects that exist between the ancient values out of which traditional Judeo-Christian marital practices were born, and modern lifestyles. In some kind of weird throwback to a long-gone era, the bridesmaids are all zipped into floor-length, corseted gowns that are as uncomfortable as they are impractical, while the bride is decked out in what Mindy appraises as a 'white monstrosity, meant to symbolise that she is undamaged goods, it's like a sacrifice!' When it comes to marriage, the characters appear to be trapped in limbo; still bound by ways of thinking and behaving dreamt up long ago, and yet aware too that the world they inhabit has moved on significantly. That's not to say that the play is an all-out critique of love, romance, or even marriage. Indeed, there's an incredibly tender scene in which Trisha, a woman so disillusioned by any man's ability to make her happy that she never sticks around long enough to let one try, falls for one of the ushers. Rather, it is the lack of honesty entailed in a big, showy, white wedding – in which even the bridesmaids can't stand the bride – that the play lampoons.

'Everybody here is so aggressively *normal*, it's like the bland leading the bland' is Meredith's analysis of her sister's wedding reception. It is this 'aggressive normality' that Ball places under the microscope, exposing Knoxville as a community quietly besieged with insecurities, dysfunctional behaviour and bigotry beneath its suburban niceties and ostensible wealth. Adultery, homophobia, child molestation, abortion, religious fundamentalism and substance abuse are just some of the murkier territories that the play zips through as champagne glasses are clinked, guests mingle on the lawn and the bouquet is thrown. It's a play that deals with individuals attempting to assert themselves in the face of a culture that demands conformity, and conformity with a smile at that. As the five very different women who have all been forced to wear the same dress hide from a wedding reception of which none of them chose to be a part, they argue, laugh and cry about what *they* want, and attempt to forge their own, individual paths towards that.

Ursula
by Howard Barker (b. 1946, UK)

First performed: The Wrestling School, tour, 1998

Cast breakdown: 11f, 1m

Publisher: Oberon Books in *Barker Plays 3*, 2007

Ursula, renowned for her beauty, desired for her yellow hair and prized for her charm, has been promised in marriage. Lucas, a prince with sad eyes and a castle on a lonely estuary, is to be her husband, and he has sent his betrothed a specially commissioned painting of himself. Hearing the voice of Christ tell her to fling the painting into the river, Ursula believes her godliness is being tested. To demonstrate her devotion to Jesus, she resolves to resist the marriage and pledges her virginity instead to Him. With ten fellow virgins, she sets sail for Lucas's kingdom to deliver the news and await the consequences. Howard Barker's play is inspired by the legend of Saint Ursula, who along with eleven thousand holy virgin attendants, was said to have been massacred following a sea voyage made to call off her engagement.

Lyrical, disturbing and darkly humorous, *Ursula* takes a deliciously complex look at the cult of virginity. Barker's point of departure for the play was an altarpiece in Dresden, *The Massacre of the Virgin Martyrs* by Lucas Cranach the Elder (1472–1553). Barker observed what fascinated him was how 'Cranach revolutionised the subject by shifting the attention of the viewer from the victims to the perpetuator, the Prince. Far from being a parody of a pagan barbarian, he is infinitely cold and beautiful, leaning on his unused sword and observing the massacre with the moral detachment of the SS Officer.' Barker moves beyond Cranach's approach to constantly redefine and realign the audience's perspective. It's not just through Lucas's eyes we see the story, but in turn through those of Ursula, the Mother Superior Placida, a beggar girl called Leonora, and any one of the virgins who attend Ursula on her journey. A sense of unease and unpredictability underlines the piece, largely due to this constant rotation of the audience's sympathies and affiliation. Furthermore, no one is ever quite what they seem for long. Should Lucas be pitied or despised? Is Placida the virgins' protector or their greatest threat? Are we to regard Ursula as a paragon of religious devotion, or a dangerously deluded fanatic who leads herself and others to their deaths? In Barker's characteristic style, few easy answers are offered; rather an ever-growing and increasingly complex range of questions are deposited one by one into the audience's minds.

Although written with a stirring poeticism that captures the play's heady mix of desire, temptation, ecstasy and devotion, the language of *Ursula* is just one element of the play's overall arresting force. Visually potent, it is packed with images that are simultaneously beautiful, troubling and subversive – Lucas struggling under the weight of a gigantic and overflowing tray of fruit; Placida, post-massacre, wringing blood from the skirts of her scarlet gown; the virgins, blindfolded and strapped to steel trolleys that are shoved onto the stage from the wings so that they career chaotically one into another. It's a play that offers outstanding opportunities to any company wanting to work physically, and the movement of the piece provides an alternative language, equal to if not even more expressive than the words that are spoken. So, too, the play has a strong musicality, the psalms sung by the virgins and the sounds of the wildlife on the estuary providing a further, expressive layer.

A provocative and uncompromising figure in European theatre since the 1970s, Barker uses the term 'Theatre of Catastrophe' to describe his work. Believing that plays – like any art – should be complex and multifaceted, his work tends to elude easy definition. There's very rarely a neat 'message' that is spelled out to his audiences; his work leaves a far longer legacy of unanswered questions and conflicting, sometimes troubling emotions. 'Theatre of Catastrophe takes as its first principle the idea that art is not digestible. Rather, it is an irritant in consciousness, like the grain of sand in the oyster's gut' is how Barker phrases the desired effect of his work, much of which is produced by The Wrestling School, the theatre company created in 1988 to produce his plays and further explore and disseminate his theories. The Wrestling School is so called because of the need to 'wrestle' with the ideas in his texts, the clue in the company's name being that no one involved in Barker's work, whether watching or making it, is in for an easy ride. *Ursula* is no exception to this principle and, whilst a challenging piece, if treated with a well-measured blend of sensitivity and tenacity, has the potential to be hugely rewarding for performers and audiences alike.

9 The Madras House
by Harley Granville Barker (b. 1877, UK)

First performed: Duke of York's Theatre, London, 1910

Cast breakdown: 17f, 8m (doubling possible)

Publisher: Methuen, in *Granville Barker Plays: Two*, 1994

Philip Madras is a man concerned with the 'Women Question'. Keen to enter politics, Philip wants to understand why society treats women the way it does, and once he's understood this, he wants to know what he can do about it. Even without extending his focus to the wider world, there's plenty of food for thought in his own sphere; six spinster cousins cooped up like eternal children under their parents' roof, an unmarried employee 'in trouble' and consequently in line for the sack, his father's active endorsement of polygamy, and a family business that treats both its female staff and customers like cattle. And that's before he's even worked out how to negotiate a marriage with his old-fashioned-values-orientated wife or agreed with her on how their daughter should be raised. Granville Barker takes his audience through thirty-six hours in the life of a would-be reformer and in the process captures a fascinating period of astonishing social change.

The Madras House is isolated within the plays in this book in that its protagonist, and indeed the characters that get the meat of the action are, in the main, men. At the same time, the female roles – many of them cameos – are of such a quality, range and depth that I felt the play warranted inclusion. In addition, the focus of the play, revolving as it does around the question of female emancipation but told, unusually, from a male perspective, seemed an interesting addition to a book exploring depictions of women on stage. Granville Barker called *The Madras House* 'a comedy in four acts' and it is – largely thanks to the cavalcade of human foibles it exhibits – very funny. But it's a play with a deadly serious intent too, an angry piece of work that refuses to pull its punches and which, even today, feels uncomfortably raw.

Very much an 'issue play', *The Madras House* possesses an admittedly slight plot, the main points of which (the selling of the Madras family's couture business, the long-awaited meeting between Philip's estranged parents, the dismissal of the unfortunate pregnant employee) are largely there to enable Granville Barker's own fastidiously detailed dissection of the Women Question. As a consequence, it's a play that may frustrate audience members looking purely for a ripping plot ('issues dominate action' was *Guardian* critic Michael Billington's dry dismissal of the Orange Tree's 2006 revival), but it will delight those who like their theatre to make them think or who possess a keen interest in social history. The play offers a range of fascinating and rare windows into contemporary gender politics, with Granville Barker providing a panoramic view of what life was like for women in Edwardian London. Change is on the horizon, female suffrage is being discussed and yet, for the majority of women, Victorian values prevail. And it is these values, Granville Barker demonstrates with ever-graver consternation, that have proved so appallingly pernicious in depriving women of autonomy, recognition or self-respect. It's a situation that proto-feminist Philip finds baffling. 'Good lord, you can't behave to women as if they were men!' his good friend Thomas remarks. 'Why not?' Philip responds, 'I always do.'

Granville Barker first wrote *The Madras House* in 1909 (and wrote a later, revised version in 1925), and it's a piece that, over a hundred years on, has proved to be remarkably prescient as far as our current consumer-based culture is concerned. Woman's emancipation will be great for business, is the gleeful prediction of Eustace Stern, the American retail magnate who is busy enlarging his women's fashion empire in hungry anticipation of the imminent growth in female spending power. His retail chain, he announces, is delighted to do the Women's Movement 'glad service', a pro-Suffrage stance that, Stern is happy to declare, has more to do with profit than equality. 'What now,' he asks, 'is the Modern Woman's Movement? It is woman expressing herself' – and Stern and his shops are ready and poised to help women express themselves with gloves, hats, skirts, jackets or anything else that he can convince them they need to buy in order to assert their new-found independence. This depiction of the genesis of the commodification of women's liberation, and the lining of rich men's pockets in the process, is one of the most thought-provoking aspects of *The Madras House*, drawing as it does a direct line between the experiences of the Edwardian woman and her modern counterpart sitting in the audience today. Ask an average twenty-first-century Western woman how much of her monthly earnings go on clothes, shoes, cosmetics, haircuts and beauty treatments, and it isn't difficult to see how shrewd the Sterns of the world were. Over a hundred years on, the business models they pioneered – and profited from greatly – continue to have an impact on how we spend our money, and how, in the process, we express ourselves as 'liberated' women.

First performed: Landor Theatre, London, 2005

Cast breakdown: 4f

Publisher: Roland Egan Press, in *Kieron Barry Five Plays*, 2005

It's the final days of Katherine, Isabel and Jennifer's penultimate year at their exclusive girls boarding school. As term draws to a close and a summer of work experience at Reuters, driving lessons and cricket on the green beckons, all that's left is the naming of next year's head girl. Katherine – captain of the lacrosse team, daughter of one of the school's major donors and undisputed most popular (i.e. powerful) girl in the lower sixth – is already practising her acceptance speech. So when scholarship girl Hetty announces that she has been asked to take on the role, Katherine and her friends are stunned. Why Hetty, a non-entity and non-fee-paying interloper, has been awarded such high office is beyond them, and to make matters worse, Hetty wants to use her mandate to make the school a fairer place. Declaring she *must* be head girl if only to save the school from Hetty's liberal values, Katherine embarks on a ferocious campaign to topple her opponent.

Anyone who has ever set foot in an all-girls school will recognise the noxious combination of competition, self-interest, insecurity and downright viciousness that Kieron Barry displays with such devastating accuracy in *Numbers,* and while the play is laugh-out-loud funny, it remains a testament to the ferocity of girls and their own particular brand of warfare against one another. Katherine, Isabel and Jennifer use no punches, slaps or kicks against Hetty, just a series of psychological blows designed to wound deeper and scar more permanently than any physical attack. The A to Z of reasons they unleash to her face as to why she shouldn't be head girl (her father works at Waitrose, she got a C in French GCSE, sometimes substantial amounts of hair is visible on her upper lip) is particularly stinging, for all its humorous connotations. Playing out in real time over the course of around forty minutes, the play is a David and Goliath narrative, telling the story of the underdog rising up with quiet courage to challenge the status quo. While its subject matter is ostensibly the minor matter of a head girl's appointment, *Numbers* makes a much larger comment. An intensely political piece, it paints in shrewd detail the battle for power, influence and control that exists at the heart of any community.

As Katherine and Hetty slug it out for supremacy, the school becomes a microcosm of society, with every house, sports team and club a potential battleground over which either girl can win control. Katherine's existing empire extends to the school newspaper, debating society, riding club, net-ball, hockey, tennis and swimming teams plus two of the houses, won through a combination of previous alliances, family connections ('her father and my father play squash together') and downright intimidation. Hetty's dominion is somewhat less impressive, consisting predominantly of 'chess club, stamps, the-go-out-on-Wednesday-and-help-the-local-community-thing'. At the heart of the contest between the two girls lies the unnamed but unalienable question of class. Scholarship girl Hetty's manifesto to make the school into a fairer, more tolerant place via a dem-ocratically elected student council is interpreted by the others as the creation of 'an average school for average people', and across the play, enti-tlement and the sharp distinction between what it is to be middle class and what it is to be upper class are ever present. While Katherine dismisses Hetty's future as involving 'living an hour and a half from work to have a big enough garden for the children, state school, NHS, packed lunches, holidays in the Lake District', for herself and her friends she predicts jobs as QCs, cabinet ministers and PR gurus. Depressingly – and despite their flagrant lack of fairness or desire to share the privilege with which they have been bestowed – it does indeed seem likely that it is Katherine, Isabel and Jennifer, not Hetty, who will go on to run the world.

Barry comments in his preface to the published version of the play, 'one is always rewarded by giving the director and actors the greatest amount of freedom of interpretation', and, indeed, stage directions and information on setting are kept to a minimum in his uncluttered text. Like many of his early plays, *Numbers* premiered in the tiny South London pub theatre, the Landor, and was originally performed alongside a companion piece, *Embassyland* (4m) which, although initially seemingly unconnected to *Numbers*, emerges as increasingly interlinked. Performed without *Embas-syland* though, *Numbers* functions entirely as a stand-alone piece. Sharp and funny, terrifying and inspiring, it is an impressive account of the cruel sophistication, wit and savagery with which young women can destroy one another.

11 Contractions
by Mike Bartlett (b. 1980, UK)

First performed: Royal Court Theatre, London, 2008

Cast breakdown: 2f

Publisher: Methuen, 2008

Emma has started working for a new company. Darren works there too, and they've had a bit of a thing. It's nothing serious and, as far as Emma is concerned, her manager doesn't need to know. Her sales figures haven't dropped and she's entitled to a personal life, right? Wrong, according to her manager. A clause in the contract Emma signed when she started working for the company states all relationships with a colleague of a romantic or sexual nature must be reported. Now Emma's seeing Darren on a regular basis and she wants to do the right thing. But as Emma's love life takes some unexpected turns and events become increasingly bizarre, it seems that her contractual obligations are of an unusually personal nature. A jet-black comedy with a decidedly surreal edge, Bartlett's *Contractions* pitches one woman against the corporate machine with diabolical results.

Contractions is a beautifully compact play. It's simple to stage, requires no more than a desk and two chairs, and in performance runs at around forty-five minutes in length. At first glance it's a neat, innocuous little play, sedentary and emotionally contained. Look deeper and you find a weighty piece of theatre and a chilling indictment of our times. It's taut, disturbing, incredibly funny, and has a huge deal to say about how we live and how we work in a world where the boundaries between private and public, personal and professional are blurring beyond recognition. Showing a succession of interviews between Emma and her manager, Bartlett depicts a workplace in which the inherent messiness and unpredictability of human emotions is viewed by management as an inconvenient nuisance, something to be stamped out of the workforce. In this otherwise streamlined, super-efficient structure, two employees falling in love could really upset the apple cart. As the 'safeguards' the manager puts in place to avoid Emma and Darren's relationship interfering with the company's productivity go from the comic to the absurd and finally to the deeply disturbing, the play asks uncomfortable questions about how little infringements of privacy here and there can ultimately snowball into something much bigger and far more dangerous.

The only predictable thing about love is its unpredictability and Bartlett pokes fun at a corporate culture attempting to forecast and control the future success of a burgeoning romance in the way it would an emerging market. At every turn, the company attempts to categorise, delineate, codify, record and analyse the exact nature of Emma and Darren's growing relationship, their increasingly pernicious attempts to define the undefinable as funny as they are grotesque. The company even issues a written statement outlining their exact definition of 'romance' ('any gesture, indication, communication (verbal or otherwise), appearance, message, understanding or organised meeting or event, which is perpetrated with a view to advancing the relationship toward love'), which ironically Emma uses in her favour to successfully argue that her initial, drunken kiss with Darren in the back of a cab was not 'romantic' under the company's guidelines but 'merely for the purpose of achieving sex' thereby avoiding disciplinary action. Although this lets the couple off the hook temporarily, as their relationship increasingly resembles the company's definition of 'romantic', their problems really begin. An initial relocation for Darren to the Richmond office, after the couple dutifully report that they have formally started dating, pales into insignificance when he's sent to Kiev after they announce the imminent arrival of their first child.

Originally broadcast as a Radio 4 Afternoon Play under the title, *Love Contract*, *Contractions* is a piece that, like much of Bartlett's work, contains an inherent musicality and fastidious rhythmic precision. In the published playscript, the text is laid out meticulously on the page in such a way as to demonstrate the various pauses, deliberate silences, trailing-off of thoughts and drifting of time that occurs between the women's words. It invariably feels that what is said by Emma and her manager is secondary to what is not. With mordant humour, Bartlett captures the sanitised world of the corporate environment and the work-speak used within it, depicting it as a thin veneer under which the chaos, unpredictability and vibrancy of human emotion and desire can always be felt, pulsating powerfully beneath.

12 Happy Days
by Samuel Beckett (b. 1906, Ireland)

First performed: Cherry Lane Theatre, New York, 1961

Cast breakdown: 1f, 1m

Publisher: Faber and Faber, 2010

The particular hell in which Beckett incarcerates the unfortunate but relentlessly upbeat protagonist of his two-act, tragi-comic drama is one of the most striking and iconic of all his dramatic works. The curtain rises on Winnie, a woman of about fifty, dressed in a low bodice, with bare shoulders, and buried entirely up to her waist in the earth. Around her exists an 'expanse of scorched earth', there is 'blazing light' and a 'very pompier *trompe-l'œil* backcloth to represent unbroken plain and sky receding to meet in far distance'. Seemingly unperturbed by her immobile state, the wilderness around her, or the indifference of husband Willie, who scrabbles about in the nearby earth, Winnie chatters away, passing the time of day with a non-stop stream of inanity punctuated by moments of searing emotional honesty.

Nothing, it seems, is capable of dampening Winnie's mood; not the mound of earth imprisoning her, not the ringing of a bell that sounds loudly every time she drops off to sleep, not the mute, gentle aggression of husband Willie. No, says Winnie, today is 'another heavenly day'. An apparent expert at keeping herself busy by doing absolutely nothing, Winnie goes through a complex process of non-stop business with the contents of her handbag, enacting a never-ending ritual of lipstick application, tooth brushing and nail filing. Sure, there's a revolver tucked in her handbag, but why would she want to use that when these are such 'happy days'? As the curtain rises on Act Two, Winnie is buried up to her neck, 'her head, which she can no longer turn, nor bow, nor raise, faces front motionless throughout'. The revolver is out of the bag and on the ground; tantalisingly close and yet, buried as she is, entirely out of her reach.

Happy Days is perhaps one of the greatest challenges a playwright has ever made to an actress. As a feat of memory alone it is an astonishingly difficult task, with Winnie's non-stop chatter lacking those comforting footholds around which the process of line-learning can be pinned; there's little action or plot development, just Winnie fixed in one spot, centre-stage, delivering a constant flow of words originating from a thought process that is far from linear or indeed, at times, logical. Into her dialogue, Beckett weaves intricate repetitions and extraordinarily complicated linguistic patterns that would test even the nimblest of minds. On top of this, he piles perhaps the most fastidiously constructed set of stage directions of any of his plays. He gives the actress directions – sometimes on a word-by-word basis – on her tone, physicality, facial expression, business with props, and timing that is detailed to the point of being obsessive. Beckett is not a writer whose work is ever open to radical (or indeed non-radical) reinterpretations due to the dedicated efforts of his estate to ensure productions of his plays follow his stage directions to the word, so any actress taking on the role of Winnie does so knowing she needs to play by his rules, or not at all.

Perhaps the most punishing of all Beckett's demands is that the actress playing Winnie be stuck to the spot, literally buried alive and immobile from the waist, and then the neck, up (in his 1972 play *Not I* (if) he would take the principle even further by clamping an actress into a chair, head and all, so that the only movement possible, and the only part of her visible, was that of her mouth). Brenda Bruce, who played Winnie in the 1962 British premiere at the Royal Court recollects the 'dreadful' moment of panic on opening night when the stage manager bolted her into the set and left her alone in 'the claustrophobia of sitting there trapped'. And where was Beckett on that opening night? He'd left by then, Bruce recollects, 'gone off to write some more torture for somebody else'. At the same time, the extraordinary hardships endured by Winnie – and the actress playing her – arguably point towards Beckett's faith in women. Asked by Bruce what inspired him to write *Happy Days*, a play in which the protagonist is buried alive, denied help from the companion who could save her, and with the means to commit suicide at hand but too great a sense of hope to end it all, Beckett replied, 'I thought, who would cope with that and go down singing? Only a woman.'

13

The Enchantment (Den Bergtagna)
by Victoria Benedictsson (*b.* 1888, Sweden)

First performed: Svenska Teatern, Stockholm, 1910

Cast breakdown: 7f, 5m (doubling possible)

Recommended version: by Clare Bayley

Publisher: Nick Hern Books, 2007

Louise Strandberg has spent the first thirty-one years of her life living a secluded existence in rural Sweden. Now, with her mother recently deceased and herself recuperating from illness, Louise has travelled to Paris where she lodges in an empty artist's studio. Initiated into Parisian artistic circles, Louise meets the charismatic sculptor Gustave Alland. Falling deeply and irretrievably in love with him, Louise begins a relationship that is both destructive and all-consuming. Terrified of his growing influence over her, she flees France and returns to her childhood home. But Gustave's appeal proves hard to resist and, when he summons her, Louise returns to Paris with dire consequences.

A contemporary of Strindberg and Ibsen and yet, today, largely unknown outside of Scandinavia, Victoria Benedictsson is a literary figure whose own story is as fascinating as it is tragic. Like Louise, Benedictsson hailed from a rural part of Sweden and, until her thirties, lived a relatively secluded life. This situation changed when, bedbound for some two years after a riding accident, she wrote a novel, *Pengar* (*Money*), which was published under a male pseudonym in 1885 and achieved wide critical acclaim. Buoyed by the novel's success, Benedictsson left her sixty-three-year-old postmaster husband and moved to Stockholm, where she mixed in the same circles as the leading artists and thinkers of the day. Here she met the highly influential critic and writer Georg Brandes, and the pair began a relationship, echoing that between Louise and Gustave. During their time together, Benedictsson wrote a second novel, *Fru Marianne* (*Mrs Marianne*), published in 1887, in which she proposed an alternative approach to male-female relationships, based on equality and mutual support, rather than women as chattels. Despite their relationship, Brandes disdained to review *Fru Marianne*, passing it instead to his younger brother, who in turn dismissed it as too much of a 'ladies' novel' to warrant serious attention.

The blow to Benedictsson was intense and, in 1888, she expressed the depth of her feeling over the failed relationship and the disparity between standards applied to male and female artists in *Den Bergtagna* (*The Enchantment*). In July of that year she checked into a room in the Copenhagen hotel where she had previously met with Brandes and cut her own throat with a razor blade.

The Enchantment is a play about the madness of love. A starkly unsentimental piece, it is not a celebration of love but a cautionary tale about the dangers of falling for someone who does not have your best interests at heart. His psychological cruelty masquerading as romance, Gustave's behaviour towards Louise is textbook manipulation. He chips away at her confidence like a sculptor at marble and reduces Louise to such a weakened, unstable impression of her former self that she is ultimately unable to cope with life on her own terms. What makes this dynamic so fascinating but also troubling for an audience, is that while Louise has seen little of the world prior to her trip to Paris, she is no fool. She understands exactly what Gustave is doing and yet goes along with it anyway. She is a largely willing accomplice in her own demise and, despite her intelligence, sense and principles, seems unable to break out of the spell cast by her lover.

Much like Nina in Chekhov's *The Seagull*, Louise falls prey to an artist who uses his temporary fascination with her to inspire his work before abruptly ending the relationship. Gustave's monument to his time with Louise is a sculpture of her lying naked on the floor, crushed, trampled and discarded. He describes it as his 'greatest work'; she calls it 'his way of saying goodbye'. The difference between Chekhov and Benedictsson's handling of the matter is that, while Nina's demise occurs conveniently offstage between acts, Louise unravels before our eyes, painfully, slowly and in full, undignified view. And while the failed affair leaves Louise utterly defeated, for Gustave it gives him a new lease of creative life and inspires work that will increase his already impressive professional profile. Herself a victim of the double standards applied to men and women in relationship to art, Benedictsson pits Louise's experience alongside that of her friend Erna, a painter still attempting to recover after her own failed affair with Gustave. His analysis of Erna's work, that 'her paintings are so good that if you didn't know better, you'd swear they were done by a man' is a comment made within the first few minutes of the action, and which strikes the key note around which the rest of the play resounds. Benedictsson, whose writing was exalted when published under a male pseudonym and dismissed when released under her own, would have been all too appreciative of the struggle facing female artists.

14

Summer
by Edward Bond (*b.* 1934, UK)

First performed: National Theatre, London, 1982

Cast breakdown: 3f, 2m

Publisher: Methuen, in *Edward Bond Plays: 4*, 1992

Forty years ago, as a young woman living in an occupied Eastern European country, Marthe was rounded up in the street and held captive by German soldiers. For a day and a half she and other townswomen sat in a windowless hut and awaited the firing squad. An intervention from Xenia, the daughter of the wealthy family to which Marthe was a servant, saved her life and, while Marthe was able to return home, the neighbours she left behind her were shot. Now both women are in their sixties, Marthe owns the house in which she was once a servant and Xenia, exiled to the West after the war, visits every summer. But this summer, Marthe is dying. Having never reconciled what happened between them all those years ago, Marthe and Xenia must confront their feelings towards one another and the political events that have changed their world.

Summer is a striking play. An unflinching yet poetic account of human brutality, it is a provocative take on the legacy of war on civilian populations. Although set almost entirely on the sunny terrace of Marthe's home during a glorious summer, that terrace overlooks an island in the sea on which German occupiers once built an extermination camp, and in which Marthe once awaited her death. Now, having 'lived a second life for forty years', Marthe faces her end again, this time sitting in a sunlit spot and gazing out at the island and the sea that surrounds it. It is an island on which bodies were once piled so high that 'they had to be sealed up in caves and pushed down cracks', and a sea into which more corpses were thrown, only to wash up on the beach with each new tide. It is now a place where holidaymakers enjoy themselves; the bullet marks in the rocks merge in with the fossils and veins of quartz. In the sunshine, the blood that once soaked into the rocks can no longer be seen, but Marthe, Xenia and all who witnessed it remain captive to the memory. The wartime occupation of the town hangs over their lives, like a shadow that becomes darker and more clearly defined the brighter the sun shines.

First performed in 1982, *Summer* is a play in which the seismic social, political and cultural shifts that occurred across Eastern Europe in the twentieth century are brought vividly into focus through the experiences of just two generations. Often through extensive monologues, Bond conjures images of Xenia's comfortable, almost aristocratic pre-war existence, the horrors of the occupation years, and what the town has become today – a burgeoning holiday resort complete with hotels, discos and drunken tourists. Like much of Bond's work, *Summer* is concerned with social justice and the relationship between the proletariat and the ruling classes. Marthe and Xenia, once servant and mistress, now live very different lives to those they did prior to the war and the arrival of Communism. In peacetime, Xenia's family owned half the town – the banks, factories, farms and newspaper. They were known for their kindness towards their employees but, as Marthe says, 'factories and banks aren't run by kindness' and, in the face of their stranglehold on the town's wealth and resources, these crumbs of 'kindness' meant little to the people. After the war, Xenia's father was stripped of his property and sentenced to hard labour while she herself was forced to flee the country. Decades later, Xenia remains unable to understand why the townspeople felt anything other than gratitude towards her father. It is a bewilderment matched by her inability to grasp why Marthe's response to the life-saving intervention she once performed is ambiguous to say the least.

Bond accompanies the script with several poems which give an eloquent insight into his thinking behind the play. The first of these, itself called *Summer*, starts with the lines:

> I wanted to show how ordinary people lived
> Married gave birth ate had holidays
> And died
> But clearly ordinary lives are strange

Indeed what the play captures so starkly is the way that ordinary lives become strange once lived during war. It examines how, even in peacetime, after the appearance of ordinariness has returned, scars remain and horrors can never be wiped from the memories of those who have seen them. But it is also a strong social commentary on the opportunity that extraordinary political events give us to reassess how we live alongside one another, and the perils that await us if we do not. As the poem concludes:

> Here is a simple story
> Of war and its aftermath
> Which shows that as we live in history
> We cannot learn to bear the unbearable but seek justice
> And praises to those who share the earth

15

The Jewish Wife (Die Jüdische Frau)
by Bertolt Brecht (*b*. 1898, Germany)

First performed: as part of *99%*, Salle d'Iéna, Paris, 1938

Cast breakdown: 1f, 1m

Recommended version: by John Willett

Publisher: Methuen, in *Fear and Misery of the Third Reich*, 2002

Frankfurt, 1935, and Judith Keith is packing. Methodically she fills a suit-case, occasionally returning an item to its original place in order to fit another one in instead. Her packing done, she makes a series of phone calls to friends and relations – she's going away for a while, a short trip to Amsterdam, nothing important, just a change of scenery and the chance to see some new faces. Then, her conversations concluded, she carefully sets light to the book from which she took the telephone numbers. Pacing the room she rehearses the possible ways she will tell her husband that she is going away. But when Fritz, a Gentile, arrives home, his Jewish wife finds it difficult to put her intention into words.

The Jewish Wife is one of the twenty-four sketches Brecht compiled for his montage piece *Fear and Misery of the Third Reich*, although it has a history of being performed as a short but stand-alone piece in its own right. It was one of the first *Fear and Misery* vignettes that Brecht wrote and it is widely believed he penned it in the summer of 1937. By that time he had already been in exile for several years himself, having fled Germany upon Hitler's appointment as Chancellor in 1933, and his simple but deeply affecting depiction of a woman preparing to leave her life behind is a remarkable and highly personal piece of work. It was originally performed in Paris in 1938 alongside four other plays that would eventually form part of *Fear and Misery* under the collective title *99%*, a reference to the proportion of the German population that had supported Hitler in the vote of March 1936.

Despite its brevity and simplicity, *The Jewish Wife* is perhaps one of Brecht's most humane and moving dramas. The seemingly innocuous opening image of a woman packing a suitcase, becomes redolent of the persecution of millions when the audience realises why it is that Judith is going away. Her false levity and the pretend nonchalance she assumes on the telephone while reassuring various friends that she is merely taking a little holiday out of the country for a matter of weeks, gives way to a far more truthful expression of her despair as she paces around the empty room, rehearsing the speech with which she will inform Fritz of her departure. It's not fair, she proposes to tell him, that he should be treated with contempt by their neighbours and dropped by their friends, that his position at work should be placed under threat and that he should endure endless sleepless nights of worry, simply because he is married to a Jew. And while it is not fair on her either that she should have to leave, now that increasingly anti-Semitic sentiments have started falling from his mouth, what else is she to do? In the devastating final moments of the play, when Fritz arrives home to their apartment, Judith's honesty deserts her. Husband and wife play-act their way through a conversation in which they both pretend she will only be gone for two or three weeks. The final image – that of Fritz passing Judith the fur coat she will not need for months to come – belies his knowledge that her absence is not the temporary one they have both been pretending it is. It's a sobering moment, the rupture between this once entwined Jew and Gentile symbolic of the much bigger chasm being driven through German society. It is made all the more terrible by the fact that Fritz has made no effort to stop his wife leaving.

Written prior to the outbreak of the Second World War and several years before the scale of the Nazi's campaign to annihilate the Jews became known, it's a play that is, of course, all the more poignant to post-war audiences given our knowledge of what awaits Judith, Fritz and their fellow Germans. A tiny play with a lot to say, *The Jewish Wife* is a fascinating contemporary document of life under the early days of the Third Reich and an enduring portrait of the crushing effects of political persecution on individual lives.

First performed: National Theatre, London, 2010

Cast breakdown: 15f, 11m (doubling possible)

Publisher: Faber and Faber, 2010

Thebes has been savaged by a brutal civil war. Now, taking tentative steps towards peace and having held its first democratic elections, the country has selected Eurydice to be its new President. Along with her mainly female government, Eurydice is about to be sworn in, an event attended by Theseus, First Citizen of Athens, who is keen to take the opportunity to import his particular brand of civilisation, democracy and economic development to the ravaged state. But as the diplomatic visit continues, things do not go well; former warlord Tydeus is threatening a coup, there is unrest on the streets, a blind seer presages disaster and Theseus has his own problems – back home his wife Phaedra is refusing to return his calls and now his son has gone AWOL from barracks. Plus Eurydice and her ministers are hardly taking the cap-in-hand attitude that he'd been expecting. But it is when Eurydice's niece Antigone disobeys the new President's orders and gives burial rites to her deceased brother, that the already perilous peace in Thebes reaches breaking point. Eurydice must employ a nerve of steel and the courage of her convictions to maintain her grasp on power.

Set in 'a city named Thebes, somewhere in the twenty-first century', *Welcome to Thebes* is a very modern reimagining of the legends of antiquity. In Moira Buffini's version of the story, King Creon – usually its central figure – is absent, killed in the war, a war in which his widow Eurydice had been working at the forefront of a grass-roots movement of women demanding peace. These women reportedly placed themselves in the line of fire, barricaded the men inside during peace talks, and 'shamed them into peace'. Now they make up the new government and Eurydice is their leader. In her programme notes for the play's 2010 National Theatre premiere, Buffini commented that, in her retelling of the story of Thebes and the relocation of Eurydice to its heart, she wanted to 'give an almost mute character a voice. I replaced a male autocrat with a female democrat'.

Written shortly after the election of Ellen Johnson Sirleaf, President of Liberia, and Africa's first female elected head of state, *Welcome to Thebes* explores the opportunities and challenges faced by a female-led government, particularly one reconfiguring a country after a violent crisis of a very male nature. While exploring gender and politics, Buffini goes beyond this to query how differently power, civilisation and society could look if traditional forms of governance were to be complemented with new models, and she uses Greek legends as the framework within which to embark on this. 'The very point of myths is that they are immutable,' she comments, 'but politics are all about transforming things. In plays, we can explore possibilities. How can the unchangeable begin to change?'

Muscular, passionate and arresting, *Welcome to Thebes* is certainly not a play in which the audience is permitted to sit back and let the action wash over them. It opens with the arrival of three soldiers, one of them just thirteen years old, who burst into the auditorium, barking orders at the audience to switch off mobile phones ('all of you make sure those fuckers don't go off'), stop reading their programmes ('put the booklets down. Don't read that shit') and not even think about getting up for a loo trip ('anyone who wants the toilet I don't care. You missed your chance'). The soldiers welcome us to Thebes, setting the scene and leaving us in absolutely no doubt as to the hellish nature of the country in which we have arrived. They talk of large-scale gang rape and mass slaughters, of children being pulled from schools, given guns and made to fight, of starvation, fighting in the forests, and mines that explode underfoot so 'you become a rain of meat'. Into this savage and infrastructure-less landscape, Theseus, his entourage of aides, security staff, their mobile phones, bottled water and paperwork arrive to dispense wisdom (and secure their own economic stake) in the rebuilding of the shattered land.

In Buffini's characteristic style, the play is rich in wit, irony and subtly subversive humour. 'I have the honour of holding the purse strings of a bankrupt state,' the Minister of Finance informs Theseus. 'I've explored the lining of this purse in case a coin or two is hiding there but all I've found is fluff and old receipts,' she continues, before handing him a cheque for the latest instalment of interest on the debts her bankrupted nation owes to flourishing Athens. A large-scale, deeply affecting, five-act epic on the horrors of war and the paradoxes of power, *Welcome to Thebes* is a play that takes no prisoners and yet in precise detail counts the cost of war on human lives. It is ambitious, urgent, and arguably one of the most important political plays of recent years.

17 Di and Viv and Rose
by Amelia Bullmore (b. 1964, UK)

First performed: Hampstead Theatre, London, 2011

Cast breakdown: 3f

Publisher: Methuen, 2011

It's 1983, and Di and Viv and Rose have all just started at the same university. They move into a house that Rose's stepdad has bought as an investment and set about making it their home, enjoying their first taste of what it is to be adults and free from parents. Initially life seems good; all dancing around the kitchen to Prince, drinking cider and going on dates. But a couple of wake-up calls lie in store for the trio, and suddenly things are no longer carefree. As the action swings forward to show snapshots of Di, Viv and Rose four, fifteen, sixteen and finally twenty-seven years after they first meet, it emerges how the relationships, experiences and decisions of that time will play a crucial role in their future lives, both together and apart.

Amelia Bullmore captures with tenderness, steely humour and a laser-like accuracy the experience of being a young person leaving home and setting off to university for the first time. Eighteen-year-old Di, Viv and Rose are excited, full of trepidation, but free. Finding themselves away from the towns and villages of their childhoods, the girls set about reinventing themselves. Everything is up for grabs and suddenly what they wear, how they talk, what they eat and with whom they sleep are all pointed acts of identity. University opens up a whole new world of possibilities, and away from the gaze of their parents and the ties of their youth, each girl can do things and be things she couldn't at home. Di can have relationships with other women, Viv can transcend the class and gender barriers that she feels curtailed her mother's ambition, and Rose can sleep with boys, lots of boys, and hopefully find some of the affection she so desperately craves along the way.

By whizzing the action forward beyond their first term at university and into future years (the second half of the action takes place at various moments between 1986 and 2010), Bullmore demonstrates potently how formative this early time together has been in defining who Di, Viv and

Rose ultimately become. Providing her audience with flashpoints through which it can catch glimpses of the trio's unfolding lives, Bullmore skilfully compacts three decades of their friendship into fleeting scenes while subtly alluding to the resonance that the experiences of adolescence continue to have years down the line. In particular she explores how powerfully the friends of our youth shape the adults we become and, although initially thrown together through the coincidence of being placed in the same student accommodation and, ostensibly at least, with little in common, Di, Viv and Rose grow to be an intrinsic and vital force in one another's lives. 'I used to think growing up together meant you just happened to shoot upwards alongside certain people,' thirty-four-year-old Di reflects on her relationship with the other two, 'but now I think the way you shoot up, the shape you shoot up in – is contingent on a few people shooting up with you.' Bullmore demonstrates how, in a friendship as close, as strong and ultimately as enduring as that between Di, Viv and Rose, what happens to one happens to all. The triumphs and tragedies each woman experiences automatically impact – directly or obliquely, visibly or nearly imperceptibly – on the other two and their trajectories, as Bullmore shows, are so entangled as to be practically fused into one.

Di and Viv and Rose opened in Hampstead Theatre's studio space in 2011 before becoming the first ever play to transfer to its main house, with a revival of the original production opening in January 2013. Both a bittersweet tale about the loss of innocence and an ode to friendship, it's a deeply moving but never sentimental piece. Its depiction of the relationship between the women is far from rose-tinted; they hurt, judge and attack one another as much as they protect, inspire and love, and for every moment of warmth, humour or shared joy between the three there is one of painful miscommunication, selfishness or pride. It's a play that will make an audience laugh, make it wince and most probably shed a tear or two. Like the best of friendships, it is rich, funny, honest and encompasses both the good times and the bad.

The Witlings
by Frances Burney (*b*. 1752, UK)

First performed: private reading, Burney family home, 1779

Cast breakdown: 10f, 7m (doubling possible)

Publisher: Broadview Literary Texts, 1999

Lady Smatter presides over the Esprit Party, a collection of wealthy yet buffoon-like individuals who, fancying themselves as Wits of their day, meet regularly in her home for a literary salon. Categorising themselves as either 'artists' or 'critics', the former offer up their latest writings for the delectation of the group, while the latter pour forth on the errors of those outside their hallowed company. Shakespeare, Swift, Pope, Prior, Dryden, none are safe from the harsh criticisms of the Esprits, and the group whiles away many a self-satisfied hour in discussing the merits of their own artistic endeavours. Their peaceful proceedings are interrupted when Lady Smatter's nephew and heir Beaumont discovers that his fiancée Cecilia has lost her fortune and is in fact destitute. Having no truck with the prospect of such a mismatched marriage, Lady Smatter does her utmost to separate the young lovers. But, unbeknownst to her, it is her own literary pretentions that will ultimately stand in her way.

Frances Burney is celebrated as a notable novelist of the eighteenth century, and yet remains lesser known for her dramas. *The Witlings* was her first play, and was penned in response to the encouragement of several leading contemporary figures including Richard Brinsley Sheridan, Samuel Johnson, Joshua Reynolds and Hester Thrale. Yet the play never saw public performance during Burney's lifetime, nor indeed for more than a hundred and fifty years after her death. An early draft received an informal, private reading at her family's home in August 1779, where by all accounts it received great praise. But despite this, Burney's father and their family friend Samuel Crisp (referred to by Burney as her two 'daddies' in her correspondence of the time) advised her to suppress the play for fear of offending the Bluestockings, a contemporary circle of influential, salon-loving intellectuals. Although she went on to further revise *The Witlings*, Burney was eventually persuaded to give up on it. She went on to spend five years working as Keeper of the Robes to Queen Charlotte, placing her in the Royal Court during the period of the madness of George III, and continued to write novels and plays during this time and after, although only one of these, *Edwy and Elgiva* (1795), was performed publically. Staged at Drury Lane it was withdrawn after one performance and, although later plays *Love and Fashion* (1798), *The Woman-Hater* (1802) and *A Busy Day* (1802) were all intended for production at Covent Garden, none were actually staged. It wasn't until the 1990s that interest in the performance of Burney's plays, as opposed to study for literary or academic purposes, was reignited and her fantastically entertaining, savagely satirical works finally began to find the audiences that they so richly deserved.

In the members of the Esprit Party and their associated servants, family members and acquaintances, Burney creates a cavalcade of larger-than-life characters who all contribute to the mixture of folly, conceit and nonsense that provide the driving energy of this ferociously funny play. Burney is merciless in her attack on the idleness, stupidity and egotism of her upper-class characters, and the gossiping, scraping, two-facedness of the social climbers who surround them. Admittedly, the plotline surrounding Cecilia and Beaumont is less enthralling than the affairs of the Esprits, but it provides a dramatic through-line to the piece along with the standard helpings of double-dealing, intrigue and ingenious plots to either separate or reunite young lovers that are characteristic of works of the period.

Written in five acts, the play could perhaps benefit from some judicious cutting, not just to compress the action, but also to remove some of the contemporary comic references likely to be lost on a modern audience. Even after such trims, *The Witlings* contains masses to delight audiences and, over two centuries after the play's creation, Burney's writing continues to sparkle, while demonstrating the timeless and universal comic potential of lampooning those who aspire to celebrity through appointing themselves arbiters of artistic excellence. Lady Smatter, along with her Esprit companions Mrs Sapient, Mr Dabler, Mr Codger and Mrs Voluble, all have their modern equivalents both inside and outside the arts world, and it's a play that pokes fun at the pretentions and preoccupations of anyone who engages in artistic endeavours with the goal of being esteemed by the public, rather than for purposes of personal enjoyment or enrichment. 'I declare, if my pursuits were not made public, I should not have any of it,' Lady Smatter tells Cecilia, 'for where can be the pleasure of reading books, and studying authors, if one is not to have the credit of talking of them?' Casting a sceptical eye over those who would be the gatekeepers of art for the attainment of celebrity, *The Witlings* remains a stinging rebuke to fools, snobs and self-aggrandising egotists everywhere.

First performed: Le Casa de Cultura, Miajadas, 2002

Cast breakdown: 5f

Recommended version: by Robert Shaw

Publisher: Oberon Books, 2005

Months into the military coup in Chile, and all over people are being 'disappeared'. Some eventually return home with reports of torture and the scars to prove it. Others are never seen again, their families left to mourn with no body to bury or any idea of what has happened to their loved one. Fermín Cabal's arresting *Tejas Verdes* is inspired by real stories of life under the gruesome early months of the Pinochet regime. Consisting of seven monologues spoken by five actresses, the play offers varying perspectives on the disappearance of a fictional young woman from Santiago. 'The Disappeared', 'The Friend/Informer', 'The Doctor', 'The Gravedigger' and 'The Spanish Lawyer' offer competing views in this impassioned, dignified and powerful piece of work.

'We don't allow ourselves to hear. If we could, life would be unbearable.' With this sentiment, an audience is welcomed into *Tejas Verdes*, Fermín Cabal's disturbing and important window into one of the darkest episodes in Chile's recent bloody history. Tejas Verdes (which roughly translates in English into 'Green Gables') was an upmarket hotel in a Santiago holiday resort. Following the coup by General Augusto Pinochet in 1973, it was requisitioned by the Chilean Army, who turned it into a detention centre. There, detainees would be taken into what used to be the music room and those who failed to reveal the desired information, or who refused to inform on friends, acquaintances and family members, were tortured. Basing his work on the accounts of surviving Tejas Verdes prisoners, Cabal opens the play with a prolonged and graphic description of the torture endured within its walls. It's far from easy listening, but is a powerful introduction to this most bracing and politically charged of dramatic responses to the Pinochet regime.

An estimated three thousand people disappeared under Pinochet but Cabal focuses on just one, a fictional character he names Colorina, whose story could be based on that of any number of disappeared young people. Colorina is middle-class, university-educated, and has a mother and sister who love her. She's been a volunteer worker in some of Santiago's poorest areas and has plans to travel south. But she also has had the misfortune of falling in love with Miguel, a militant Marxist involved in the Revolutionary Left Movement (MIR) and, as a consequence, has attracted the attention of the security forces. Imprisoned in Tejas Verdes, she is brutally tortured and finally killed, her body dumped in the sea. Now, described by Cabal as a 'Soul in Torment', she can only watch from afar as her mother weeps daily for her. She knows that the charred remains her mother mourns over are not hers, but belong to another girl, accidentally taken to be Colorina in a case of mistaken identity. But, as far as Colorina is concerned, her mother's ignorance over the remains proves better than the alternative, for if she 'didn't believe she had found them she would still be as desperate as so many women, so many mothers, searching for a body receding further and further into the distance'.

By offering five perspectives on the same event, Cabal keeps his audience's wits, and sympathies, constantly on the move. As soon as we feel we have a handle on what happened to Colorina and why, the parameters shift once more and our expectations and assumptions are thrown into the unknown. It's a dark and disorientating world that Cabal takes us into, one in which humanity appears to have been so vilely abused that normal concepts of what is right and wrong feel increasingly difficult to defend. When we learn that The Friend who comforted Colorina in Tejas Verdes was actually the person who informed on her, it is a complicated moment for us to comprehend. As The Friend then reveals that it was the sound of her small son's fingers being crushed in a nutcracker that made her betray Colorina, our moral gauge goes into free fall. What, we cannot help but ask ourselves, would we have done in her situation? But perhaps most troubling of all is The Spanish Lawyer who, speaking to the audience as if journalists at a press conference, defends her client General Pinochet, 'a poor, sick, tired, old man'. And that's before we even consider the motives of those states – Britain and the USA among them – who for so long enabled Pinochet to wreak such misery on his own people.

20　The Mai
by Marina Carr (b. 1964, Ireland)

First performed: Peacock Theatre, Dublin, 1994

Cast breakdown: 7f, 1m

Publisher: The Gallery Press, 1995

On the bank of Owl Lake, a woman who everyone simply refers to as 'The Mai', has built a magnificent house. Five years ago her husband Robert left and, scooping their children up along with what remained of her pride, The Mai took her family away from the town and to the solitude of the lake. Always certain that Robert would return, The Mai has built the house for him and now on its completion, as if by magic, he has appeared. The Mai is hoping they can pick up where they left off, but Robert's capacity to hurt her is greater than ever. It would seem that fate has other plans in store.

Marina Carr's haunting tragedy *The Mai* takes a tale of marital infidelity and explodes it into a drama of epic proportions. Celtic mythology, ghost stories and fairytales meld with the details of domestic life in 1970s rural Ireland to make a rich and arresting piece of work that bears the hallmark darkness and wild passion of Carr's writing. The legend of Owl Lake, so Carr tells us, revolves around Coillte, daughter of the mountain god who, discovering her lover's supposed unfaithfulness, wept so much that her tears formed a lake, in which she then drowned. Into this mournful landscape The Mai, herself bereft for the man who has abandoned her, brings her family, builds a house and waits for him to return. Told with a desolate beauty and steely humour, *The Mai* is a fierce and mysterious play from one of Ireland's most distinctive contemporary dramatic voices.

When the action begins it is the summer of 1979. The house is newly completed, Robert is back and The Mai is ecstatic. It is a happiness that is short-lived. By the second act it is 1980, Robert is preparing to leave once more, and this time The Mai isn't sure she'll survive. Millie, their daughter, remains omnipresent throughout the unfolding drama, a shadowy presence on the fringes of the stage, sometimes participating in scenes as her teenage self, and at others speaking directly to the audience as a grown woman in her capacity as narrator. Very much The Mai's story, Carr's choice to tell it in flashback through the eyes of her daughter, now a mother herself, reflects the play's preoccupation with the legacy of parents' actions on their children's lives. 'Our children are haunted,' The Mai warns Robert as he threatens to leave the family for a second time, and, indeed, even as an adult, Millie strives but fails to be free of the legacy of the house by the lake. Now, a mother to a child who was conceived during an extra-marital affair, Millie regales her son with tales of his absent father's dark eyes, but carefully omits the $5,000 cheque she received in return for seeking no further contact.

The play is composed with a dreamlike quality. Characters drift in and out of the action, there is cello music and dance, and time appears to be flexible and non-linear. Always surprising, *The Mai* features an unlikely mixture of influences and conceits woven expertly together; a fairytale set in a London hairdressing salon and stories of the Nine-Fingered Fisherman, the husband of The Mai's one-hundred-year-old, opium-pipe-puffing grandmother proving among the more unexpected threads in this most intriguing and unusual of dramatic tapestries. Like much of Carr's work, the play is influenced heavily by the constructs of Greek tragedy, and the idea that an irrefutable destiny awaits The Mai pulsates throughout. What ultimately makes her such an intriguing protagonist, though, is her collusion in her own destruction. Entirely alert to the damage that Robert can, and almost surely will, do to her, she refuses to let go. Doggedly pursuing a doomed relationship, she rushes headfirst and eyes open towards her own annihilation.

Cast breakdown: 12f, 8m (doubling possible)

Publisher: A.Warren, in *Playes Written by the Thrice Noble, Illustrious and Excellent Princess, the Lady Marchioness of Newcastle*, 1662 (available to read via the British Library)

The 'Sociable Virgins' are a group of intellectual young women who meet on a daily basis to discuss their views on the world. Disinterested in homemaking, marriage and breeding – the primary pursuits of their female contemporaries – the Sociable Virgins would rather spend their time engaging in rhetoric, political debate and the study of great works of literature. Despite their rebuttal of marriage, one of the Virgins sees an opportunity for an interesting domestic experiment when the recently widowed Monsieur Malateste starts casting his eye around for wife number two. Marrying him, and turning his household upside down in the process, she introduces him to an entirely new model of conjugal life.

'May your house be your hell, and your wife be your devil' is the parting shot which Nan, servant to Monsieur Malateste, delivers upon being thrown out by his new wife. Having driven the first Madame Malateste to an early grave by spending more time in Nan's bed than his own, Malteste is all but helpless as his startlingly proactive second wife rearranges his household to suit her tastes. Offering an unusual spin on gender relations, *The Unnatural Tragedy* is an impassioned and admittedly odd piece of work. It's fragmentary, is less than ideally structured, needs a hefty edit and, by the end, is pretty preposterous. And yet there's something to it that makes it worth reading. There's a fire to Cavendish's writing, a shrewd wit and the play, in a radical reinterpretation, contains material that deserves to be seen by modern audiences.

Alongside the Sociable Virgins and Malateste storyline runs the parallel plot – and one that seems to owe a debt to Ford's *'Tis Pity She's a Whore* – of the unfortunate Madame Soeur. Having not seen her brother, Monsieur Frere, since the two were children, he returns home after an extended period away, only to fall madly, and highly inappropriately, in love with her. Initially determined to keep his incestuous longings to himself, Frere eventually buckles and embarks on a campaign to win her acquiescence.

When it becomes evident that the virtuous Soeur is far from convinced, he contrives a plot to get everyone else out of the house and rapes her. He then stabs her to death before falling on his sword and the whole sorry affair ends with high drama as their father and Soeur's husband discover their corpses, the former 'falls down dead at the sight' while the latter 'tears his hair, and beats his breast, and being as distracted, rises hastily, and catches up the bloody sword to kill himself'. It's only the quick-thinking of his servants that prevent him from adding to the trio of corpses already littering the stage, although those who like their tragedies to end in a gore-fest will be relieved to hear there's more death to come when Frere's betrothed, Mademoiselle Armour, spontaneously perishes upon hearing news of his death.

Margaret Cavendish, Duchess of Newcastle, is an intriguing figure and one who, perplexingly, is often left out of histories of early female play-writing. Perhaps this omission is in part due to the breadth of her accomplishments in other fields, her better-known achievements as a scientist, poet, essayist and as one of the first writers of science fiction somewhat overshadowing her playwriting. Regardless, her collected plays were published in 1662 (under the somewhat grandiose title *Playes Written by the Thrice Noble, Illustrious and Excellent Princess, the Lady Marchioness of Newcastle*), a rare feat for a woman at the time, more unusual still given that her works were published under her own name, rather than a male nom de plume. Her position as an aristocrat and her possession of a husband who was clearly interested enough in his wife's literary pursuits to have her work published no doubt helped. However, the fact that Cavendish's plays have survived only leaves us to wonder how many other women were writing at the same time, perhaps seeing their plays performed in the privacy of their own homes, but without the means to have their works laid down for posterity. Yes, *The Unnatural Tragedy*, like Cavendish's other plays, is a somewhat zany piece of writing, but there's an energy to it that is undeniable. Taking a large pair of scissors to them may be the only way to stage her works today, but the oeuvre of this most intriguing of playwrights is certainly worth a look.

22

Top Girls
by Caryl Churchill (*b*. 1938, UK)

First performed: Royal Court Theatre, London, 1982

Cast breakdown: 16f (doubling possible)

Publisher: Methuen, 2008

Marlene is celebrating her promotion to managing director of the Top Girls employment agency. She hosts a dinner party which an eclectic mix of women from history and myth attend: Isabella Bird, a Victorian explorer; Lady Nijo, a thirteenth-century Japanese courtesan; Dull Gret, the subject of a Brueghel painting; Pope Joan, who, concealed as a man, is thought to have been Pope in the ninth century and gave birth on the way to her coronation; and Patient Griselda, a character from *The Canterbury Tales*. Post-dinner party, Marlene is back in the office. Her busy schedule is interrupted by Angie, her unprepossessing teenage niece who arrives unannounced and keen to chat. The final scene of the play skips back in time to a year earlier and to an encounter between Marlene and Angie that explains the teenager's subsequent visit.

The first scene of *Top Girls*, the fantastical dinner party in which various fictional and historical figures argue, discuss and laugh across their Waldorf salad, profiteroles and Frascati, is perhaps one of the most iconic in modern theatre. Besides the fascinating juxtaposition of the real and the imaginary, the past and the present, the scene is notable for Churchill's innovative structuring of dialogue in which characters constantly interrupt and speak across one another, denoted in the script through a vast quantity of slashes and asterisks. In doing so, Churchill authentically captures the rhythm and flow of a dinner party in which guests constantly break off into smaller conversations, talk at cross purposes, come back together as one, and then splinter off into subdivisions again. The result is a shrewdly observed and cynically funny depiction of that very worst kind of dinner party – one in which the guests spend far more time bringing the conversation around to themselves than they do listening to each other. The fact that the discussions roll back and forth between tales of life in mediaeval England, thirteenth-century Japan, Victorian Edinburgh and ninth-century Rome operates as an additional, quirky layer. Over the course of the meal, the group gets increasingly enmeshed in talk of those two dinner party taboos: religion and politics, between them exhibiting an irreconcilably wide range of theological, social and religious perspectives. Their backgrounds and opinions could not be more disparate, and yet they find themselves unwillingly united as victims of male subjugation.

Perhaps better than any play of its era, *Top Girls* dramatises the seismic shifts that occurred in the world of work at the tail end of the twentieth century. Evoking the aggressive individualism promoted by Margaret Thatcher upon her entry to office, *Top Girls* depicts a landscape in which competitiveness is the order of the day, and a job is no longer for life. Despite being younger and newer to the company than her colleague Howard, Marlene has pipped him to a promotion. No longer operating in a climate in which longevity and being male guarantee advancement, everything is up for grabs for the most capable and the less so will be left to fall by the wayside. For a high-flying, ambitious operator like Marlene, Thatcher's Britain is ideal. 'I think the eighties are going to be stupendous,' she tells her sister Joyce, 'I'm going up, up, up.' Joyce, a single parent living outside Ipswich and juggling four cleaning jobs, is not so convinced. A firm believer that 'anyone can do anything if they've got what it takes', Marlene epitomises the upwardly mobile, individualistic stance of Thatcher's world view, having transcended her working-class roots to enjoy a jet-setting lifestyle and transatlantic career. But Joyce, left behind in the sisters' childhood home and having dedicated her life to looking after Angie, the daughter Marlene abandoned, sees a very different future. Angie is on the cusp of leaving school but with no qualifications, little intelligence, and unemployment at three million, all that awaits her is the dole queue. Angie is not someone that Marlene's employment agency would look at twice. 'She's not going to make it,' Marlene's simple analysis of the sixteen-year-old's future is depressingly bleak in its finality.

Thanks to finding its way onto the A-Level Theatre Studies syllabus, *Top Girls* is perhaps the best-known English language play for an all-female cast. Somewhat a victim of its own success, and like a number of literary works now largely associated with exams and school work, just the mention of the play's name can incur a groan among those who have been introduced to it in this way. This is a shame because it is a remarkable piece of theatre, cutting edge in its day and still impressively powerful decades on. For all its humour and bite, watching or reading *Top Girls* is a sobering experience. A startlingly honest piece of social documenting, it is a benchmark against which to measure how much has changed for women since Marlene and co first sat down to dinner in 1982, and, depressingly, how little.

23

Three Women and a Piano Tuner
by Helen Cooper (b. 1954, UK)

First performed: Minerva Theatre, Chichester, 2004

Cast breakdown: 3f, 1m

Publisher: Nick Hern Books, 2004

Then: a young woman lies on a clinic bed, awaiting anaesthetic. A moment of decision: keep the child growing inside her; give birth and hand it over for adoption; or go through with the termination for which she is now being prepared. Which is the brave choice? Which the cowardly? And how will she ever again be fully herself once that decision has been made?

Now: Ella has written a piano concerto. She wants Liz to perform it and needs Beth's money to finance it. Three very different women, one shared set of memories, and an incredibly public performance. And then there's Harold, the young man who tunes the piano around which the women's dreams, fears, pasts and futures coalesce.

Three Women and a Piano Tuner is an extraordinary piece of writing. Lyrical, taut and infinitely moving, the play takes as its departure point 'Elizabeth', an eighteen-year-old who, at the point of deciding whether to keep an unplanned pregnancy, fractures and splits into three separate women; Ella who becomes the child's mother, Beth who gives him up for adoption, and Liz who has a termination. The three different choices made as a teenager send the three versions of Elizabeth spinning away from one another into vastly different lives and directions. Ella gave up her aspirations of a career in classical music and, instead, turned the child into her 'life's work'. Beth became a professional wife, caught in a passionless marriage to William and she now lunches, wears Prada, and prefaces most sentences with 'William says…' Liz has had the sparkling career and is a world-class pianist, revered, desired, and apparently unencumbered by family commitments. Aged around forty, the three reconvene for the first time in Ella's chilly kitchen, plan how to perform her concerto and, inevitably, compare how their lives have turned out against one another's.

While commenting on the often-fraught relationship between motherhood, creative fulfilment and career progression, Helen Cooper's perceptive play goes much further to take a highly original look at the crossroads we all encounter in life. With a playfulness that is combined with a deep poeticism, *Three Women and a Piano Tuner* examines how we become vastly different people simply as a consequence of electing to take one path over another. 'There are so many "might-have-beens" in everybody's life,' Liz comments, and while the play explores this principle it also looks into how, once paths have been chosen and decisions made, some of the 'might-have-beens' in our lives are left to wither and die, while others are preserved, fiercely and loyally, as a much-needed way of justifying the person we have become. Despite sharing one set of memories and eighteen years' worth of common experiences, Ella, Liz and Beth can't agree on many of them. Each woman has reserved the version of events that suits her, the one that justifies her present choices and allows her to defend who she is now. As Ella attempts to tell the story of their early life through her concerto, the three women's recollections of what happened, and how events should be interpreted, vary dramatically.

Despite the differing details in the three women's accounts of Elizabeth's life, what remains a constant is a sense of an unhappy, sinister and stifling home life. Oppressive family meals around an oblong table, a mother whose dreams 'were big and so the loss of them must have been big too', their father 'the man without ambition', a suicidal older sister, and dark family secrets appear to have characterised Elizabeth's youth. Snippets of childhood memories – the stalking of a stork, fish and chips eaten with ketchup, a trip to an island in a lake – are visited and revisited by the women, recurring stories that they interpret differently but which, motif-like, thread throughout the entire piece. In this way, the play itself is scored not unlike a piece of music, with sections of language, images, ideas, indeed even the characters themselves, serving as themes that recur and are varied throughout. Perpetually exploring the relationship between emotion, memory and music, the play concludes with a stage direction that calls for the appearance of a female orchestra made up of 'might-have-beens', a bizarre assemblage of 'hippies, hookers, hostesses, librarians, dykes, nuns, executives and Muslims in burkas'. It is a surreal image (and, admittedly, not a stage direction the original production of the play followed), yet, somehow, an entirely fitting crescendo to this most unusual, ambitious and arresting of plays.

First performed: Royal Court Theatre, London, 2000

Cast breakdown: 19f, 1m (doubling possible)

Publisher: Methuen, 2000

Prix is at the top of her game. Only sixteen and already she's managing a highly effective Bronx girl gang, masterminding their operations and earning the fear and respect of all around her. Sure, there's the odd spell in juvenile detention and a bit of unpleasant business to take care of along the way, but prison seems a million miles away and adulthood even further. And when it comes to making their way in the world, what alternatives do Prix and her 'sisters' have? As the years tick by and the crimes of her youth begin to catch up with her, Prix is forced to reconsider. But when life in a gang is all you've known, it's hard to turn your back and even harder to walk away.

Located in a world of food stamps, teenage pregnancy, unemployment and poor educational prospects, Corthron's violent and striking play is a provocative look at the suffocating effect of poverty on talent and drive. Living in the Bronx, Prix and her 'sisters' are just a short subway ride away from one of the world's biggest centres of wealth, culture, progress and opportunity, but Manhattan might as well be on the moon for all the benefit they get from it. Yet, despite the odds stacked against her, the sixteen-year-old Prix is an impressive figure. She's a member of the criminal underclass and not above authorising vicious attacks on even her closest friends, but her incisiveness, organisational skills, focus and raw charisma are attributes that in another teenager might have secured a top university place or bright career prospects. What makes *Breath, Boom* so tragic is its depiction of potential going unrecognised and unfulfilled. Implicit in Corthron's play at all times is the provocation: what could a young woman with Prix's demonstrable talents have achieved if only she had been born into a different life?

In some ways a piece about growing up, and in others a conventional 'rise and fall' tale, the play flashes through key moments in Prix's life between the ages of sixteen and thirty as we watch her ambition, confidence and capability gradually erode. Having reached her peak by her late teens, the only way is down, and by the end of the play, Prix is merely an echo of the assertive alpha female we first encounter. 'Ain't twenty-eight bit old for the gangs?' a cellmate asks when Prix, well past the prime of her criminal career and fast losing her nerve, has bungled a drugs delivery. Not knowing when to quit and developing a 'fuck-up habit' is not good and Prix's descent from queen bee to has-been is slow and painful to watch. In one particularly humiliating episode she is savagely beaten in a toilet cubicle by a group of teenagers from the juvenile wing, including Jupiter, whose christening Prix attended, having been a gang-mate and former friend of the girl's mother.

The play jolts from scene to scene in Prix's ever-darkening life, almost like the turning of pages in a scrapbook, the action rushing on from one bleak but formative episode to the next. For the actress playing Prix, this demands a carefully plotted physical and emotional journey as she gradually transforms before our eyes from a formidable teenager to a weather-beaten thirty-year-old. Although Prix's story forms the narrative through-line of the play, *Breath, Boom* is a large-cast piece populated by the friends, family, gang-members, fellow prisoners and correction officers who move in and out of her path. In any scene, the majority of the talking is done by these other characters and Prix rarely gives voice to her emotions or offers any kind of explanation for her extreme behaviour. Rather, the audience is left to draw their own conclusions as to why she does what she does. Not easy to like and yet almost impossible to condemn, Prix is a complex and troubling figure for us to be confronted by. Vicious, controlling, damaged and brilliant, *Breath, Boom*'s inimitable anti-heroine is likely to provoke ambivalence on the part of the audience, as will the trail of destruction she leaves behind.

First performed: Opera House, Manchester, 1941

Cast breakdown: 5f, 2m

Publisher: Methuen, in *Noël Coward Collected Plays: Four*, 1979

Charles Condomine is looking for material for his next book. He wants to write about a fake psychic, a 'real professional charlatan'. Both firmly sceptical of anything supernatural, he and his wife Ruth invite one such 'imposter', local medium Madame Arcati, to perform a séance in their home. Expecting nothing more than a bit of smoke and mirrors and finding the whole thing incredibly amusing, the Condomines are stunned when the seemingly hopeless Arcati succeeds in conjuring the ghost of Elvira, Charles's seven-year-deceased first wife. Deciding she is back to stay, Elvira merrily settles into her former home, rearranging the garden, criticising her successor's taste in soft furnishings and demanding outings to the local cinema. As the two Mrs Condomines vie for supremacy, it becomes increasingly clear that Elvira has set her sights on getting Charles back. Nothing – living or dead – is going to get in her way.

Subtitled 'An Improbable Farce', *Blithe Spirit* is a decidedly frothy look at death and the afterlife. One of Coward's most finely achieved comedies, the three-act play's humour is largely derived from the incredibly matter-of-fact way in which Coward drops the ghostly presence of Elvira into Ruth and Charles's cosy suburban existence. From the manner of her early death ('She was convalescing after pneumonia and one evening she started to laugh helplessly at one of the BBC musical programmes and died of a heart attack'), to her re-entry into the realm of the living (interrupted part-way through a game of backgammon with 'a very sweet, old Oriental man, I think his name was Genghis Khan'), Coward's depiction of Elvira is entirely unsentimental. There's no wafting, floating or sighing for this ghost, she's a full-blooded spirit who stomps around the house, has a penchant for throwing missiles and yet isn't adverse to a nice spot of flower arranging. Unable to be seen or heard by anyone other than Charles, she delights in getting him into all sorts of trouble and is routinely unimpressed by Madame Arcati's botched attempts to send her back to the afterlife. Faced with an enraptured Madame Arcati mystically stretching out her arms and asking 'are you happy, my dear?', Elvira's response is to stamp her foot and proclaim, 'Tell the silly old bitch to mind her own business!'

But, this being Coward, there is substance beneath the froth, and a depth of feeling discernible in the characters no matter how hard they try to hide it beneath their bons mots. The warring couple who can't live with one another but can't live without one another is a familiar vein through several of Coward's plays, but is given an additional emotional twist in *Blithe Spirit* by being extended beyond the grave and into the afterlife. When asked by an exasperated Ruth why she has come back from the other side, Elvira's reason is simple: 'because the power of Charles's love tugged and tugged and tugged at me.' Such a plainly structured sentence and sentiment stands out amid the whirl of witticisms, florid anecdotes and sparkling put-downs that characterise much of the play's language. It hints at a far deeper attachment between Charles and his first wife than he himself could ever admit to in words, and reveals an intensity of feeling he still carries for her years after their parting. While the play fully exploits the comic effects of Charles being made into 'a sort of astral bigamist', so too it plugs into much more potent emotional depths – the ecstasy, agony, irresistibility and ultimate impossibility of exhuming a long-dead love affair.

The play contains one of Coward's most vivid, idiosyncratic and best-loved creations, the indefatigable Madame Arcati. The stage directions for her initial appearance in the action – 'Madame Arcati enters. She is a striking woman, dressed not too extravagantly but with a decided bias towards the barbaric' – is an appropriately opaque comment with which Coward brings this most slippery of characters onto the stage. Madame Arcati is a mass of contradictions; enthralled with mysticism, likely to be spotted out and about in Indian robes on Midsummer's Eve and yet with the stoic, no nonsense vernacular of the English upper classes. The focal point of any scene in which she appears, with a fizzing energy and a delicious line in veiled compliments, it's easy to see why Arcati remains the role of choice for older leading actresses. Ruth, whose morbid fascination with Charles and Elvira's past relationship comes back to bite her, is a wonderful comic character whose every word and action is informed by a noxious blend of jealousy, egotism and insecurity. But it is Elvira who is the driving force behind the play's action, wreaking havoc and having a marvellous time terrorising everyone in the household, from her former husband down to the servants. It's a fantastically powerful role and one that sees the character alternately manipulate, charm and bulldoze her way through the play in an utterly single-minded attempt to get what she wants.

26 Attempts on Her Life
by Martin Crimp (*b.* 1956, UK)

First performed: Royal Court Theatre, London, 1997

Cast breakdown: unspecified – could be performed by a cast of any size and gender

Publisher: Faber and Faber, 2007

A constantly shifting kaleidoscope of genres, perspectives and narratives, Martin Crimp's structurally innovative *Attempts on Her Life* (*17 Scenarios for the Theatre*) is a piece that eludes easy definition. A collection of un-named, unidentified voices discuss, debate and narrate the experiences of 'Ann', an elusive figure on whose exact nature the speakers appear unable to agree. As the seventeen scenarios play out, Ann morphs from persona to persona, changing age, nationality, physicality and occupa-tion. Variously described as an international terrorist, particle physicist, mother of three, porn star, even a car, the play offers no single explana-tion of who or what Ann is, only (as declared in the lyrics of 'The Girl Next Door', one of the play's two songs) 'all the things that Ann can be'. Ricocheting between snappy scenes that reference the lingo of modern news reporting, advertising, light entertainment, cop shows and block-buster movies, *Attempts on Her Life* is a play evocative of a media-saturated, information-overloaded world.

Depending on how you look at it, *Attempts on Her Life* is either a dream or a nightmare to stage. An incredibly 'free' piece, the script contains few stage directions and little information regarding where or when the play is set, who the people on the stage are, why they are discussing 'Ann', or what their relationship with her is. The only suggestion Crimp makes regarding casting is that 'this is a piece for a company of actors whose composition should reflect the composition of the world beyond the theatre', and it's a play that could just as easily be performed by four actors as forty. Lines of dialogue are not assigned to specific characters; rather a simple dash on the page indicates a change of speaker.

Although no linear narrative links the seventeen sections of Crimp's text, the play is perhaps not unlike a music score, with themes that are established, developed and then subject to variation. Motifs are abundant, whether thematic, visual, or expressed in certain words and phrases that pop up relentlessly across the scenarios. A strong sense of symmetry is at work, with the two halves of the play rough mirror images of one another – in each half there is a song, a scene spoken in a foreign language and translated into English, a scene located in a landscape devastated by civil war and a number of other echoes and resonances.

Key to an appreciation of *Attempts on Her Life* is the understanding that it is not a play in which the audience is *shown* a story, but rather one in which they are *told* a story. Dramatic events are not enacted on stage, but are described by the collection of speakers Crimp has created. We never actually get to see Ann, we only hear varying accounts of what she's like, and the drama of the piece comes not from the revelation of who Ann is, but from the conflicts that emerge in the various tellings of her story. Crimp prefaces the text with a quote from French cultural commentator and philosopher Jean Baudrillard: 'No one will have directly experienced the actual course of such happenings, but everyone will have received an image of them.' In many ways, what Ann is, is not the point – how she is represented is.

Appropriately for a play that captures the helter-skelter multiple narratives of contemporary life, *Attempts on Her Life* is not one way of telling a story, but seventeen. Its analysis of consumer culture, global capitalism, media, communications, war, violence and depictions of women is in turn funny, outrageous, sobering and downright depressing. The play zooms from continent to continent, takes in various political ideologies along the way and is perhaps something like the experience of flicking through channels on a TV set at high speed. Ann is just as likely to be found driving a tank as running a country pub, posing for the cover of *Vogue*, or planting bombs in shopping centres. She is a victim of war, the reason for war, a consumer, a commodity, a politician and a pin-up. She is everywoman and no woman. When I interviewed Crimp in 2007, I asked him what qualities a director of *Attempts on Her Life* should possess. He paused for a moment before replying 'a sense of humour. A sense of irony. A sense of despair. Those are the things that are required.'

First performed: Royal Court Theatre, London, 1986

Cast breakdown: 14f, 5m (doubling possible)

Publisher: Methuen, in *Sarah Daniels: Plays 1*, 1991

While Civil War rumbles on across England, the female inhabitants of an Essex village have their own, more pressing battle at hand. The Pricker, a man charged with identifying and arresting witches, is in the area and very much at large. No woman is safe from his accusatory attentions, nor the gruesome end that his suspicions almost certainly guarantee. Childlessness, spinsterhood, outspokenness, physical blemishes, old age; anything and everything can be used as evidence of a woman's collusion with the Devil. And, after all, given that women are descended from Eve, the originator of all human sin, how much more evidence is needed? Seventeen-year-old Rose and her friends can no longer bear the threat of a ducking in the local pond. They make a pact to stand up, either by covert or direct means, to the terror facing them.

'Certainly sad to say 'twas better when we was all Catholics' is an observation made by Grace, the seventy-year-old wise woman of Rose's village, 'at least the Virgin Mary was sacred. There's not a good word to be said about Eve.' Grace has every reason to look back on the past with reluctant warmth. Change is marching side by side with Cromwell's armies through the counties of England and, for Rose, Grace and their female neighbours, the knock-on effects are far from pleasant. There's a new drive for public purity and pamphlets that have recently appeared are condemning all womankind for innate wickedness and their sinful bodies; just one indicator of a growing misogyny. Although the women in the play dismiss the pamphlets as offering 'more truth of the writers' blighted minds than of women's nature,' the increasing suspicion around them – that they are all fixated on running amok with the country's morals – is having a pronounced effect on their already fragile sense of liberty. In this intensifying climate of fear and hostility, the conditions are ripe for a large-scale witch-hunt.

Pertinent to the potency of Daniels' sprawling and fiercely perceptive play is her choice to locate it at a moment in history when women's freedoms were beginning to be eroded (admittedly beyond their already limited state), rather than in the period *after* that erosion had already taken place. In particular, she focuses on the shift that occurred in the seventeenth century over control of female reproductive health and, in particular, the manner by which childbirth was conducted. Whereas women such as Grace, who acted as self-appointed midwives and were proponents of natural plant-based medicines, had traditionally cared for women before and during birth, in the seventeenth century this began to change. A relatively new invention – the doctor – had arrived on the scene, and with him he brought forceps, a medical innovation trumpeted by the medical profession, but with an often less than desirable effect on the health of women. Given that women were barred from training as doctors, and knowledge of natural medicines was jumped upon as evidence of witchery, the shift to the control of women's health from female to male hands was swift, decisive and, as Daniels suggests, something that lingers on centuries later.

One of the leading British playwrights of the 1980s, Daniels placed contemporary feminist debate imaginatively, humorously but uncompromisingly on stage. When feminism became a somewhat taboo subject in the theatre programming of the later 1990s and the 2000s, so too unfortunately did Daniels' work, and opportunities to see revivals of her plays, and in particular her earlier plays, became increasingly rare. While it remains unusual to find her work programmed in theatres (although the female-heavy nature of many of her plays means she continues to have a healthy following in university drama departments), with the recent emergence of a new generation of playwrights – E V Crowe, Sam Holcroft, Lucy Kirkwood, Duncan Macmillan and Penelope Skinner among them – who are keen to write about issues of gender and engage in feminist arguments, a renewed interest among theatre audiences in trailblazer Daniels' work feels timely. Always prepared to be outspoken whilst writing bloody good plays in the process, Daniels placed an anger and a passion at the heart of her work that will continue to resonate with anyone who wants to live in a fairer and more equitable world.

28

Playhouse Creatures
by April De Angelis (b. 1960, UK)

First performed: Sphinx Theatre Company at the Haymarket Theatre Studio, Leicester, 1993

Cast breakdown: 5f (see note at the bottom of this entry regarding a later version written for 6f, 2m)

Publisher: Samuel French, 1994

Young Nell Gwyn dreams of a life on the stage. It beats selling oranges for a living, and now that women are allowed to act professionally, why shouldn't she carve a career for herself as an actress? She can't remember her lines or speak clearly, but she's great at a jig and, when it comes to flashing her ankles, is more than willing to oblige. With the King cheering her on from the audience, what can possibly stand in Nell's way? Inspired by the experiences of the first English actresses, April De Angelis's *Playhouse Creatures* is an affectionate but unsentimental imagining of the onstage and offstage lives of Nell Gwyn and her contemporaries.

Steeped in theatre history, dramatically playful and constantly giving the audience a knowing wink, *Playhouse Creatures* is a real theatre-lover's play. Although certainly not averse to focusing on the seedier aspects of the industry, the play is in many ways a celebration of theatres, particularly their spirit, resilience and dogged determination, often against the odds, to play a role in popular consciousness. 'Not so long back they burnt these places to the ground and pissed on the ashes,' Doll Common, one of Nell's fellow actresses and a sort of narrator figure in the play, tells the audience, 'they swore they'd seen the last of them. But they sprung up again. Like mushrooms.' Set around 1670 and not long after the playhouses of London began reopening their doors after nearly twenty years of closure during the interregnum, the play takes place at a moment in which theatre was bouncing back, experiencing a new surge of energy. De Angelis focuses on the women who carved a place for themselves at the heart of this resurgence.

Funny, poignant and spikily subversive, *Playhouse Creatures* illustrates with suitable levels of theatrical aplomb the double-edged sword that legalisation offered to the earliest English actresses. While Nell and her fellows are pioneers, the first women allowed to earn a living on the stage, navigating this new territory is far from straightforward. 'Actresses' they may be, but audiences don't seem particularly interested in their acting ability. Rather, baring ankles, legs and even the occasional breast (how could a play about the Amazons be complete without them?) and bestowing sexual favours on the aristocracy are the greatest determinants of how an actress's career will develop. Hence it is the attractive sixteen-year-old Nell who enjoys a stratospheric rise to the top, while middle-aged Mrs Betterton is unceremoniously dumped by the theatre company to which she has dedicated her life. Of course, Mrs Betterton's predicament – finding herself in her fifties and facing a dearth of roles she can (or perhaps more importantly, would want) to play – is one not unfamiliar to actresses today. Indeed, De Angelis depicts these early actresses facing similar hurdles to those often encountered by their modern descendants. A lack of decent roles, sexual harassment in the workplace, low pay and lack of autonomy over creative decisions characterise Nell and her fellows' working lives. It's no coincidence that the play was commissioned and originally produced by Sphinx – formerly the Women's Theatre Group – which since the early 1970s has been seeking to highlight the comparative lack of creative opportunity offered to women in the theatre.

Having started out as an actress herself, De Angelis may not have been entirely unfamiliar with the trials and tribulations experienced by the women of *Playhouse Creatures*. She made the move into writing in 1989 with her first play *Ironmistress* (2f), an exploration of the relationship between women and power in the face of industrialisation. Since then she has gone on to write a proliferation of plays that feature strong, complex and, above all, funny roles for women of all ages. Having had her work produced with impressive frequency by companies such as the National Theatre, Out of Joint, the Royal Court and Hampstead Theatre, as well as in the commercial West End, De Angelis has become one of the most visible and enduring British female playwrights of the past twenty years.

A revised version of *Playhouse Creatures* was written by De Angelis in 1997. Conceived for London's Old Vic, it expanded the cast to 6f, 2m and adapted the original script (intended for performance in studio spaces) into a piece large enough to play on a main-house stage. This version is published by Faber and Faber in *April De Angelis: Plays* (1999).

29 The Woman in the Window
by Alma De Groen (*b.* 1941, New Zealand)

First performed: Melbourne Theatre Company at The Fairfax, Victorian Arts Centre, Melbourne, 1998

Cast breakdown: 7f, 5m (doubling possible)

Publisher: Currency Press, 1999

Constantly flipping back and forth between 1951 and 2300, *The Woman in the Window* is a fantastical account of a relationship between two women, one real and one fictional, both living in surveillance states but separated by continents, political ideologies and hundreds of years. The poet Anna Akhmatova (1889–1966) languishes in Cold War Russia. She is forbidden from writing poetry (except in praise of Stalin), watched by the authorities, informed on by her neighbours, and forced to witness those close to her being arrested and dispatched one by one. Rachel lives in 2300 in Australia, a stultifying dystopian future in which technology has evolved to the point where it can analyse whether a person's smile evokes authentic joy, or is merely the performance of pleasure. As Rachel begins to question her world, a mysterious bond forms between her and Akhmatova across the boundaries of time and space. Akhmatova helps Rachel understand how poetry – long-since forgotten and dismissed in the latter's futuristic world as non-profitable and hence non-useful – can be a powerful but dangerously galvanising influence on the human soul.

Anna Akhmatova was a writer the Soviet Government perceived as a threat. Her writing had been lauded for rousing the spirits of the Russian people during the dark days of the Second World War but, fearful that the influence of her poetry on the nation's psyche may not prove so useful during the Cold War, the Government placed Akhmatova under a weird kind of house arrest. She was ordered to appear at her window for MGB officers in the morning and evening, and was forbidden from writing her own verse. In De Groen's highly unusual and at times thrillingly unpredictable imagining of the great writer's incarceration, she pairs Akhmatova's trajectory with that of Rachel, a fictional young woman living in the far future. When Rachel exhibits worrying signs that she has started to 'feel things' after being introduced to the work of John Milton, Gerard Manley Hopkins and Henry Newbolt, she too becomes something of a renegade figure in the eyes of the authorities.

De Groen's play explores the power of art. It celebrates its boundless capacity for expressing the infinitude of the human experience, but also highlights its subversive qualities. Embracing art as a medium through which to reflect upon the world truthfully and freely is far from de rigueur in the environments in which Akhmatova and Rachel find themselves, and the women's respective attempts to do so are met with responses that are far from encouraging. 'Comrade Stalin tells us life must be depicted as it should be, not as it is,' is a sentiment expressed by a MGB agent to Akhmatova while he ransacks her one-room home for contraband literature. Indeed, her poetry having been considered too likely to describe life 'as it is', she is ordered to limit her creativity to translating the work of a list of writers personally approved by Stalin, a process she dryly describes 'like eating one's own brain'. By 2300, poets aren't even the translators of work, let alone its creators. Instead, 'poet' is the term given to someone who excavates poems from online literary archives. Even this weak link to poems of the past is under threat as the Government decides to 'de-list' poets and delete the literary archives for not being economically viable. When ninety per cent of the population spends the majority of its time almost permanently plugged into anaesthetising virtual reality games, who needs poetry? As Sandor, Rachel's 'poet' friend who awakens her interest in the form, states, 'my parents wanted me to create games so I'd always have a job – I didn't have enough imagination. I became a poet instead.'

The Woman in the Window is fragmentary in structure, a series of detailed but brief scenes gliding one into the next, sometimes overlapping, sometimes occurring concurrently, reflecting perhaps the experience of being on the internet. It's a piece that presents a tantalising challenge to a director and design team, and demands a thoughtful approach to its staging, with the play's two strands of Cold War Russia and futuristic Australia dancing an unlikely duet. A play that makes bold statements, while maintaining a dreamlike feel, *The Woman in the Window* is an engaging reflection on the interplay between art, humanity and technology.

First performed: Hip Pocket Theatre, Fort Worth, Texas, 1987

Cast breakdown: 13f, 9m (doubling possible. Could also be performed with the addition of a non-speaking ensemble)

Publisher: Nick Hern Books, in *The Resistance Trilogy*, 1998

The women of a tragic, dust-blighted valley tend the land, look after their homes, and wait. They wait for the return of their men, every one of them mysteriously 'disappeared' by the totalitarian regime that is holding the country in its grip. Fathers, husbands, brothers, sons and nephews, all have been taken from their homes and have seemingly vanished without a trace. One of the oldest women, Sophia, decides she has waited long enough and begins a vigil by the river. Suddenly, strange dreams begin to haunt the women of the valley and, sure enough, the river yields up the bloated, faceless corpse of a man. Sophia is adamant it is the body of her father, but who's to tell it's him and not some other woman's father, husband, son or lover? Another corpse appears, then another, and soon the decomposing, always faceless and entirely unidentifiable bodies of men flood the river and the surrounding fields. As the authorities struggle to maintain control in the face of this bizarre plague, the women become ever more determined to bury their men.

Written during a long period of exile from his Chilean homeland during the Pinochet regime, Ariel Dorfman's dreamlike story of female resilience is a powerful, magical, yet disturbing piece. Developed partly in collaboration with the playwright Tony Kushner, the play *Widows* is a dramatic reimagining of Dorfman's 1983 novel of the same name. The novel itself had been prompted by a poem Dorfman had been inspired to write after being struck by the image of an old woman doggedly waiting by a river until it yielded up the bodies of her lost men. Finding a suitable way to bring the spirit of his poem, and then his novel, to the stage was a lengthy process Dorfman has subsequently described as 'one of the longest and most arduous creative odysseys of my existence'. The poem had been written in one overnight rush, the novel across a twelve-month period, but the play was to 'bedevil' Dorfman for nearly a decade. Although several earlier versions had been staged in the USA and then the UK from 1987 onwards, the 1997 revised edition of the text is the one considered by

Dorfman to be final and definitive. It is published by Nick Hern Books alongside Dorfman's best-known work *Death and the Maiden* (1991) and his 1995 play *Reader*, under the collective name *The Resistance Trilogy* (1998).

Although *Widows* is the only play in *The Resistance Trilogy* to feature a predominantly female cast, all three have at their heart a protagonist (or, to use Dorfman's words, 'a detonating factor') who is female. This, as Dorfman observes in his introduction to the trilogy, is no coincidence, but is driven by the fact that, as often the most disempowered members of society, when women 'do revolt, they do so with a determination, fury and dignity which cracks the world open, which compels authority to reveal itself in all its arbitrary ugliness'. It is indeed the stand-off between the women and the military authorities who would supress them that forms the dramatic heartbeat of *Widows*. An insecure Captain, freshly appointed to the region, finds he's met his match in Sophia and her neighbours. No matter how ardently he and his colleagues dismiss, demean or attempt to degrade the local population of 'mentally underdeveloped emotionally overdeveloped superstitious mindless peasants', the women are not going to back down quietly.

One of the few surviving men of the valley, the local priest, describes the women as living in 'a peculiar form of Hell'. Indeed, it is the sense of not knowing whether their men are alive or dead that characterises and blights the women's existences, a situation which, as Dorfman knew, was all too familiar to his countrymen and women under Pinochet. Unable to grieve but also unable to summon much by way of hope, the women of the play inhabit the worst kind of limbo, and Dorfman expresses their experiences with a lyricism that sets *Widows* apart from some of his more naturalistic works. An expansive, ambitious and important piece of drama, *Widows* captures with terrible vividness the torture of a community left unable to bury its dead.

First performed: Royal Court Theatre, London, 1982

Cast breakdown: 4f, 2m

Publisher: Methuen, 2000

Fifteen years old, best friends, and a force to be reckoned with, Rita and Sue receive a sexual awakening at the hands of Bob, a twenty-seven-year-old who employs them to babysit his children. Going for drives on the moors and then taking it in turns to have sex with Bob in the front seat of his car is a welcome diversion for the girls from the boredom of school, the bossiness of parents and the largely unimpressive prospects exhibited by the teenage boys around them. But like all three-way relationships, competition and jealousies start to develop, and the girls' loyalty towards Bob, and to one another, is tested.

Andrea Dunbar first came to prominence as a nineteen-year-old when her play *The Arbor* (1980) was performed at the Royal Court Theatre. Begun three years earlier as part of a school assignment and submitted to the Royal Court on biro-covered pages ripped from her exercise book, *The Arbor* deals with the story of a teenager who becomes pregnant the first time she has sex and then suffers a miscarriage. In *Rita, Sue and Bob Too*, Dunbar continues to explore the consequences of sexual activity on young girls' lives, but from a standpoint that is unexpected to say the least. While a play revolving around the grooming of two minors by a man with an apparently unhealthy attraction towards teenage girls might be expected to deliver a sombre or sinister experience to an audience, *Rita, Sue and Bob Too* couldn't be further from this.

The play is an exuberant, freewheeling piece of drama, bold, brash and incredibly funny in its entirely unsentimental depiction of sex. Dunbar's two young protagonists, Rita and Sue, aren't susceptible innocents waiting to be corrupted. Rather, they are refreshingly feisty, powerful young women, uncompromising in what they want and, as it turns out, even more insatiable than Bob. Yes, there is an incredibly dark side to the play. The poverty, domestic violence and lack of opportunity that characterises Rita and Sue's world is far from amusing. But Dunbar doesn't dwell on this bleakness, nor seem particularly interested in foregrounding it for the audience's attention – it's simply the way things are. Herself a single parent living on a depressed Bradford estate by the time she wrote *Rita, Sue and Bob Too*, Dunbar would have been entirely au fait with the circumstances in which Rita and Sue find themselves.

There is a naivety to Dunbar's writing; it's unclear where certain scenes take place, how they could be physically staged, and the messiness of the play's structure would most likely provoke raised eyebrows from most playwriting tutors. Yet the shear vitality of the writing shines through and encourages one to forgive, and even enjoy, the play's rough edges. Certainly not for the prudish, much of the play's humour is derived from the girls' wholly unromantic approach towards their relations with Bob and their candour upon first encountering the wonders and weirdness of sex. 'Jesus! It looks like a frozen sausage!' Rita exclaims on first glimpsing Bob's erect penis, while Sue's response to his efforts to teach them about the facts of life ('we haven't got eggs inside us. We're not ducks you know') shows how woefully unprepared the girls have been by their parents and school sex-education classes for any kind of physical relationship. The scene in which Bob fails to achieve an erection is illuminating of the girls' no-nonsense stance on sex, and reflective of the totally undaunted manner with which they take each new step into this previously unchartered territory. While Bob nurses his wounded ego, Sue laughs and Rita asks simply 'does that mean I can't have a jump then?' before pragmatically continuing 'oh never mind, get dressed. I want to go home.'

Given the tagline 'Thatcher's Britain with her knickers down', *Rita, Sue and Bob Too* was made into a film in 1987, directed by Alan Parker. The film was awarded a cheerier ending than the play, the eponymous trio joyfully continuing their ménage, rather than being driven apart by their actions. What both stage and film versions have in common, though, is a ferociously sharp sense of humour and totally unabashed stance. The girls' relationship with Bob isn't romantic, it isn't sensual, it doesn't even seem particularly passionate; it's simply sex, and something to do, to get them out the house for a few hours. Whether they are Bob's victims or not is debatable, but what is clear is that *Rita, Sue and Bob Too* is no ordinary coming-of-age drama.

First performed: Royal Shakespeare Company at the Swan Theatre, Stratford-upon-Avon, 2012

Cast breakdown: 7f, 5m (doubling possible)

Publisher: Nick Hern Books, 2012

Mexico, 1690s. From her convent cell, Sister Juana Inés de la Cruz, a woman of superior intellect, writes prolifically. A favourite of the court, her poetry and plays have won her fame and adulation, along with the patronage necessary for her to continue writing. But with the election of a new Archbishop, everything changes. A 'war on decadence' is declared and its target is anything of a secular nature. Soon books are being burned in the town square, theatrical performances are banned, and Juana's literary pursuits are attracting all the worst kinds of attention. Suddenly a nun writing plays – and secular plays at that – is a far from acceptable phenomenon. But when Juana argues for her right to think and speak freely, she sets in motion a vicious plot; one that intends to silence her exceptional voice.

Juana Inés de la Cruz (date of birth disputed, thought to be between 1648 and 1651–1695) was an extraordinary figure. That a seventeenth-century woman – and not just any woman, but a nun – had her work so widely read and performed, and was so ardently patronised by the court, is testimony not just to her talent, but to what must have been an astonishing strength of character. In 2004, the Royal Shakespeare Company staged her 1683 play *The House of Desires* as part of its Spanish Golden Age season, and it was upon seeing this production that Helen Edmundson became fascinated by de la Cruz. She read everything she could find about the nun and her life, and what she discovered was intriguing. Here, according to Edmundson, was 'a conundrum: a nun who wrote comic plays and secular poetry; a beautiful woman who shut herself away from the eyes of men; one of the greatest intellects of her time who ended by renouncing her right to a life of the mind'. In 2012, the RSC produced the fruits of Edmundson's interest, *The Heresy of Love*, an imagining of the final, dramatic period of de la Cruz's remarkable life.

The Heresy of Love is a big play with a huge scope, and Edmundson certainly packs plenty in. Politics, religion, sex, power and imperialism; it's all going on and the consequence is a meaty, provocative and powerful play. Set at a time when Mexico was part of the Spanish Empire, and the scrutiny of the Inquisition remained a very real disincentive to any kind of alternative thinking, the play takes its temperature from the tumultuous climate of the day. Shipped over from Spain after a not entirely reliable election process, the new Archbishop is on a mission to instil some decorum in the land that he calls New Spain, and everyone else in the play calls Mexico. As tensions within the population grow, he becomes all the more determined to impose swingeing changes, no matter that he hasn't been given a mandate to do so, nor that the shifts he is bent on imposing appear to have more to do with ideology than faith. At times an angry piece, Edmundson writes powerfully against those who take it upon themselves to dictate the terms by which others should live their lives – especially when they have been given no invitation to make such an imposition.

Introducing the play, Edmundson states she wanted to dramatise de la Cruz's story 'rather as a seventeenth-century Spanish playwright might have done'. Stylistically, the play certainly leans in this direction, as characters shift in and out of direct address and speak in a heightened language ordered into distinct rhythmic structures, reminiscent of de la Cruz's own work and that of her contemporaries. Likewise, Edmundson employs certain familiar tropes – there are the scheming servants and the malcontent figure who, despite initially appearing inconsequential, ultimately provides the touchpaper with which our protagonist's more apparent enemies can ignite her demise. While Edmundson gives more than a nod to the dramatic form of seventeenth-century Spain, *The Heresy of Love* remains capable of speaking eloquently, urgently and persuasively to modern audiences. The themes of the play are universal and the political intrigue and jostling for power in which its characters engage are all too recognisable to us today, and probably will remain so for all eternity. In the surprising shape of Sister Juana Inés de la Cruz, Edmundson conjures a fantastically original victim of – and, arguably, victor against – such timeless human ambition and frailty.

First performed: Athens, 415 BCE

Cast breakdown: 5f plus a chorus of women, 4m

Recommended version: by Don Taylor

Publisher: Methuen, 2007

Troy is ablaze. Invaded by the Greeks, the city has been destroyed, its men slaughtered and now its women, imprisoned, wait to hear their fate. The Queen, Hecuba, has been dethroned and receives the most horrifying of news from the victors; she is to be sent to Greece to become the slave of the General Odysseus. Her son Hector and daughter Polyxena have been killed and now a surviving child Cassandra (already afflicted by a curse that allows her to see the future but prevents anyone from believing her) is to be made concubine to Agamemnon. Some comfort remains in the form of Astyanax, Hector's baby son. But, flinging the baby from the battlements of the city, the Greeks ensure that Hecuba's despair is complete. Left to bury the child, Hecuba laments her fate and bereft of all choice, sets sail for Greece.

Women of Troy (sometimes translated as *The Trojan Women*) is an anguished cry against war. There is no glamorising of violence here, no suggestion that warfare is a valiant act or the maker of heroes. Rather, the play is a relentless, grimly detailed and highly emotive piece, and one that offers an unreserved condemnation of the acts of aggression perpetrated by one state towards another. In the winter before Euripides first staged the play, Athenian forces had besieged the Island of Melos and, in the face of unrest amongst its citizens, slain every man and boy from the age of fifteen upwards then enslaved the women and children. *Women of Troy* is widely thought to be Euripides' response to this act. Possibly a further galvanising factor was the apparent fracturing that began around this time of the fragile truce that had existed in Athens' war against Sparta. On the cusp of a return to fighting, and with news of the genocide on Melos still fresh on the streets of Athens, Euripides served up to its people an anti-war play of devastating bleakness and bite.

It is, of course, both high praise for the play, and a deeply depressing thought to linger on, that *Women of Troy* remains as startlingly relevant and phenomenally powerful for audiences today as we can imagine it would have been for those who first saw it tens of centuries ago. Indeed, the remarkable turbulence of the twentieth century, and in particular the proliferation of images that documented its horrors, offer modern audiences a new, fresh range of reference points around which they can construct their interpretation of the play. 'One is reminded at times of the memoirs, on film and in print, of Auschwitz survivors and the strangely compelled sense of horror that keeps us watching and reading,' Don Taylor wrote in 1990 in the introduction to his translation of the play. Just five years later, images of the Srebrenica massacre would be broadcast on television screens around the globe; yet another Troy or Melos to connect the modern world to the ancient.

To this end, the play offers theatre-makers a broad canvas upon which they can pin their own particular interpretation. Katie Mitchell's 2007 production at the National Theatre located the action in an austere modern-day ferry-terminal building. A chorus of women in evening gowns awaited in terror the recurring appearance of clipboard-wielding Greek officials, come to deliver yet another piece of devastating news. This relationship between the imprisoned women and the men who have been given the task of holding them is, according to Mitchell, at the heart of the drama and gives the play its moral complexity. 'The real conflict is between these Greek officials and Trojan women,' she commented in a 2007 *Guardian* interview, 'how these civil servants cope with what their masters have done. They are now on the ground having to deal with collateral damage.' It is this idea of the women of Troy as 'collateral damage' that makes Euripides' play so poignant, so terrible, and so incredibly indignant. Not responsible for the conflict in any way, it is these women who, as the survivors facing what could quite fairly be termed a fate worse than death, must bear the brunt of the horrors that have been entirely beyond their making.

First performed: Landestheater of Darmstadt at the 'experimenta 4', Frankfurt am Main, 1971

Cast breakdown: 6f

Recommended version: by Anthony Vivis

Publisher: Amber Lane Press, 1984

Petra von Kant seems unstoppable. A celebrity fashion designer with a gathering momentum of success, money and influence, her star seems firmly in the ascent. She's just freed herself from a defunct second marriage, is on good terms with her mother and teenage daughter and is firmly in control of her life. But when an old friend pays an unexpected visit, Petra's secure existence goes spiralling out of control. With her, the friend brings Karin Thimm, a young woman recently returned to Germany and keen to make a new life for herself. Petra falls suddenly, completely and dangerously in love with the younger woman. Offering her a modelling career (and a place in her bed in return), Petra enters into a relationship that is perilously unequal.

Born near Munich in May 1945, just weeks after Germany conceded defeat to the Allied forces, the actor, writer and theatre and film director Rainer Werner Fassbinder would become one of the most controversial and brutal chroniclers of the German post-war experience. Although his creative career was cut short by his early death, it was a prolific one, and Fassbinder repeatedly delivered works that were unflinchingly frank in their depiction of extreme emotion and human dysfunctionality. Unafraid of showing the ugly side of romantic love, Fassbinder depicted characters enmeshed in grim, nihilistic and sometimes downright disturbing relationships. No social niceties here, this was an artist happy to stick his finger deep into the wound of a society already struggling to come to terms with its recent record on human cruelty. In Petra von Kant, Fassbinder creates an arresting anti-heroine who, blindsided by the sheer force of desires she has never previously experienced, pitches herself head first into a relationship of utter and terrifying toxicity.

Petra's story is not an easy one to watch. The demonstration of her love for Karin is grotesque to behold, with Petra repeatedly debasing herself before the other woman in the hope of achieving some respite from the gnarled mess of arousal, jealously and adoration that consumes her. The fact that her protestations are received with barely concealed contempt by the largely disinterested Karin only serves to make Petra's vulnerability all the more painful for an audience to witness. In the play's dramatic crescendo, an ill-fated birthday party in which Petra's nearest and dearest gather to wish her many happy returns (other than Karin, who, conspicuous by her absence, has skipped off to see her ex-husband), Petra descends into a violent breakdown. Sobbing, drunk and enraged, she lurches around throwing punches and slinging glasses. Not content with smashing up her apartment, she seems dead set on smashing everything of importance to her and does her very best to destroy her career, livelihood and relationship with her mother and daughter in one fell swoop.

What makes Petra's deranged behaviour so uncomfortable to watch is the sneaking suspicion that any one of us could fall prey to the same sickness. When we first meet Petra she is an entirely sane woman who, although a little self-obsessed and somewhat self-important, is essentially of sound mind and logical action. Fassbinder's depiction of the speed and potency with which Petra falls into such a damaging and dangerous type of love is unsettling precisely *because* of this very contrast between Petra before and then after Karin's appearance. It is exacerbated by the apparent extent of Karin's mediocrity. 'She is a bit…well, ordinary, isn't she?' is Petra's daughter's simple analysis of the object of her mother's affections.

Fassbinder made a film version of the play in 1972 and it is this version of *The Bitter Tears…* for which he is better known. That said, for a sheer emotional hit, getting up close and personal with Petra and her despair can't be beaten. Different English translations of the play do exist, although for playability, truth and fluency, Anthony Vivis's version, first performed in 1976, is worth a look. It leaves intact movingly and with crushing force the terrible tragedy of a proud woman brought low by love.

35　Fefu and Her Friends
by María Irene Fornés (b. 1930, Cuba)

First performed: New York Theatre Strategy at the Relativity Media Lab, New York, 1977

Cast breakdown: 8f

Publisher: PAJ Publications, 1990

Innovative, poetic and always surprising, María Irene Fornés's rich dramatisation of an encounter between eight women is divided into three parts and takes place in 1930s New England. Fefu has invited a group of her friends to her home so they can plan a presentation they are to give as part of an education initiative for which they are raising funds. *Part 1* takes place in Fefu's living room. In *Part 2*, Fornés divides her audience into four groups and sends them to various locations around Fefu's house and garden, where they follow the unravelling strands of various characters' stories. *Part 3* brings the audience back together and returns to the living room, taking on an increasingly meta-theatrical turn as the women not only prepare, but rehearse their presentation.

There's a decent chance that many people coming to *Fefu and Her Friends* for the first time will find it frustrating, if not excruciatingly so. If you like your theatre to come with a clearly defined narrative arc, easy to understand characters, a logically plotted sequence of dramatic events and a discernible 'message', Fornés's enigmatic and sometimes troubling work is probably not for you. If, however, what you enjoy about theatre is being posed conundrums, and if you prefer your drama to ask you questions, rather than offer answers, *Fefu and Her Friends* is absolutely worth exploring. With its quicksand quality and unpredictable direction, the lines of thought pursued by its characters are endlessly shifting, swirling between hard-edged political rhetoric, philosophical debate, and dreamlike mysticism. Darting between meticulously detailed naturalism and moments of high surrealism, it's a play that never allows an audience to settle into comfortable territory. Just as Fefu's house guests are unable to entirely relax in their hostess' eccentric and at times downright dangerous company, the audience is left in a state of alertness, never able to predict what Fornés has up her sleeve next, an experience that can be draining on the intellect as much as it is intriguing to the imagination. Provocative, unsettling, funny and impossible to define on a cerebral level, it's a play that makes us *feel* something deeply, even if we couldn't quite give a name to what that feeling is.

Fefu and Her Friends is often termed a 'feminist play'. Whether it was given this title by critics and commentators simply because it happens to feature a cast of eight women who – shock horror – spend more time talking about themselves than the men in their lives, is open to debate. Regardless of whether the play was written with the intention of expressing a feminist viewpoint, penned in the 1970s, it is certainly the product of a time when feminism was a vocal, recognised and organised force in Western society. However, set in New England in 1935, it is located in a time and place when this was not the case. Just fifteen years after the Nineteenth Amendment made votes for women law in the USA, Fefu and her friends are still trying to work out what their status as women entitles them to, and also what it denies them. Most of the characters are highly educated, immensely articulate, emotionally and intellectually intelligent, and yet seem to struggle for the words with which to describe their predicament, or, indeed, the wherewithal to know how to transcend it.

With sensitivity, insight, and dark humour, Fornés captures this moment in American history when the understanding that change ought to and could occur for women had become tangible, but before the language or knowledge had been established to signpost how this might occur in individual lives. The women of the play seem somewhat stuck, caught between an all-too painful awareness that they are trapped in an unjust situation, and yet largely paralysed when it comes to knowing how to free themselves from it. A sense of bewilderment, anger, loss, loneliness, confusion and frustration variously afflicts them and each in her own way adopts coping mechanisms of varying bizarreness. For Fefu, regularly firing a shotgun through the French windows in a somewhat Hedda Gabler-like manner (and dabbling in the odd bit of domestic plumbing) is the way to express the disconnection she feels between who she wants to be and the role prescribed for her. Fornés shows us how Fefu and her friends, whilst planning a presentation designed to inspire the betterment of others, are searching, scrabbling, and longing to find a way to secure their own.

First performed: Abbey Theatre, Dublin, 1990

Cast breakdown: 5f, 3m

Publisher: Faber and Faber, 1990

In an isolated house in rural County Donegal, the five Mundy sisters – Kate, Maggie, Agnes, Rose and Chris, none of them married and all of them living on Kate's schoolteacher salary – do their best to get by. With Chris's illegitimate son Michael to care for, their older brother Jack returned after twenty-five years working as a missionary priest in Uganda, and the constant battle to make ends meet, the sisters have little time to think of themselves. But with industrialisation marching ever closer and change on the horizon, the sisters have a choice: stay as they have always been, or strike out in a bold new direction. Set in the summer of 1936, *Dancing at Lughnasa* is a mesmerising snapshot of a way of life poised on the brink of change.

Brian Friel frames the action of *Dancing at Lughnasa* with the narration of Michael who, now appearing to the audience as a grown man, recollects the summer in which he was seven, reliving those few extraordinary weeks in which fate briefly brought his entire family together. In the appearance of his formerly absent travelling salesman father Gerry, the return of the much lauded Father Jack, and the arrival of a temperamental radio set beaming Irish dance music 'all the way from Dublin', the outside world appears finally to be knocking on the door of the Mundy household. But while these outside influences bring a breath of fresh air, they also bring a sense of danger and a destabilising influence that will fracture the sisters' bond.

The play captures beautifully the moment in the lives of its female protagonists when possibilities seem to open up, dreams hover on the edge of fulfilment and life, despite its harshness, temporarily takes on a golden sheen. When music bursts into their lives via the arrival of their prized radio set, the stagnancy of the Mundy sisters' lives is thrillingly disrupted and Michael can only watch its 'voodoo derange those kind, sensible women and transform them into shrieking strangers', as they dance around the kitchen and the adjoining yard. Crammed into their cut-off home and shackled by the suffocating effects of poverty, duty and religious propriety, dancing becomes a much-needed way for the sisters to release steam in their pressure-cooker-like existence. But while those heady days of music and dancing that coincide with the festival of Lughnasa (named for Lugh, the Celtic God of the Harvest) offer the bewitching prospect of love, fulfilment and the possibility of personal expression, the reality, as it turns out for the sisters, will be something entirely different.

An incredibly funny, sometimes irreverent and occasionally raucous depiction of family life in pre-war rural Ireland, *Dancing at Lughnasa* is a bittersweet glance at the past, but not a rose-tinted one. By employing the unusual technique of having his narrator telling the audience what fate awaits each of the characters in the days, months and years after the action of the play ends, but doing so *while* that action is occurring, rather than at its conclusion, Friel ensures his audience's view can never be obscured by a fuzzy glow of nostalgia. The final scene of the play in particular, a seemingly innocuous al fresco meal that the family share in the evening sun, is underpinned by a sense of tragedy, Michael having already informed the audience of the future of illness, poverty, death, loneliness and unfulfilled dreams that awaits them. In fact, what we in the audience are observing are the final moments of relative peace and contentment that the Mundys will spend in one another's company. Although set during a summer of possibility, when so much seems so tantalisingly close for several of the sisters, the play shows how these possibilities are one by one missed or cruelly swept away from their grasps. The play concludes on a sombre note, August having given way to September and the impending winter months seeming representative of more than just cold weather.

The play opened at the Abbey Theatre, Dublin, in April 1990, before transferring to the National Theatre in London in October of that year. It was made into a film in 1998, starring Meryl Streep as Kate, Michael Gambon as Father Jack and with Bríd Brennan as Agnes, reprising her Tony Award-winning role from the original stage production.

First performed: Théâtre Athénée, Paris, 1947

Cast breakdown: 3f

Recommended version: by Martin Crimp

Publisher: Faber and Faber, 1999

Sisters Solange and Claire are maids to Madame. When Madame is out they like to dress up in her clothes and pretend to 'be' her, venting their hatred towards their employer by acting out sadistic fantasies of her death. With a bad habit of getting carried away by the 'preliminaries', Solange and Claire never quite get to the point where they can murder Madame, and the time always comes to stop the game and tidy up before they can get to the final fatal act. Tonight is different. Madame is at the police station where Monsieur has been imprisoned because of anonymous letters written by the sisters and, hearing he has been bailed and is imminently due home, Solange and Claire know they are about to be found out. Determined to take their game to its grizzly conclusion while they still have the chance, the sisters agree that this is the night Madame will be killed. But when their mistress returns home, the realisation of the sisters' long-rehearsed fantasy does not go entirely to plan.

Jean Genet's modern classic *The Maids* is a fantastical yet steely piece that remains an explosive dissection of the relationship between servant and employer, as well as a journey into the darker recesses of human desire. It was partly inspired by the real-life case of the Papin sisters, Lea and Christine, who spent six years under the employ of a Le Mans solicitor before one night unexpectedly attacking his wife and daughter, gouging their eyes out and bludgeoning them to death. While Wendy Kesselman would later dramatise the case in a more direct and biographical manner in her 1981 play *My Sister in This House* (4f), Genet's 1947 take on the terrible tale of the Papin sisters is a far looser approach, but incontestably the richer and more theatrically imaginative. Deeply unsettling, darkly funny, poignant and occasionally just breathtakingly odd, Genet somehow manages to create a piece that is as compelling to watch as it is repugnant. As Solange and Claire engage in their depraved and deeply private role-play, the audience is forced to witness the outward expression of an erotic, vengeful and perverse hatred usually kept locked safely away in the privacy of the human brain. The fact that the boundaries between what is an act and what is reality are consistently being dismantled in ever more wily ways by Genet makes the viewing of these clandestine acts all the more disconcerting.

Shattering dramatic form and then reconfiguring it to create an effect that is both startling and beguiling, *The Maids* is characteristic of Genet's renegade approach to the rules of structure. As much about the constructs of performance as it is about the sisters' actual attempts to literally or figuratively 'murder' Madame, it's a piece that feels a bit like a hall of mirrors – a performance within a performance within a performance. Jean Paul Sartre described Genet's expert manipulation of an audience's sense of artifice and reality as figurative 'whirligigs', likening it to 'when a multicoloured disc is spun quickly enough, the colours of the rainbow interpenetrate and produce white'. Impossible to pin down (or indeed, ever entirely know what's going on), *The Maids* is a play constructed from a narrative that constantly reshuffles and, in which time, stretches and warps in weird ways. The consequence is a somewhat nightmarish and yet utterly engrossing experience as, among the lace, Louis Quinze furniture and overflowing flower arrangements of Madame's almost grotesquely gorgeous boudoir, the grubby interactions of the three women take on a bizarre logic of their own.

A play in which the threat of violence is always present but in which no direct act of physical aggression ever takes place, *The Maids* is all the more arresting, sitting as it does on a perpetual knife-edge of tension. Skimming the boundaries of decency yet not directly explicit, it plays upon the darkness of the human imagination for much of its effect. Arguably too, it takes advantage of an audience's preconceptions of the capacity that well-turned-out young women have for brutality, wilfully contrasting constructs of femininity against articulations of the most debased behaviour. Despite their penchant for evening gowns and Madame's face powder, Solange and Claire turn out to be every bit as terrifying as the worst sadists. The dainty cup of poisoned tea with which they attempt to murder their mistress (served up in the best china, of course) stands in delicious contrast to the cesspool of their thoughts.

A Chat with Mrs Chicky
by Evelyn Glover (*b.* 1874, UK)

First performed: Rehearsal Theatre, London, 1912

Cast breakdown: 2f

Publisher: Methuen, in *How the Vote Was Won and Other Suffrage Plays*, 1985

Mrs Holbrook doesn't believe in all this nonsense about women getting the vote; just because a group of silly women with too much time on their hands want to start meddling in politics, doesn't mean England should be allowed to go to rack and ruin. Keen to demonstrate how many women share her views, Mrs Holbrook is seeking the signatures of one hundred women from all walks of life so she can post a petition in the papers. Setting her sights on her brother's charlady as a useful addition from the working classes, Mrs Holbrook arrives for a chat. But the mischievous Mrs Chicky isn't quite the walkover Mrs Holbrook had expected, and soon the brief conversation she'd been anticipating turns into something altogether more challenging.

In 1908, frustrated by the limited range of roles available to them in Britain's almost exclusively male-led theatres, a group of actresses formed the Actresses' Franchise League. The League was designed to improve conditions for women working in the theatre and its first meeting, held at the Criterion restaurant in London, was attended by four hundred actresses including leading figures such as Ellen Terry and Violet Vanbrugh. As well as wanting access to a greater quantity and an improved quality of roles, many of the actresses were engaged in the suffrage movement, and the League began making work that responded to these dual ideals, creating an interesting intersection between art and activism. A specially created 'play department' in the League toured a variety of performances – ranging from monologues, recitals and sketches to full-length plays – to the meetings and events of various suffrage societies. Generally written by women and on the topic of suffrage or gender equality, these political works became extremely popular, while offering the women who worked on them an unprecedented level of creative freedom. Perhaps the best known of the plays, *How the Vote Was Won* (1909, 8f, 2m) by Christopher St John (the pseudonym of Christabel Marshall) and Cicely Hamilton, went on to receive a critically acclaimed and commercially successful run in the West

End. In 1985, Methuen published a collection of these works, which, along with *How the Vote Was Won* and *A Chat with Mrs Chicky*, features five other suffrage plays. The volume provides an insight into this thriving movement, one that is strangely often excluded from histories of women's theatre and of twentieth-century political theatre.

'*You* haven't got time to trouble your head with politics, have you?' is Holbrook's condescending opener to the charlady busily working around her. On the contrary, Chicky cannot help but have a head troubled with politics, given that her gender and class have left her at the bottom of the pile of Parliament's priorities, the effects of which are sorely apparent in every aspect of her day-to-day life. Going along with Holbrook's preconceptions by playing dumb and asking a series of seemingly innocent questions, the wily Chicky spends the subsequent half-hour tying the other woman into ever more complex knots. Only in the final moments of the play does she reveal her true feelings, whipping a 'Votes for Women' handbill from her petticoats and launching into a dazzling tirade of mockery against those who feel women such as herself shouldn't demand a say in the laws that control their lives.

Glover's satirical short play draws attention to a fascinating aspect of the fight for universal suffrage – that those in favour of it were at times not only attempting to influence the opinions of men, but also to change the minds of women. By the time that *A Chat with Mrs Chicky* premiered in 1912, the Anti-Suffrage League had more than a hundred branches around the UK and thousands of paying members. It claimed that only a tiny but organised and disproportionately vocal minority of women actually wanted the vote and its female members focused much of their energies on collecting signatures of other women to provide evidence of this. As an energetic proponent of emancipation herself, Glover's feelings of contempt towards such women are not disguised in *A Chat with Mrs Chicky,* and the play revels in the intellectual rings the stoic charlady runs around the Anti-Suffrage canvasser. Dealing specifically with class in the context of the fight for emancipation, Glover brings together two women whose usual contact would end with one silently clearing away her cleaning equipment and making herself scarce if the other entered the room. In the ensuing battle of wills, Glover leaves her audience in little doubt of the affront done to working-class women by their middle-class counterparts telling them not to demand the vote. It's more of a sketch than a play, but it's a masterfully executed one at that, is incredibly funny and has lost none of its zeal, wit nor passion in the century since it was written. Above all, it is a fantastically vivid and valuable snapshot from a revolutionary moment in history, the effects of which have altered our lives in a profound and permanent way.

First performed: Nezlobin Theatre, Moscow, 1911

Cast breakdown: 7f, 6m

Recommended version: by Cathy Porter

Publisher: Methuen, in *Gorky Plays: 2*, 2003

Vassa Zheleznova is a woman of business. Ever since her abusive husband nearly lost everything in a game of cards, she has been managing the family shipping company single-handed. Never shy about paying the odd bribe if it keeps an official quiet, or firing a worker if he voices dissent, Vassa's business empire is robust, if not entirely ethical. While she would like to manage her wayward family with the same efficiency, they're so dysfunctional it would be hard to know where to start. Her husband is under enquiry for the rape of a twelve-year-old girl, one teenage daughter is an alcoholic and the other trapped in a bizarre, child-like form of arrested development. Her lecherous older brother maintains an unhealthy interest in the female household staff and then there's Rachel, the revolutionary firebrand and Vassa's daughter-in-law, on the run and determined to take back the child Vassa has stolen from her. Gorky's depiction of the seediest of set-ups masquerading under the guise of a respectable family business is stunningly dark and laced with a brutal wit.

Maxim Gorky wrote an earlier version of *Vassa Zheleznova*, which he completed in 1910 and was premiered in Moscow the following year. But in 1935, a year before his death and suffering from extreme depression prompted by the sudden death of his son and an apparent discomfort in the lavish, high-profile life he had come to lead, Gorky returned to the play. Alexei Maximovich Peshkov (who assumed the pen name Gorky or 'the bitter' at the age of twenty-four) started life as the son of an impoverished joiner and ended it as one of his country's most celebrated literary figures, residing in a state-funded mansion complete with car and servants. It was a lifestyle that the aged Gorky, a committed and vocal socialist since his youth, found hard to reconcile. His decision to rewrite *Vassa Zheleznova*, a play that among all of his writing takes one of the most critical looks at the corrosive effects of money and influence, is an interesting one. Despite all of Vassa's hard work, determination and tenacity, the apparent success she has flogged herself nearly to death to achieve does not make her, or her family, happy. Rather, it drives rifts between them, fosters a culture of suspicion, back-stabbing and envy, and, most visibly, equips them with an eternal, low-level terror that it might all come toppling down around them tomorrow. Acquisition of property, reputation and power, Gorky shows, does not necessarily bring the peace of mind or moral autonomy one might expect.

Vassa Zheleznova is a play that is astoundingly sinister, and what Gorky dishes up to his audience in the first ten minutes, many playwrights would spend an entire evening building up to. As the curtain rises, Vassa is attempting to hush-up her husband's arrest for child molestation, offering to bribe the court and buy evidence. Having accepted that even the biggest of bribes won't get the case thrown out, she proceeds to produce a conveniently handy dose of poison and orders her husband to commit suicide to spare the family the shame of a public trial. She then either leaves him to take it or bumps him off herself – Gorky leaves it up to the audience's imagination to decide which. Such an explosive opening may well leave an audience wondering where on earth Gorky will take the drama next, but by the end of the evening it's clear there are few depths to which the Zheleznova family will not stoop. Murder, rape, suicide, kidnap, alcoholism, violence, blackmail and sexual perversion are all in the mix, and presented by Gorky with unflinching starkness and gallows humour.

'What do you lawyers call this – sort of thing,' Vassa asks the contact who she is attempting to bribe, 'messing about with children?' 'We call it depravity, madam,' he retorts, before handing her police photographs of one of her husband's young victims, taken after the attack. While Vassa is chilled by her husband's behaviour, it is not startling to her. Twenty years her senior, he first made advances towards the young Vassa when she was just fourteen, married her by the time she was sixteen, then regularly beat, neglected and humiliated her, even during the nine pregnancies that followed. Now, mother to three surviving children and grandmother to a boy on whom she pins all her hopes for the future, Vassa is determined to create some kind of legacy that will honour the struggle she has faced. But Gorky's swift three-act play (perhaps performed most successfully straight through without an interval) remains a wholly unsentimental one. It offers little optimism that the future of Vassa's progeny will be any less sullied than her own.

First performed: Royal Shakespeare Company at The Other Place, Stratford-upon-Avon, 2004

Cast breakdown: 3f

Publisher: Nick Hern Books, 2005

> 'Before you even finished your first straight-up-and-down-high-balled-economic-transaction of a drink / he had you sussed. Sussed – clocked an categorise. Thass what that was for. *Thass* what you were for.'

debbie tucker green's darkly humorous and quietly brutal meditation on female sex tourism is an astute and compelling piece of work. Looking at the implicit indignities inherent in international trade, it does so through the lens of first-world women visiting a third-world resort in search of sun, sea, sand and something special. Travelling abroad with purses stuffed with local currency and British Kitemark condoms, everything is available to the tourists at an astonishingly low price. But what, green asks, is the real cost? At times an uncomfortably perceptive dissection of the wealthy West's relationship with the developing world, *trade* is an epic piece of writing tied up in a neat fifty minutes.

Constructed in green's signature dramatic prose, *trade* offers its performers something to really get their teeth into. The play is written for three black actresses who between them enact a total of eleven characters, all entangled in some way in the transactions between a local man and the white British women who spend time with him. Slipping from character to character whilst maintaining the precise rhythm, timing and direction of green's language, it's a play that demands agile, technically assured and highly versatile actresses. The play consists of one continuous verbal encounter between the three as they assume the personas of typical holidaymakers, the 'Regular' (visits twice a year like clockwork) and the 'Novice' (first time there and enjoying a 'plastic fuckin fantastic' fortnight of luxury living she couldn't afford back home). Both have been having a relationship with a local man, but as the play unfolds, his professional interest in them (and their cash) comes cringingly, depressingly and heart-wrenchingly to the fore. Casting an unimpressed eye over the tourists' behaviour is the local woman who earns a meagre living offering a beachside hair-plaiting service and who is more involved in the situation – emotionally and economically – than she would like. As the sun beats down and another 'highball glass of su'un sweet' is consumed, disturbing transactions are taking place; sex and romance, consumer and consumed, victim and perpetrator become ever more difficult to tell apart.

green's adept creation of rich, dramatic, and politically charged aural compositions has singled her out as one of the most original voices in contemporary British playwriting. 'No playwright makes you sit up and listen like debbie tucker green' was Lyn Gardner of the *Guardian*'s response to the 2006 London production of *trade*. 'While others struggle to find a distinctive voice, green has developed her own unique way of saying things. There is something both beautiful and jagged about her theatrical collages: they are poetry laced with shards of broken glass.' Often largely noncommittal about the visual elements of her plays – something a director will find either endlessly frustrating or fantastically liberating – in *trade*, green offers absolutely no information about what the audience sees. Instead she provides an immaculately detailed vocal score, one that in turn assaults and charms the ear of the listener.

Viewed in the micro, *trade* is about three women involved with the same man. In the macro, it is a searing and depressingly adroit analysis of world trade and global inequality. In the Caribbean resort that green conjures, 'tourism' is the title under which indignities thrust by one culture onto another are permissible in the name of commerce, and for the alleged betterment of a flailing economy. It's a piece that is likely to speak to anyone who has ever experienced the alluring yet troubling temporary opulence that taking a luxury holiday in a developing country can offer, and will appeal to those who like their theatre to examine the grey areas of human ethical behaviour. Taking the themes of exploitation, pride and greed and exploring them on a global scale with insight and a ferocious wit, green delivers a piece of writing that is important and chilling. A play for our times and penned by arguably one of the most extraordinary and arresting dramatic voices to have emerged in recent years, *trade* is a work that deserves to be performed and seen widely.

41 Just to Get Married
by Cicely Mary Hamilton (*b.* 1872, UK)

First performed: The Little Theatre, London, 1910

Cast breakdown: 5f, 4m

Publisher: Kessinger, 2011

Things are not looking good for Georgiana Vickary. Twenty-nine at her last birthday and still resolutely un-proposed-to, Georgiana knows that remaining reliant on the charity of her extended family is an increasingly untenable option. Keen to get Georgiana off their hands, her family have latched onto Adam Lankester, an eligible but pathologically shy man, as Georgiana's best – and most probably final – opportunity to marry. But after a two-week stay at the family seat, the practically mute Adam has failed to pop the question, no matter how many chances to be alone with him Georgiana has contrived. As the last night of Adam's stay draws to a close, Georgiana announces that she has resigned herself to a life of spinsterhood, penury and the companionship of cats. Then, at the eleventh hour, Adam finally finds his voice. But having secured her proposal, Georgiana discovers that, as the future Mrs Lankester, her troubles are only just beginning. Cecily Mary Hamilton's sharp comedy is a smart, outspoken and refreshingly unsentimental satire on the bizarre etiquette of Edwardian marriage.

By the time *Just to Get Married* appeared on the London stage, Cicely Mary Hamilton's views on marriage were far from secret. Having published her book *Marriage as a Trade* in 1904 (the title says it all), audiences were unlikely to attend her 1914 comedy in anticipation of rose-tinted romanticising, nor a celebration of marriage as a state that, as far as Hamilton perceived it, signified the beginning and end of female aspiration and achievement. What audiences may not have been prepared for, though, is the fantastic humour of Hamilton's decidedly offbeat take on love and marriage, nor the uncompromising and at times bracingly direct wit with which she systematically dismantles the niceties of Edwardian matchmaking. Georgiana, despite describing herself as 'a distinctly prosaic person', is a fantastically outspoken character who calls a spade a spade. She can see her engagement to Adam exactly for what it is – a charade designed to save her family the financial burden of keeping her fed, watered and clothed, and an opportunity for him to acquire something nicely decorative to look at around the house. But she's also a woman with a strong moral compass, and as the wedding day approaches, her queasiness at the idea of taking religious vows with a man she feels just the faintest of warmth towards becomes increasingly uncomfortable.

'I should be very sorry for myself if I had to sit opposite Mr Adam Lankester at breakfast for the term of my natural life,' Georgiana's friend Mrs Macartney concedes, before adding with faint optimism, 'but he may improve on acquaintance.' No one thinks Adam is a good match for Georgiana in any respect other than his three thousand pounds a year. He is considered shy to the point of being uncouth and appears to lack charm, sensitivity, passion or any other kind of attribute that may recommend him as decent husband material. And yet, the household's coordinated attempt to ensnare this particularly cold fish for Georgiana proceeds with a fervour that is as entertaining to watch as it is patently ridiculous. Everyone from the scullery maid up to the head of the household is in on the game and, although news of the couple's eventual engagement brings with it a flood of wedding gifts and much excitement over the minutiae of the big day and subsequent honeymoon, no one actually believes the match between the young couple has anything to do with affection. It is a strategic alliance between two socially, if not emotionally, compatible individuals and a highly sensible arrangement for both of them to enter into.

Where Georgiana becomes unstuck is on discovering that her betrothed is, unfortunately, the only person not in on the game. Adam is in love with her, madly, deeply and head over heels, an unfortunate situation that his taciturn ways had hidden during his apparently passionless wooing. Keen on having her own home, social respectability and a secure future Georgiana may be, but she's not heartless, and having realised that her own lukewarm feelings are met with an ardent fire of passion from her fiancé, she decides to throw a monumental spanner in the works. Of course, this being a comedy, there's a happy ending in store for both Georgiana and Adam and a delightfully romantic scene in a chilly railway waiting room sees the apparently mismatched couple discovering they might just have a future together after all, although not the one either of them had envisaged. At its close, *Just to Get Married* is a play that finally speaks out warmly in praise of marriage – although only when it's a state in which both partners enjoy equal rights, respect and responsibility, and not as the loveless and imbalanced one into which Georgiana and Adam so nearly fell.

First performed: Maxine Elliot Theatre, New York, 1934

Cast breakdown: 12f, 2m (doubling possible)

Publisher: Kessinger, 2010

Karen Wright and Martha Dobie are old college friends who have spent the last eight years building up their own business, a boarding school for girls. After the years of dedication, hard work and frugality, their investment is finally beginning to pay off – they have a full register of students, are adored by the girls they teach, and respected in the local community. But one student, a troubled child called Mary Tilford, seems determined to disrupt the harmonious way of life at the Wright-Dobie School for Girls. She starts a rumour about the two young teachers that triggers a frenzy of paranoia and prejudice within the town, threatening to undermine the future of the school, and all that Karen and Martha have worked for. As parents begin to withdraw their daughters one by one, Karen and Martha fight to defend themselves against the accusations of a child.

The Children's Hour premiered in November 1934 and ran for 691 performances – a record at the time for the longest single-venue run of a play. It attracted controversy, dealing as it does with the allegation of lesbianism between its two lead characters. The selection panel of the Pulitzer Prize refused to attend and the play was banned in Boston, Chicago and London. When the play was made into a film in 1936, it was retitled *These Three* and in place of lesbianism, the focus of Mary's accusation was on the suggestion that Martha was having an inappropriate relationship with Joseph, Karen's fiancé. Twenty-five years later, Hellman and William Wyler, the director of *These Three*, collaborated on a second film adaptation of the play, which resumed the original title, *The Children's Hour*, and reinstated the alleged lesbian relationship. Released in 1961, it starred Audrey Hepburn as Karen and Shirley MacLaine as Martha.

Hellman was partly inspired to write *The Children's Hour* after coming across the story of two Scottish schoolteachers, Jane Pirie and Marianne Woods, who in 1810 were accused by their pupil Jane Cumming of having a lesbian relationship and of doing so in view of their students. Jane Cumming's grandmother was a powerful figure who, like Agatha Tilford – Mary's grandmother in the play – used her influence to mobilise the local community against the teachers. Pirie and Woods sued and won their case against the Cummings, but neither their livelihoods nor their reputations ever entirely recovered. In *The Children's Hour*, Hellman includes an additional cruel twist in which the teachers' innocence is proven only once it is too late.

While the idea of homosexuality between two adults is unlikely to trouble a modern audience (and certainly not be seen as something to be 'accused' of), the idea that Karen and Martha have engaged in sexual activity in view of their young charges might, given how sensitive the interface between children and sex inevitably remains. The play asks difficult questions about the extent to which we believe – or want to believe – that our children are unaware of sex, giving *The Children's Hour* a provocative edge that continues to bite some eighty years after its premiere. Mary's account of the girls in her dormitory being unable to sleep because of the 'strange' and 'frightening' noises coming from the teachers' room next door is preposterously melodramatic, and yet Agatha and the town choose to believe it, perhaps because it is easier to do so than question the ethical integrity and level of sexual awareness possessed by their own children. Mary's claims of having seen and heard her two teachers engage in sexual activities is what cements their guilt in her grandmother's mind, largely because Agatha can't believe the girl could possibly be aware that such acts could take place between two adults unless she had witnessed them at first hand. Her assumption of her granddaughter's innocence of sex is unfounded, misguided and, as it turns out, dangerously naive.

So, too, Agatha's blindness to the dishonesty and manipulative cries for help of her clearly damaged granddaughter serves as one of the propelling forces of Hellman's tense drama. Adults who are unable or unwilling to see any fault in the children they have reared – even at the expense of the children themselves – are both universal and timeless figures in drama and, by the play's conclusion, Mary's lies have finally come to light, and her grandmother's faith in the child, as well as her own prowess of perception, have been destroyed. Agatha recognises that she herself must bear the brunt of the behaviour of the indulged but highly dysfunctional child she, in the absence of Mary's parents, has raised. 'Whatever she does, it must be to me and no one else,' Agatha tells Karen. The teacher replies philosophically, 'She's harmed us both, but she's harmed you more, I guess.' *The Children's Hour* is not just an illustration of how unchecked lies can destroy lives, but how failing to acknowledge wickedness in our own children can do so too.

43

Cockroach
by Sam Holcroft (*b*. 1983, UK)

First performed: Traverse Theatre, Edinburgh, 2008

Cast breakdown: 4f, 2m

Publisher: Nick Hern Books, 2008

Opening with an explosive row between sixteen-year-old lovers Lee and Leah, *Cockroach* bursts onto the stage with all the adrenaline and anger of an irate teenager. She accuses him of cheating and locks herself in a classroom; he smashes the door down in an effort to get to her; both are stopped by the arrival of their science teacher, Beth, who seems to be operating more like a security guard than a teacher, whipping a walkie-talkie from a holster and radioing for help. But *Cockroach* is no straightforward drama about teenage aggression or declining standards in schools. What emerges is a far darker piece about war, and one that examines young people's relationship to it in a highly original and complex way.

Constantly playing with the audience's perceptions, Sam Holcroft's brutal, intelligent and intensely moving *Cockroach* repeatedly leads its audience to think it knows exactly what is going on, before shedding a little more light onto the picture to show that, actually, the stakes are far higher than they could possibly have imagined. Using the Darwinian theory of natural selection as the lens through which she examines the effect of warfare on reproduction within a civilian population, Holcroft offers an unusual spin on what could happen were today's younger generation plunged into war.

The young people in *Cockroach* aren't driven to having sex with one another through run-of-the-mill teenage curiosity or overactive hormones; they're fighting for the survival of their species and trying to ensure their presence (or at least the presence of their genes) in the new world order. While the school football team is left in disarray as the strongest and healthiest of its members are conscripted, an interesting new world of possibilities opens up for the less anatomically gifted peers they leave behind. Suddenly, being a boy with a limp, asthma, or a predisposition to ear infections becomes a huge evolutionary advantage if it keeps you away from the battlefield. As Beth urgently endeavours to impress on her wayward class in preparation for their forthcoming Biology exam, while it is the strongest and fittest of any species that will survive to pass on their genes, ' "strongest and fittest" does not necessarily mean physically strong and physically fit.' After using the cockroach as an example of a species that has evolved to a point where it can successfully survive side by side with humans by becoming smaller, flatter and less easy to squash, one of her students, Mmoma, is drawn to point out, 'Well, it's like cockroaches, isn't it, this war? It's the biggest and strongest that's going to get squashed... we're not going. So, we're the ones who survive. We're the fittest.'

The reason that Mmoma isn't going to war is that she's a girl, and the circumstances in which the female characters in *Cockroach* find themselves is an interesting one. By setting up the males as fighters and the females as stay-at-home civilians, the play takes a provocative look at what happens to gender politics in a time of war. With three girls to any one boy at school, there's strong competition. Even Martin from 12C, 'the one with the cracked face and the ear infections so bad that he's got to lie with his head on the ground', has reportedly hooked up with Sue Ellen, one of the prettiest girls in the school. While in these circumstances the basic human urge to reproduce takes on a sinister significance among a group of already sexually volatile teenagers, the ramifications for adults are hinted at too. A motif that runs through the piece is Beth's increasingly focused attempts to make herself sexually attractive to her fiancé, exchanging comfortable shoes for high heels, applying make-up and perfume, and finally exchanging her knickers for a seductive thong; and all this after she conducts Biology lessons on how various females in the animal world make themselves attractive to their male counterparts during the most fertile parts of their menstrual cycles. But *Cockroach* goes beyond a reductive approach to reproduction to ask big, provocative and at times disconcertingly challenging questions about gender and power. As the girls find themselves forming an ever-growing majority in the school, they are left to ask some difficult questions about how a female-dominated society may look and function.

44

Hedda Gabler
by Henrik Ibsen (*b.* 1828, Norway)

First performed: Residenztheater, Munich, 1881

Cast breakdown: 4f, 3m

Recommended version: by Jens Arup

Publisher: Oxford University Press, 2008

After a six-month honeymoon with Jorgen, a husband who bores her stiff, Hedda Tesman, formerly Hedda Gabler, is home. Installed in the expensive villa her husband mistakenly believes to be her idea of a dream house, Hedda is facing a deathly dull future, broken up only by the suffocating attentions of her new in-laws. The appearance of Thea Elvsted, an old schoolmate of Hedda's, promises to shake things up, arriving as she does with interesting news about Ejlert Lövborg, a writer who, some years ago, played an important role in both Hedda and Jorgen's lives. Identifying the relationship between Thea and Ejlert as a possible focus for her frustration, vengeance and despair, Hedda engages in a sadistic game designed to ensure the downfall of those around her.

No one in the play, himself included, can quite believe that the thoroughly uninspiring Jorgen Tesman has won the hand of the beautiful, proud Hedda Gabler. Previously considered outside of the lowly Tesman family's league, as one of them, Hedda finds she is idolised and fawned over by her new husband and his family, a situation that provides ample fuel for her instinctual cruelty towards those who admire her. The play is, of course, called *Hedda Gabler*, not *Hedda Tesman* or even simply *Hedda*, and in a work that illustrates so clearly how the actions of one's past set the stage for the conditions of the present, perhaps Ibsen considered it apt to foreground how Hedda Gabler made the bed in which Hedda Tesman must now lie. Or perhaps it was Hedda's dogged insistence in having her own way and refusing to be subsumed into her husband's identity that made her creator feel she would always be Hedda Gabler, albeit Hedda Tesman in name. A preoccupation of much of Ibsen's work, marriage is shown not as a glorious state of mutual support, understanding or comfort between a man and a woman, but a malfunctioning structure, built on the rocky ground of delusion, secrecy and emotional inarticulacy, perverted by the stultifying restrictions of social correctness. Suffocating for both husbands and wives, the marriages within *Hedda Gabler* are formed on the basis of economic advantage and practical usefulness, not a remotely genuine affection evident between the personalities involved.

The soap-opera-like blend of previous relationships, unfinished business and unrequited desire that exists between the main characters of *Hedda Gabler* is as combustible as it is knotty. While the play itself takes place over the course of thirty-six hours, it is dealing with the fallout of fifteen years of festering resentment, spurned love, unresolved conflict and constrained longing within a group of people whose lives have been irrepressibly entangled. Ejlert, still preoccupied with Hedda despite the ending of their relationship some years before, is now the lover of Thea, who was herself previously the object of Jorgen's affections; Hedda and Thea were at school together where they existed in an antagonistic bully/victim relationship, and now as adults find themselves both married to men they don't love; Jorgen and Ejlert were contemporaries but competitors in the world of academia until Ejlert's alcoholism rendered him incapable of working, although his recent return to health through Thea's support has made him once more a dangerous professional rival to Jorgen. To add to the mix, Judge Brack, a trusted friend of Jorgen and former suitor of Hedda's, is now proposing that the three enter into what he enticingly calls a 'triangular' relationship. Ibsen creates a complex web of interrelationships and interdependence between his lead characters in which the decisions, ambitions and misdemeanours of their youth conspire to create tragic consequences.

Pistol-toting Hedda is understandably recognised as an iconic role for an actress. For someone who is so concerned with her inability to drive her own destiny or those of the people in her world, she certainly drives the action on stage. Described by Ibsen as 'demonic', Hedda is one of his most complex creations. She is a force of nature, a law unto herself and a seething ball of fury, despair and humour, buttoned neatly within a smart morning gown. Those who pass through her sphere seldom do so without falling prey to her wrath, deviousness or charm. She is an enigma, the reasons for her marriage to the uninspiring and socially inferior Jorgen never entirely revealed, nor the motivation for her wilful destruction of Ejlert, Thea and ultimately herself. She is a bleakly funny character, dry in her humour, caustic in her wit, and devastatingly brutal in the horror she smilingly wreaks on those who fall in her path.

First performed: Sweet Desserts Theatre Company at Battersea Arts Centre, London, 1997

Cast breakdown: 2f

Publisher: Faber and Faber in *Charlotte Jones: Plays 1*, 2004

Persephone Baker has fallen in love with a married man thirty years her senior. Dora Kitson likes wearing men's clothing and smoking cigars. Both are moral imbeciles, or at least, as far as their files at St Dymphna's Hospital for the Criminally Insane are concerned. The year is 1924 and young women who exhibit signs of deviancy need to be locked away. Persephone and Dora try to make the best of it; after all, surely it's only a matter of time before someone comes to get them out? In another reality and decades later, 'Porph' and 'Dorph' inhabit an odd world of fantasy, play-acting and an obsessive interest in the oeuvre of Doris Day. They may have made it out of St Dymphna's, but are they any closer to reality?

A sentence Charlotte Jones came across in a book – 'A Miss Kitson and a Miss Baker were placed in a Hospital for the Criminally Insane in the 1920s for bearing illegitimate children and not released until the 1970s' – sparked her interest in writing *Airswimming*. With sensitivity, humour and a healthy dose of theatrical flair, Jones gives an unexpectedly flamboyant treatment to the story of an imaginary Miss Kitson and Miss Baker, who, like their namesakes, have been locked away for decades for 'moral degeneracy'. It's similar territory to that covered by Valerie Windsor in her poignant drama *Effie's Burning* (2f, 1987) in which a burns-unit doctor is stunned to discover that an elderly patient has been in an institution since giving birth at the age of thirteen. While both plays throb with an underlying anger at the injustice done to such women, stylistically they couldn't be more different. *Airswimming* never ceases to surprise and, despite (or perhaps because of) the direness of her two protagonists' predicament, Jones creates a gloriously exuberant piece that is as weird as it is wonderful.

Jones's plays can be characterised by the improbable mix of ideas and influences that populate them (her best-known play, *Humble Boy*, is an unlikely combination of *Hamlet*, gardening, beekeeping, astrophysics and plastic surgery), and *Airswimming* is no exception. Doris Day, synchronised swimming, historical battles, trepanning and a Moulinex hand-mixer are recurring features. Likewise, references to Greek mythology are threaded throughout the piece, although rather than being kept in the Underworld by Hades, the fate of *Airswimming*'s Persephone seems to be that of perpetually having to clean the same tiled, institutional bathroom. Still, things could be worse according to her companion, the eternal optimist Dora: they could be on laundry duty ('the delirious wash, the imbeciles carry the linen to dry, the melancholy iron it and the monomaniacs fold it and put it away. And we have to sleep on those sheets. No wonder we all have nightmares'). It is this unusual combination of influences that lends *Airswimming* much of its emotional power. In comparison to the saccharine sweetness of Doris Day and the plastic glamour of synchronised swimming, the play's more sombre themes – mental illness, suicide, imprisonment and dehumanising medical treatments – seem all the more grim. Without taking us into any of St Dymphna's rooms besides the tiled bathroom that Persephone and Dora continually clean, Jones successfully evokes the brutality of these institutions, in which the mentally ill, physically impaired, social nonconformists and those considered to be of dubious morality were thrown in together, forgotten about, and left collectively to go slowly crazy.

Jones began her theatre career as an actress but, frustrated by the lack of roles open to her, turned to writing. *Airswimming* was her first play and in the original Battersea Arts Centre production she played Dora, a role that, as it turned out, would be her last on stage. Swapping acting for writing, Jones had an astounding and impressively speedy trajectory. Within four years of *Airswimming*'s appearance on London's fringe, *Humble Boy* had opened at the National Theatre, from where it transferred to the West End. While her move away from acting has been a permanent one, her largely unedifying early experience of the profession continues to resonate in the roles she writes for others. 'I can't write walk-on parts, probably because I played so many myself,' she commented in 2001, 'all my characters have a journey.' Her other predominantly female plays include *In Flame* (4f, 2m, 1999), a time-travelling drama about senile dementia, tap dancing and the dilemmas of being a thirty-something woman at the turn of the twenty-first century, and *Martha, Josie and the Chinese Elvis* (4f, 2m, 1999) a laugh-out-loud comedy in which a bizarre birthday party is made all the odder by the arrival of a Chinese Elvis impersonator.

46 | 4.48 Psychosis
by Sarah Kane (*b.* 1971, UK)

First performed: Royal Court Theatre, London, 2000

Cast breakdown: can be performed by a cast of any number or gender. The casting of the original production was 2f, 1m

Publisher: Methuen, 2000

Sarah Kane's exposition of a mind gone into overdrive as its owner teeters on the edge of suicide is an astonishingly honest, brutal and poetic literary achievement. Performable by a cast of two, two hundred or any number in between, it is an undeniably challenging and yet hugely beguiling piece of work. Delivering an hour-long hit of an unflinchingly raw depiction of mental anguish, it also captures the brilliance of the human brain. Kane's protagonist – simultaneously gifted and cursed by the clarity of her perception – unpacks the contents of her mind and there finds a consciousness that in its sophistication cannot help but prove her undoing.

'A piece for voices' is how Michael Billington of the *Guardian* described *4.48 Psychosis* at its 2000 premiere, 'it is not a play in the familiar sense of the word. It is more… a dramatised poem.' Billington wasn't alone among the critics in expressing a vague sense of bafflement over how to describe *4.48 Psychosis*, a play that spiritedly eludes categorisation. In the text, Kane gives no information as to what the audience sees happening on stage, who the people are that are speaking the words, nor how many of them are doing so. What she does give is a forensically detailed vocal score, rich in intricate aural patterns, which alternately assaults and seduces the ear of the audience and has a structure that is somehow both playful and desperately sad. Fragments of narrative do emerge; there's a patient who has formed an emotional attachment to a doctor who adamantly keeps their relationship on professional grounds, and a gradual, increasingly futile journey taken by that patient through a range of drug treatments (or 'chemical cures for congenital anguish,' as she calls them), each more damaging than the last. James Macdonald's original production at the Royal Court used just three actors, all of them in turn speaking the words of the protagonist and the doctor(s) trying to save her. At the same time, the text could be interpreted by a team of theatre-makers in a thousand different ways and by its audiences in even more.

Recognised as one of the most innovative voices of late-twentieth-century British theatre, each of Kane's plays saw her explode the accepted parameters of playwriting in some new and unexpected direction. *4.48 Psychosis* is no exception and it is testament to Kane's skill as a playwright that, while abandoning the conventional rules of plot, narrative, form and structure, she still creates characters and a world that an audience will care about deeply. Perhaps like a painter capturing the shape and quality of an object through painting the negative space around it, rather than the object itself, Kane conjures the central character so vividly in the audience's imagination largely by dint of what she *doesn't* write about her. We are told absolutely nothing about this person beyond the details of how she experiences her illness (is it an illness? The patient herself describes it as an 'anger') and yet there she is, vivid, recognisable and disturbingly real. Maybe it is Kane's decision to leave the canvas bare of almost all extraneous detail that makes *4.48 Psychosis* so moving, allowing as it does each audience member to project their own personal reading of the situation onto its central figure.

Throughout the play, Kane guides her audience by the hand into the dark recesses at the back of the human mind, recesses that all of us have but which most of us, depending on how you look at it, are either too wise or too stupid to spend much time digging about in. It's an unnerving journey to be taken on, one that at times feels harrowing and, at others, blessedly brief. The play offers no neat narrative, comforting resolution or cathartic release to help its audience digest the experience, there's just what there is – a horrifically painful and yet florid mental state. The playwright Mark Ravenhill, a friend and contemporary of Kane's, has identified this as a common theme in her work, suggesting 'it is quite confrontational because it doesn't reassure you with social context or Freudian psychology – it doesn't explain things. It just presents you with these austere, extreme situations.' As 'austere' and 'extreme' as the situations she depicts may be, for Kane, an overwhelming sense of goodness always permeated her work, despite what the critics may have said about it. 'I don't find my plays depressing or lacking hope,' she once commented in an interview. 'To create something beautiful about despair, is for me the most hopeful, life-affirming thing a person can do.'

Goodbye, My Fancy (originally titled Most Likely to Succeed) by Fay Kanin (b. 1917, USA)

First performed: Morosco Theatre, New York, 1948

Cast breakdown: 11f, 7m (doubling possible)

Publisher: Samuel French, 2010

Agatha Reed – successful war correspondent and now Congresswoman – is visiting her old college, Good Hope. She's being awarded an honorary degree, somewhat ironically given that she never actually graduated; the young Agatha was expelled when it was discovered she'd stayed out for the night with a man. But Good Hope is more than happy to overlook such a minor detail in the wake of all the positive publicity a renewed link with such a notable alumna will bring. Agatha's own motives for returning to Good Hope extend beyond a simple desire to take a stroll down memory lane. Jim Merrill, once a young professor at the college and the man over whom Agatha was expelled some twenty years ago, is now Good Hope's Principal. Agatha wants him back, but while she has spent the last two decades travelling all over the world, Jim has been comfortably ensconced in the quietude of a wealthy American women's college. As their political principles (or, in Jim's case, lack of political principles) clash, Agatha comes to realise that the man she has always loved was more a fiction of her imagination than a reality, and one to whom it is time to say goodbye.

Goodbye, My Fancy is an intriguing proposition. It's a solid piece of writing and does everything that a good, well-made American play of the 1940s could be expected to do – secure narrative structure, excellent plotting, fizzing dialogue, great gags, rounded characters and so on. But it's the play's political perspective, and its unusual combination of setting and subject matter that makes it stand out so strikingly from other plays of its period. Robert Garland, one of the founding members of the New York Drama Critics' Circle, described *Goodbye, My Fancy* as an 'earnest, adult play with laughter on the surface and underneath, a fierce, almost frightening cry for common sense'. It's a piece that, just three years after America dropped the atomic bomb, asks breathtakingly important questions about individual and collective responsibility in the face of foreign atrocities, about big-business profiteering in wartime, about wealth, the luxury of apathy that it brings, and the role of education in ensuring that the young never repeat the mistakes of their parents. That it does all of this from the single setting of a girls' dormitory room makes *Goodbye, My Fancy* all the more unusual.

The collision between Agatha's proactive stance on world affairs and the carefully cultivated inertia that Good Hope instils in its staff and students provides the dramatic touchpaper from which the events of the play ignite. Central to the plot is a disagreement over whether a graphic anti-war film Agatha has made should be shown to the students. The school's trustees feel that young people – and in particular young women – should not be exposed to such horrors, suggesting instead their focus should be kept firmly on more appropriate pursuits, such as attending dances and thinking about homemaking. The college's apparent squeamishness at opening its students' eyes to the reality of their country's recent violent past is something that shakes Agatha, not just as a politically engaged human being, but as a woman. Part of a generation that thrived on the opportunity that wartime conscription gave them to get into the workplace, she is surprised by the healthy doses of propaganda being meted out to the girls of Good Hope, encouraging them back into lives of domesticity and frivolity. 'Let their daughters bring their knitting to classes and read movie magazines inside their notebook covers' is the defeated stance of jaded Physics professor Pitt, who has had his attempts to teach about nuclear armament quashed by the school's governors, 'let them all be wiped off the face of the earth without even knowing why. Like the pigs and the mice at Bikini. Maybe it's better to die stupid, like an animal.' The ability to remain 'stupid' is something the affluent young women of Good Hope can afford to do.

Despite belonging to an incredibly specific moment in time, *Goodbye, My Fancy* continues to resonate powerfully today. It's a travesty that the play isn't performed more frequently, giving as it does a perspective on women's relationship with education, war and political activism that is rarely seen. Likewise, its comments on the inherent conservatism that patronage in the education system brings are as adroit as they ever were. 'Give a college a science building – then tell the professors what they can say in it. Give them a motion-picture machine but tell them what to run on it. That's not generosity. That's an investment – with damned good dividends!' is Agatha's parting salvo to the college's main donor. It is a sentiment that remains relevant today and, as big business becomes an increasingly powerful force, likely to be evermore so. Both an astonishing document of its time and a powerful piece today, *Goodbye, My Fancy* is a play that urgently deserves to be seen by audiences again.

48 · it felt empty when the heart went at first but it is alright now by Lucy Kirkwood (b. 1984, UK)

First performed: Clean Break with the Arcola Theatre, London, 2009

Cast breakdown: 2f

Publisher: Nick Hern Books, 2009

Welcome to the world of Dijana. She's early twenties, lives in London and dreams of swimming in the sea at Brighton. She's good at maths, likes nice shampoo and reads *Cosmopolitan* magazine. She's also a sex slave, trafficked from Eastern Europe. Lucy Kirkwood's gorgeously imaginative and, at times, devastatingly graphic depiction of one trafficked woman's story is anything but predictable. There's more to Dijana than her status as victim and in a breathtaking collision between fantasy and reality, degradation and aspiration, Dijana has a journey to take us on. A magical landscape awaits and as we chase Dijana through time and space, her trail takes us on a precarious route, traversing the fragile boundary between a nightmare and a dream.

Originally conceived as a promenade piece, *it felt empty...* sends its audience in chase of Dijana as she dashes through a contorted Alice in Wonderland-esque landscape from one form of prison to the next. She darts through air ventilation shafts, coughs up tiny golden keys in her phlegm and flies through airports, police stations and detention centres. Kirkwood created the piece in 'close collaboration' with the original production's director and design team, and the published playtext documents meticulously the exquisite worlds, jam-packed with sights, sounds and smells in which they immersed their audience. Carefully plotted in such a way as to constantly challenge the audience's expectations, the piece slides further along the scale from naturalism to surrealism the deeper we get into Dijana's story, and by the final scene, when we find ourselves in a wide-open cornfield (complete with door in the horizon) and discover Dijana diligently vacuuming it, we entirely accept the reality of the situation. Originally staged in a large warehouse, Kirkwood feels there is ample flexibility in the text to relocate it: 'I think it would be just as possible to produce the play simply in a single studio space.' Executed almost as a solo performance (a second role – Gloria, Dijana's cellmate – appears as a brief cameo in the middle of the play), *it felt empty*... offers a challenging, but fantastically rewarding opportunity to a young actress.

As Clean Break's Writer in Residence, Kirkwood had worked with women in and leaving the criminal justice system and had spent 'a lot of time thinking about what captivity does to you'. But it was learning about the experiences of trafficked women held in detention centres such as Yarl's Wood that gave her the inspiration for *it felt empty*... Just as Dijana, having surrendered her passport to her trafficker-turned-'boyfriend'-turned- pimp Babac, escapes his captivity only to find herself swiftly landed in a detention centre, so many of the women Kirkwood interviewed in her research for the play had undergone a similar trajectory. 'The idea that someone might be incarcerated, punished for being the *victim* of crime was breathtaking to me,' she reflects in her introduction to the play.

Early in the action, Dijana delivers a pastiche of a L'Oréal advert, shaking her hair out of its ponytail in slow motion while announcing the slogan 'Because I'm worth it.' Actually, Dijana does know exactly how much she's worth: one thousand euros was the fee Babac paid to obtain her from her cousin, a figure which she helpfully informs us 'is like two-and-a-half iPhones'. Now, finding herself forced into sex slavery to repay a £20,000 debt she inexplicably owes to Babac, another price has been put on Dijana's head, one that will line another man's pockets, and of which she herself will fail to see a penny. The thirty pounds with which a client can buy Dijana's time, body and submission is a further demeaning price tag to apply to her, no matter how many times she tells us she is 'real high-class'. The play's closing moments, in which the London skyline is illuminated just beyond Dijana's East London flat – complete with the Houses of Parliament, London Eye and Canary Wharf on the horizon – delivers a final emotional bite. These, Kirkwood observes in the play's closing stage directions, are 'Seats of money and power. Places full of tourists and men in suits, with money to burn and wives that don't understand them.' Their fleeting appearance offers us a sobering reminder of the proximity between these engines of our society, our culture and our identity, and the trade in human lives that is flourishing in their – and our – midst.

First performed: Society Hill Playhouse, Philadelphia, 1962

Cast breakdown: 8f, 2m

Publisher: Methuen, 1969

Queen Isabella of Spain, Constanz Mozart, Joan of Arc, Gertrude Stein, Osa Johnson, Pearl White, Amelia Earhart and Susan B. Anthony are gathered in a room. Convening the 'Sixth Annual Meeting of the Duly-Elected Grievance and Someday-Governing Committee of Wing Five, Women's Section', they discuss what is to be done about a perceived threat emanating from the neighbouring men's ward. No one seems to know exactly what that threat is, or indeed, quite when an attack might come, but they're determined to be organised. Susan B. Anthony is the Chair, Gertrude Stein is taking minutes, and if she can only stop bickering with Joan of Arc long enough for anyone else to get a word in edgeways, a clear plan of action might be achieved. But as things become increasingly heated, order breaks down and the committee meeting takes an unexpected turn.

Nearly twenty years before Caryl Churchill sat an assortment of female historical figures around a table in *Top Girls*, Arthur Kopit had done so in his absurdist one-act play *Chamber Music*. Much of the intriguing oddness of Kopit's piece comes from the perpetual and never-answered question of whether the eight women around the table are who they say they are, or are merely eight unexceptional individuals suffering from delusions of grandeur. Kopit refers to the characters throughout as Woman Who Plays Records, Woman in Safari Outfit, Woman with Notebook, Girl in Gossamer Dress, Woman in Aviatrix's Outfit, Woman in Queenly Spanish Garb, Woman in Armour and Woman with Gavel, rather than Constanz Mozart, Osa Johnson, Gertrude Stein, etc., despite this being how the women address one another. The brief appearance halfway through the action of a smiling white-coated doctor, who chastises the 'girls' with patronising charm for causing too much noise, adds to the confusion. Whether the audience is meant to conclude the women are patients on a mental ward (with admittedly impressive costumes – 'Joan' appears in a full set of armour and carrying a seven-foot-tall wooden crucifix), or whether the asylum set-up is a metaphor for the way ambitious women have traditionally been treated by history, is something on which Kopit remains beguilingly non-committal. Not that it matters either way – much of *Chamber Music*'s appeal comes from the weird world it presents. To attempt to rationalise what is going on is in many ways to miss the point.

Chamber Music has regularly been identified as an analogy for the Cold War, focusing as it does on a self-important committee obsessed with the possibility of an impending attack by an unknown adversary, basing their fears on evidence that is inconclusive to say the least. In a report haltingly read out to the committee by Pearl White (a star of silent movies, she appears to be having trouble with some of the bigger words in her notes), it seems members of the Women's Section of Wing Five have experienced 'definite sensations of belligerency', and seeing no immediate source for such feelings, have concluded that the only place they can be coming from is the mysterious men's wing that lies on the other side of the wall. Their tactics for addressing the issue range from the ridiculous to the sublime (why not kill the men then eat them? explorer Osa Johnson suggests), although the prevailing fear of losing their 'privileges' prevents the women from leaping to action. What, after all, would life be without bowling, movie screenings or the annual Christmas party?

As the meeting hits dead end after dead end, tensions mount and pandemonium ensues. Finally concluding that the best way to warn the men off making an attack is by sending the slain corpse of one of them over the wall to show they are not to be messed with, the action escalates into an animalistic frenzy as each woman attempts to attack another, rather than herself becoming the sacrifice. In the end, poor Amelia Earhart gets it and is violently dispatched by her fellow committee members, who then leave her mangled corpse in a heap on the floor. The most surreal of meetings is concluded with Joan still complaining about having rusty pants, Pearl wearing Amelia's goggles as a bra, and absolutely nothing having been done about the problem of the men.

50 — Men Should Weep
by Ena Lamont Stewart (*b.* 1912, UK)

First performed: Athenaeum Theatre, Glasgow, 1947

Cast breakdown: 11f, 6m

Publisher: Samuel French, 1994

Ena Lamont Stewart's portrait of life in a Glasgow slum is both an extraordinary document of working-class life during the depression of the 1930s and a widely regarded classic of twentieth-century theatre. Maggie Morrison, mother of seven, wife of a long-term unemployed husband and carer to his elderly mother, scrapes by on her meagre charlady earnings, the favours of neighbours and the charity of her childless sister. Having struggled on in such a way for years, Maggie is resigned to poverty and its inherent degradations. But as her increasingly wayward brood kick against the hand that fate has dealt the family, Maggie's head-in-the-sand attitude looks less and less tenable. She must decide whether to watch her beloved family disintegrate, or fight to secure a better life for them all.

Written entirely in Glasgow's idiosyncratic dialect, *Men Should Weep* gives audiences an insight into Lamont Stewart's youth in the city. 'I have always loved the speech of the Glasgow people,' she once commented. 'It is marvellously rhythmic; it lends itself to pathos and humour.' The daughter of a minister, Lamont Stewart's own early life was a comfortable one, although through her father's role in the community she would have been all too aware of the less fortunate circumstances among which Glasgow's poor found themselves. Attending a theatre performance in the early 1940s she 'came home in a mood of red-hot revolt against cocktail time, glamorous gowns... I asked myself what I wanted to see on stage and the answer was life. Real life. Ordinary life.' An early play, *Starched Aprons*, inspired by her experiences working behind a hospital counter, was produced by the Unity Theatre in 1946, and *Men Should Weep* followed the subsequent year. It was a runaway success, popular with audiences and critics alike and yet, bizarrely, Lamont Stewart struggled to secure productions for her subsequent plays. Despite the widespread trumpeting of *Men Should Weep* as a defining moment in Scottish theatre, its author was practically ignored by the establishment. She continued to work as a librarian whilst writing plays that were to be rejected one by one by the theatres her earlier work had influenced. It wasn't until the theatre company 7:84 revived *Men Should Weep* at the Citizens Theatre thirty-five years after its original production that Lamont Stewart once again received the attention she so richly deserves. After years of practical invisibility, *Men Should Weep* was appreciated for the significant role it played in bringing working-class voices, and particularly female ones, to the stage.

Men Should Weep is a play about what happens to self-worth and self-interest at a time of economic depression. When limited resources mean some will sink while others swim, being one of the few to stay afloat often means doing so at the expense of those around you. Maggie's sister-in-law Lizzie gets by through her dubious loan-shark activities and is reviled for it, while Alec, Maggie's oldest son, and his wife Isa derive their income from mugging women in the streets. At the same time, Maggie and her husband John's more ethical, although largely inert, approach of sitting it out in poverty and hoping some external force will alter their circumstances is one which is increasingly challenged by their children. 'Some men gets on an makes money, depression or no. Ithers hasna the brains' is teenage daughter Jenny's stinging criticism of her unemployed father when she demands to know why he hasn't been more enterprising in his efforts to provide a decent home for her and her siblings.

With both humour and a level of detail that is at times painful to watch, Lamont Stewart depicts the explosive family dynamics of the expansive Morrison clan, packed as they are into three dirty and insufficiently furnished rooms. 'I didnae ask to be born' is a rebuke slung by Jenny at her father – one that will have been heard by many parents of teenaged children – but the manner in which the Morrison family are subsisting undoubtedly makes family life harder to survive than if they were afforded the dignity of reasonable living standards. It was being born 'intae this midden,' Jenny tells her parents, that she particularly resents, 'the kitchen's aye like a pig-sty, there's never ony decent food, an if there wis, ye'd hae nae appetite for it'. Her decision to leave the chaotic family home in search of a better life is one an audience will understand, but also appreciate as emotionally complex. While pragmatically, having one less mouth to feed and person to house should be a relief, to her doting parents it is a stinging rejection by their beloved daughter and an all too apparent demonstration of their inability to provide. Insidious, suffocating and desperately hard to escape, Lamont Stewart captures with sharpness, anger and wit the wretched effects of poverty.

51 **More Light**
by Bryony Lavery (b. 1947, UK)

First performed: in schools and youth theatres across the UK as part of National Theatre Connections, 1997

Cast breakdown: 17f, 2m (doubling possible)

Publisher: Faber and Faber, 2001

Approaching death, an all-powerful Emperor commissions the finest thinkers, artists and craftsmen in his kingdom to build him a spectacular tomb, one that will be a work of art and a monument to his greatness. Fearful that after his death his body will be disturbed, he decrees that all who have worked on the tomb shall be sealed up inside it with him. The Emperor's concubines have been awarded the dubious honour of accompanying him to his final resting place, and now, after his death, find themselves effectively buried alive in the vast mausoleum. Feeling increasingly peckish and deciding to put the Emperor's corpse to good use, the women embark on a campaign of cannibalism, perfecting their cooking skills as they make their way through their former master, before moving on to the ever-declining legion of thinkers, artists and craftsmen who have been buried alongside them. As the dwindling supply of human meat keeps the women alive, their creativity flourishes and they construct a mini-empire of their own. Inspired by their new-found autonomy, but knowing their supply of food won't last for ever, these previously silenced women determine to make their mark before it is too late.

More Light was written for Connections, the National Theatre's scheme which annually commissions ten new plays from leading playwrights, written specifically for performance by thirteen- to nineteen-year-olds. Over the years the Connections plays have included some strong pieces for female-heavy casts. In particular Moira Buffini's *A Vampire Story* (2008), Isabel Wright's *Blooded* (2005), Lucinda Coxon's *The Ice Palace* (2003) and Sarah Daniels' *Dust* (2003) offer great roles for girls. Similarly, Lavery's 2002 play for Connections, *Illyria*, is a hard-hitting piece about Maria, a British journalist who travels to a war-torn nation to interview the wife of a dictator and finds herself quickly caught up in dangerous events. All the Connections plays have been published in annual anthologies with copies being placed in every secondary school in the country.

Although written for young people, *More Light* isn't a play that shies away from the darkest of subject matter. Cannibalism, castration and prostitution (including child sex – the youngest of the Emperor's concubines is just six) aren't usual material for plays for young people, yet Lavery never sensationalises the women's sorry predicament but instead creates a lyrical, dignified piece that foregrounds the beauty of their final weeks over and above their ugliness. It's true that the accounts of how the concubines performed sex acts on the Emperor may put the play off-limits for some drama teachers and youth-theatre directors, but these sections of the play are as poetic as they are explicit. Written entirely in verse and with a fairy-tale quality, it's a play that is firmly allegorical and, although it steps into complex territory, does so with a great deal of vivacity, warmth and sensitivity. So too, a hefty helping of humour diffuses the darkest aspects of the play, and as the women perfect their casseroling technique it is hard to take their macabre cannibalistic activities entirely seriously. Unlike so many plays for young people set in the 'here and now' and revolving around topical concerns and contemporary youth language, *More Light* is that rare thing – a play for young people that is unlikely to date. It is just as fresh, just as funny, relevant and provocative as it was when first performed in the 1990s. There is no reason why *More Light* should not go on to entice and charm future generations coming to it for the first time. Although originally written for young people, the play has received numerous productions by adult and professional companies.

More Light's dissection of the relationship between art and power makes it an unexpectedly subversive and political piece of work. While the women's previous opportunities to be creative began and ended with pleasuring the Emperor, in his absence they discover the terrific scope of their artistic abilities and engage in a jubilant period of drawing, sculpture, dancing, poetry, music-making and cookery. The tools available to them are meagre, cobbled together from the items in the tomb, and the women know their drawings, origami birds and clay models will crumble and disintegrate long before the man-made mausoleum. Yet they continue anyway, and the play's comment on women's ongoing struggle for their art to receive the same recognition, visibility and resources as men's remains a pertinent subject for professional theatre-makers as well as a fascinating topic with which to engage future generations.

52 Summer of the Seventeenth Doll
by Ray Lawler (*b.* 1921, Australia)

First performed: Union Theatre, Melbourne, 1955

Cast breakdown: 4f, 3m

Publisher: Samuel French, 2000

For the last sixteen summers, cane-cutters and best friends Roo and Barney have spent the 'layoff season' down south in Melbourne in the company of Olive and Nancy. Inseparable for the duration of the boys' annual five-month stay, the four friends' summers have become the stuff of legend, filled with a magical blend of fun, sunshine and romance. But on the seventeenth summer everything is different. Nancy has married and moved away and in her place is Pearl, a widow and workmate of Olive's who isn't entirely convinced by the set-up, nor her apparent role as Nancy's replacement in Barney's bed. Roo and Barney seem to have fallen out, there are problems with money, and Olive's cantankerous mother Emma appears even more intent on dispensing doom and gloom than usual. Holed up in the house Olive and Emma share, the foursome can't seem to get along, let alone have a good time, no matter how intently Olive tries to jolly the party along. As the sun beats down and tensions reach breaking point, there's no way to avoid facing up to the fact that they have outgrown one another.

'It was a queer experience to hear Australian place names and idiom being used in a big theatre after years of Bournemouth boarding house settings and brittle West End chatter.' So commented the *Sydney Morning Herald* the day after *Summer of the Seventeenth Doll*'s 1956 Sydney premiere. Credited with creating a turning point in Australian theatre, Ray Lawler's three-act drama was revolutionary. Whereas Australian audiences' experiences of theatregoing had previously consisted largely of imported British and American dramas, this new play showed Australian characters, speaking in Australian accents and in an Australian setting. It caused a sensation and the play, which had already moved to Sydney from its original home in Melbourne, went on to tour the country before receiving productions in the UK and USA. Now regarded as a classic of Australian theatre, *Summer of the Seventeenth Doll* was in many ways at the vanguard of the Australian cultural explosion of the 1960s, '70s and '80s, an extraordinary period of artistic activity in which the film, theatre and television of the country redefined how Australia saw itself, and how the world saw Australia.

A play about getting older, *Summer of the Seventeenth Doll* is a cautionary tale about the dangers of trying to defy time and the disillusionment that any attempt to do so will inevitably bring. All approaching their forties, but behaving as they did in their twenties, Olive, Roo and Barney have doggedly ignored the passing of the years, a foible which is now reaping horrible rewards. Roo, previously assured of his own virility, is still reeling from the shock of being outdone on the work field by a man nearly fifteen years his junior, while Barney, a former Lothario introduced to us by Lawler as a man 'with the beginning of a pot belly', is coming to terms with the realisation that his advances are now more likely to make girls laugh than go weak at the knees. Olive is devoted to Roo but cannot bring herself to accept his proposal of marriage, unable to conceive of their relationship as anything other than a constantly revisited five months of summer romance followed by seven months of abstinence in which every waking moment is focused on awaiting his return. Her misplaced attempt to draft Pearl in as a replacement for Nancy has inadvertently shone a light on the cracks in the gang's formerly happy exterior, rather than hide them, and now, with Pearl's eyes gazing with a mixture of condescension, pity and bemusement on the unconventional set-up, Olive is horrified to discover it is long past its sell-by date. Only Nancy, it seems, had the good sense to get out 'while the going was good'.

A master of dramatic plotting, Lawler ratchets the tension up notch by notch so that by the beginning of Act Three the living room of Emma's Victorian terrace is a veritable pressure cooker. It's a play that's incredibly dark and, for the mid-1950s, unquestionably racy, featuring ambiguous expressions of sexuality and focusing on the relationships of couples rejecting marriage in favour of living in sin. Even in less demure times, *Summer of the Seventeenth Doll* is a piece that maintains a bewitching quality and at times a desperately sad edge. In an increasingly youth-obsessed world, there is an argument that the play is an even more powerful comment on our times than when it was first performed. A salutary reminder of the impermanence of youth, *Summer of the Seventeenth Doll* remains an exquisite depiction of the folly of those who fail to relinquish it.

First performed: Royal Court Theatre, London, 1967 (written in 1912)

Cast breakdown: 3f, 2m

Publisher: Penguin, in *Three Plays by D.H. Lawrence*, 1969

'Let *her* make him as good a wife as I made him a mother!' was the gauntlet laid down by Mrs Gascoigne upon hearing of her son Luther's intention to marry Minnie Hetherington. Now, six weeks after the wedding, Mrs Gascoigne remains a forceful presence in her son and new daughter-in-law's lives, despite Minnie's determined efforts to claim Luther for herself. When news that Luther has got a local girl pregnant reaches Mrs Gascoigne, she uses it to drive a wedge between the young couple. As Minnie and Luther's already tumultuous marriage reaches breaking point, Minnie takes decisive action to unite her husband and herself in the face of her mother-in-law's unwanted interventions.

Like his other early plays, *A Collier's Friday Night* and *The Widowing of Mrs Holroyd*, *The Daughter-in-Law* is set in a Nottinghamshire mining community similar to the one into which D.H. Lawrence was born. Although he wrote the play whilst working as a schoolteacher in Croydon, Lawrence clearly carried a strong impression of the dialect and speech patterns of Nottinghamshire families such as the Gascoignes with him to Surrey; the language of the play is rich, highly idiosyncratic and, when heard spoken aloud, both deeply expressive and wryly humorous. During arguments (and the characters of *The Daughter-in-Law* do spend the overwhelming majority of the play arguing), when 'snaggin' and snarlin'' at one another, the language the Gascoignes use is like a weapon, wonderfully pointed, endlessly inventive and, at times, enjoyably obtuse. 'You're neither salt nor sugar' is Mrs Gascoigne's observation of Minnie, who in turn suggests 'a gramophone in breeches' would be as much good to her as Luther, given that all he can do is 'shilly-shally and crawl' to his mother. Not just a snapshot of life in a now-transformed industrial community, *The Daughter-in-Law* captures a unique and long-disappeared manner of speech.

But for all their words, the characters of *The Daughter-in-Law* suffer from a crippling inability to express themselves. The tragedy of the Gascoigne family is that they cannot articulate how they really feel, either to themselves, or to one another. As a group, they are stuck; appalled by the scale of their feelings, and yet somehow unable to ask even those nearest to them for help. This is a community that doesn't talk about emotions. Certainly, they may smash a few plates and throw the odd object into the fire in an effort to make their feelings known, but when it actually comes to saying what they are experiencing, whether it be burning love, gut-wrenching jealousy or grinding disappointment, they are at a loss. In particular, Minnie and Luther, the newly married couple who have wooed and agreed their engagement largely through the writing of letters, now find themselves entirely ill-equipped to be in a relationship. They are baffled by one another, and their inability to communicate, paired with a healthy dose of stubbornness and almost entire lack of empathy, means that just six weeks into their marriage they are almost constantly at war. As the backdrop to a marriage stymied by what is either the inability or refusal of either party to communicate, Lawrence positions contemporary industrial disputes between the pitmen and their bosses. These disputes descend, over the course of the play, from stalemate strikes to rioting, mirroring the increasingly volatile relationship between Minnie and Luther.

Already a published writer at the time of *The Daughter-in-Law*'s completion in 1912, Lawrence failed to secure a production of the play within his lifetime. Even with the release of novels such as *Sons and Lovers*, *The Rainbow* and *Women in Love* in the years that followed, the play received little attention. This was the case for all of Lawrence's works for the stage, a situation more indicative of the tastes of the contemporary theatre establishment than the quality of the plays themselves. Getting plays produced that focused on the experiences of working-class rather than middle-class people, and which revelled in the inherent messiness of authentic speech patterns, was beyond even this successful young novelist. It would not be until later in the twentieth century – and after his death – that Lawrence's plays would begin to find the audiences of which he was always so confident.

First performed: Steppenwolf Theatre, Chicago, 2007

Cast breakdown: 7f, 6m

Publisher: Nick Hern Books, 2008

Alcoholic poet Beverly Weston and his pill-addicted wife Violet have been living a chaotic existence in their sprawling but decaying house in Osage County, Oklahoma. A few days after hiring Johnna, a young, Native American woman as a live-in house help, Beverly disappears and is subsequently found drowned in a local lake. Violet's three adult daughters, her sister and their respective husbands, fiancés and children arrive from far and near in the wake of Beverly's disappearance. It is a swelteringly hot August and, as the extended family crowds under one roof, tensions rise, old disputes reignite and secrets emerge.

With its blend of family discord, crumbling veneers, abandoned dreams and gasp-inducing revelations, it is easy to trace a line between Letts's 2007 *August: Osage County* and the 'greats' of the early-twentieth-century American playwriting canon. The influence of Eugene O'Neill, Tennessee Williams and Arthur Miller hangs heavy over the play, but that is not to define *August: Osage County* as pastiche. It is in itself an impressive piece of drama, skilfully crafted, expertly balanced, and above all, a deeply engrossing act of storytelling. Running at over three hours in length, it is a big, solid play that revolves around a richly textured ensemble of thirteen characters, all of whom are exquisitely detailed, with sharply defined dramatic arcs and the opportunity to play both the humour and the pathos of the piece. Writing in the first decade of the twenty-first century, Letts's focus on the women's stories – and in particular his creation of a wide range of female roles which are all complex, challenging and vital to the action – reflects how much women's place in society has changed since O'Neill, Williams and Miller were writing. It is arguably the foregrounding of the women's voices that above all else injects fresh energy into this familiar genre.

August: Osage County is a play about a fictional extended family, but it is also a play about America – about its landscape, its geography, its values and its aspirations. Shortly before disappearing to take his own life, Beverly refers to the contents of his house as 'all this garbage we've acquired, our life's work'. Like Miller's *Death of a Salesman*, a sad sense of disillusionment in the American Dream resonates throughout. For the older generation of the Weston family, this seems to hinge on an inability to understand why the material benefits they struggled to acquire have failed to make their children and grandchildren happy; just as *Salesman*'s Willy Loman wonders why his hard work has failed to make his children successful. So, too, the American landscape which once would have held such potential and such promise becomes a source of disappointment. Returning to her childhood home on the Oklahoma plains, Violet's oldest daughter Barbara stares bleakly into the distance and asks 'we fucked the Indians for *this*?' The Weston's impressively large house, once the pride of the successful Irish homesteaders who built it, is now decaying, having been neglected for decades. Since her arrival, it is kept in a habitable state thanks entirely to the efforts of Johnna, the Native American who, more than a century after her forefathers would have been forced off the land, moves quietly in and out of the rooms, cooking, cleaning, and fetching cold beers for the Westons when bidden.

The play premiered at the Steppenwolf Theatre in Chicago in June 2007, before transferring in December of that year to Broadway, and winning the Pulitzer Prize in 2008. The critics were almost universal in their praise, forgiving Letts even for his unsparing use of theatrical tropes in recognition of the overall accomplishment of the piece. 'The list of pathologies afflicting one or another of the Weston family is seemingly endless, and in some ways wearily familiar,' *The New York Times* observed, 'but Mr Letts's antic recombination of soapy staples is so pop-artfully orchestrated that you never see the next curveball coming, and the play is so quotably funny I'd have a hard time winnowing favorite lines to a dozen.' As well as receiving widespread acclaim for Letts, the original production scooped a range of awards for its director Anna D. Shapiro, including a Tony for Best Director of a Play. Since 2007, *August: Osage County* has gone on to have an impressively broad international presence, receiving productions in Argentina, Australia, Austria, Denmark, Germany, Holland, Israel, New Zealand, Sweden and at the National Theatre in the UK. A film version, starring Meryl Streep and Julia Roberts, brought the trials of the warring Weston family to the big screen in 2013.

First performed: Women's Theatre Group at the Oval, London, 1985

Cast breakdown: 4f

Publisher: Methuen, in *Deborah Levy Plays: 1*, 2000

Deborah Levy's highly original *Pax* deconstructs the twentieth century via the most surreal of house visits. A group of women – the embodiments of the past, the present and the future – come together under one roof and, over meals of boiled eagle eggs and a recently dispatched pet rabbit, seek to establish the role they have played in the terror and brilliance of the century. Existing in an alternate reality that hovers somewhere between memory, a dream, and the mundane day-to-day, the women engage in their own kind of cold war. Edging towards an understanding of one another and, crucially, of how they are related, they conceive a fragile form of peace.

Deborah Levy was originally commissioned by the Women's Theatre Group to write an 'anti-nuclear' play. But, as she comments in her preface to *Pax*, felt an intense dislike for 'those "last two minutes in a bunker"-type scenarios so decided to write about twentieth-century Europe instead'. The result is an astounding piece of work; sharp, profound, wry, weird and wonderful. It was Levy's first full-length play, written at just twenty-three, and in many ways exhibits the rough, untamed abandon of a first-time writer who has little to lose and so throws herself head first at a subject matter of near-impossible scale and complexity. And while it's a play that is messy in places and difficult in others, there's a sharp intelligence at work and an understanding of theatrical form that is sophisticated enough to subvert normal conventions to thrilling effect. The vividness and poeticism with which Levy captures the grief, anguish and idealism of a century's worth of progress and self-harm is a remarkable achievement, and one that has lost little of its urgency, anger or awe. Lily Susan Todd, the director of the play's 1985 premiere, remembers receiving the script: 'I knew I was looking at something genuinely innovative.' It is testament to the quality and uniqueness of Levy's writing that a director coming to *Pax* for the first time, some thirty years on, could quite legitimately feel the same way.

The action takes place in what Levy describes as a 'large desolate house in the wilderness'. In it, the Keeper, an impossibly old, silver-haired woman shuffles around clanking keys, serving schnapps and carding the dogs for wool. The Mourner has come to stay, an archaeologist who is as bereft at the recent loss of her mother as she is over the state of her own life and, following her, a second house guest, the Domesticated Woman, all bleached hair, chirpy smile and fathomless internal angst. Each of the women is, according to Levy, an archetype representing a different aspect of the twentieth century's tumultuous trajectory. The Keeper is 'the past... Europe herself', the Mourner 'the present', and the Domesticated Woman 'both the present and the past'. Completing the quartet is H.D. or Hidden Daughter, Levy's depiction of the future, who is 'trying to make sense of the present.' The child of the Keeper, H.D., according to Levy, is 'a young woman who trusts the evidence of her eyes and ears and is dismayed by that evidence'.

Around the house visit of the Mourner and the Domesticated Woman, the play takes a whistle-stop tour of the highs and lows of modern history, darting from one decade to the next, between continents and world orders and taking in politics, religion, war, science, ideology, art, technology and popular culture along the way. There are reminiscences of breakfasts with Dalí and Freud, opium smoking with Madame Mao, and talk of Berlin cabarets, leukaemia, the Third Reich, Elvis Presley, missile bases, Capitalism, Communism, revolution and face cream. It's a dizzying hotchpotch that Levy skilfully crafts into one exhilarating, evocative and often achingly poignant theatrical mosaic, one that will send audiences out of the theatre with heads swimming and hearts touched. Grimly funny, and at times wilfully overwhelming, *Pax* remains a startlingly tenacious first play. Admittedly flawed, but brilliant in spite of it, it's a gem of a play which may have a hundred things wrong with it, but a thousand things right.

First performed: Avenida Theatre, Buenos Aires, 1945 (written in 1936)

Cast breakdown: 12f, plus a group of non-speaking women

Recommended version: by David Hare, 2005

Publisher: Faber and Faber, 2005

'Not far from Granada, there is a tiny village where my parents owned a small estate: Valderrubio. In the neighbouring house lived an old widow Doña Bernarda, who practised a tyrannical and relentless control over her unmarried daughters. They were like prisoners, deprived of any free will; I never spoke to them at all but I used to see them going by like shadows, always silent and always dressed in black... at the end of the courtyard there was an interconnecting well, which didn't have any water in it. I used to go down into it to spy on this strange family whose curious behaviour intrigued me. From there I could observe them. It was a cold and silent hell in the middle of the African sun, like a tomb of living people under the iron rod of their warden. And this is how *The House of Bernarda Alba* was born.' – Federico García Lorca, speaking in 1936

Lorca's story of Bernarda Alba, a ferocious matriarch who exerts a tyrannical rule over her five daughters, is arguably one of the best-known all-female plays. The action takes place immediately after the funeral of Bernarda Alba's second husband as she battles to maintain control over her increasingly fractious brood. In the unbearable heat of a ferociously hot summer, Bernarda decrees an extended period of mourning will be observed by her daughters. All of them will be locked inside the sweltering house, their already limited interactions with the outside world even more restricted than usual. The only exception is Angustias, the oldest sister, who is permitted to talk for a time every night between the bars of her window with Pepe el Romano, a local man whom she will shortly marry. It's a union clearly born out of Pepe's interest in Angustias's impending inheritance, rather than any personal or physical attraction between the pair, and is a relationship that Adela, Angustias's spirited and youngest sister, is determined to prevent. In Bernarda's ham-fisted attempts to retain order in the face of Adela's increasingly desperate efforts, tragedy ensues.

Lorca's depiction of a human spirit fighting against the appalling curtailments imposed by the very authority figure who should be nurturing it, is an enduringly potent piece of drama. Written as Fascism descended on Spain, it is a poignant and powerful cry against any regime that threatens to crush independent thought or desire.

Lorca completed *The House of Bernarda Alba* in June 1936. It was the third in what is now considered to be a trilogy of tragedies focusing on the experiences of women, the first being *Blood Wedding* (8f, 6m, 1933) and the second, *Yerma* (18f, 6m, 1934). The play was finished just weeks before the outbreak of the Spanish Civil War and Lorca – already a well-known poet and playwright with the combustible credentials of being a known homosexual, a member of avant-garde arts circles and a vocal supporter of leftist politics – travelled from his home in Madrid to his native Granada, fearing an outbreak of violence. It was a move that proved to be impotent and on 16th August 1936 he was arrested by Fascists. Two days later he was taken to the hills of Fuente Grande and shot dead, his body left in an unmarked grave. His final work, which in its subject matter foreshadowed his own imminent silencing, was premiered in Argentina in 1945, but would remain unperformed in Spain for a further twenty-eight years.

The House of Bernarda Alba has enjoyed a career of constant reworking and multiple English translations of the text are available. Although so clearly rooted in the customs and geography of early twentieth-century Andalusian society – and many productions do locate the action in accordance with Lorca's original vision – the play has frequently and successfully been reconceived by generations of theatre-makers to different places and moments in history. A 2012 production at the Almeida Theatre in North London used Emily Mann's relatively faithful 1997 version of the text, but relocated the action to rural Iran, while Rona Munro's radical reinterpretation for the 2009 National Theatre of Scotland production whisked the play to modern-day East End Glasgow as Bernarda (or 'Bernie') attempts to speed through the marriage of her eldest daughter in the wake of her husband's recent gangland death. Whatever the political, ideological or religious prisons within which a society can impound its citizens, *The House of Bernarda Alba* remains a resonant parallel. In an interview in *El Sol* published weeks before his death, Lorca commented, 'The day we stop resisting our instincts we'll have learned how to live.' Whether in a tiny Spanish village, contemporary Iran, or a Glaswegian crime family, under the watchful eye of Bernarda Alba and within the suffocating walls of her house, her children struggle for the right to follow their instincts in defiance of a regime fanatically determined to deprive them of life.

First performed: Ethel Barrymore Theatre, New York City, 1936

Cast breakdown: 44f (doubling possible)

Publisher: Dramatists Play Service, 1966

Clare Boothe Luce's all-female, large-cast play *The Women* is an acerbically funny take on the social mores of the upper classes. Sassy, sparky, wise-cracking and with a rich vein of visual humour, the play takes us to Park Avenue of the 1930s where it seems that everybody's husband is having an affair with someone, somewhere. Mary Haines, happily married for twelve years, is so grateful that her beloved Stephen would never do anything like that. But Mary hasn't bargained on the wiles of Crystal Allen, a beautiful young sales assistant who has managed to get her nails into Stephen (and a whole new wardrobe and her own apartment in the bargain). Discovering that the marriage she had thought to be so strong is in fact in jeopardy, Mary must decide how – or if – she's going to fight to keep her man.

The remarkably prolific, almost fantastical life of Clare Boothe Luce, a play-wright largely unheard of in the UK, could itself be the subject of a play. A successful journalist, screenwriter, editor, politician, diplomat and socialite, writing hit Broadway plays was just one item on the long list of Luce's impressive accomplishments. Her early life was unconventional. The daughter of an unmarried and subsequently separated dancer and violinist, her childhood included a stint understudying Mary Pickford on Broadway and a period living in France. By the age of twenty she was married to the heir to a New York clothing fortune who was more than twice her age, by twenty-one she was a mother, and by twenty-six a divorcee. At twenty-seven she embarked on her first career in journalism and, after joining *Vogue* as an editorial assistant, she achieved a remarkable ascent that saw her rise to Associate Editor of *Vanity Fair* within a year, and Managing Editor by the age of thirty. A marriage to Henry Robinson Luce, publisher and founder of *Time*, *Fortune*, *Life* and *Sports Illustrated* followed in 1935, the year her first Broadway play, *Abide with Me* opened. With the arrival of the Second World War, Luce's focus turned to the international stage and she travelled exten-sively across Europe as well as Africa, India, China and Burma for *Life*. Running for a seat in the US House of Representatives in 1942, Luce was duly elected to represent the Congressional District of Connecticut, serving for two terms and being appointed to the Military Affairs Committee, during which time she acted as a key player in the creation of the Atomic Energy Commission. In 1953, she was appointed ambassador to Italy by Dwight Eisenhower, serving until 1956, when arsenic poisoning from paint chips falling from her bedroom ceiling forced her to resign. While ill-health ensured Luce adopted a somewhat quieter life, she remained actively involved in the work of the Republican Party and was appointed to the President's Foreign Intelligence Advisory Board by Ronald Reagan. Not content to limit herself to politics, playwriting and journalism, Luce also entered the world of film, winning an Academy Award nomination for her screenplay *Come to the Stable*.

A relentlessly active, socially engaged, highly intelligent polymath, Clare Boothe Luce couldn't be more different to the characters at the centre of *The Women*. Epitomising shallowness, self-interest and wasted potential, these pampered socialite ladies appear to dedicate their entire existences to shopping, preening, soaking in the bath and gossiping. Only Nancy, Mary's unmarried writer friend, appears to be doing anything useful with her life. As she departs for a trip to Africa, Mary sweetly tells her: 'Goodbye Nancy, I'll miss you.' 'I doubt it' is Nancy's retort, 'practically no one ever misses a clever woman,' before exiting the play until the final scene. With Nancy out of the way, the play is left to revel in the knots the women tie themselves up in whilst attempting to keep hold of their men, whether that's engaging in ridiculous health and beauty regimes, dressing themselves in the most ludicrous of fashions, or hatching impossibly convoluted intrigues. Written for a cast of forty-four characters, with a range of sets that include opulent Park Avenue mansions, beauty salons, luxury bathrooms (complete with a giant bubble bath in which Crystal spends most of the scene immersed), department stores and maternity wards, *The Women* is likely to make most modern producers balk. But of the huge cast, only about ten characters recur and among the numerous cameos that support these, there is ample opportunity for doubling (or tripling or even quadrupling as the case may be). What is so marvellous about *The Women* is that even the most fleeting characters get their moment to play the rich comedy of the piece, whether that's '2nd Hairdresser' discovering a bottle of whisky in a wealthy client's handbag, or 'Girl in Distress' pleading for assistance in a hotel powder room after a broken shoulder strap leads to a brief loss of dignity ('It practically popped out into the soup. If only it had been the left one. It's so much better'). It's a play that, if directed with skill and performed with panache, will continue to win audiences over with its feisty charms, exuberant wit and pithy humour.

First performed: The Camden Theatre, London, 1904

Cast breakdown: 12f, 5m (plus up to a further 15 non-speaking female roles, doubling possible)

Publisher: Manchester University Press, in *Plays and Performance Texts by Women*, 2012

Madame Stéphanie, a 'genius with an aggressive personality' and an entirely fabricated French accent, rules her dressmaking business with a rod of iron. Business is booming, but for the hundred or so girls she employs, conditions are appalling. Skilled workers who keep the wealthy ladies of London kitted out in a never-ending supply of fantastic gowns, Stéphanie's employees are dead on their feet. Dinner breaks have been cut from an hour to ten minutes, sleep has all but been abandoned and now, with the Duchess of Berkshire's ball that evening and a slew of evening dresses to produce by 10 p.m., the pressure is on more than ever. Drowning under a sea of tulle, lace and sequins, Stéphanie's exhausted workforce stitch on into the night with little option to complain or disobey. Nothing, it seems, not even a visit from HM Inspector of Factories, can stop Stéphanie on her determined march to keep her customer's happy and her profits high.

The political agenda in Edith Lyttelton's impassioned drama *Warp and Woof* is not hard to miss. Presenting the dressmaking business as one that is irredeemably rotten, Lyttelton paints a bleak picture of an industry fuelled by the intimidation and disempowerment of its workers, and in which conditions amount to little more than slave labour. Lyttelton's interest in the predicament of workers was one to which she was fiercely committed. A notable social reformer and activist, as well as playwright, she and her husband, the MP Alfred Lyttelton, were prominent campaigners for the ending of sweated labour and in particular spoke out passionately about poor working conditions endured by women. Taking her fight to the stage, Lyttelton presents in *Warp and Woof* a behind-the-scenes exposé of what the dressmaking business entailed for its workers, an altogether different reality to the one presented to its moneyed clients. While the play opens amid the opulence of Madame Stéphanie's plush showroom, Act Two takes us into the engine room of her business, a cramped, austere workroom in which twenty exhausted and, in some cases, dangerously ill women are driven mercilessly on to meet unrealistic deadlines.

Although one of the play's key plot points hinges on an anonymous report being made against Stéphanie, the appearance of Miss Donaldson, His Majesty's Inspector of Factories, would have done little to reassure Edwardian audiences that the workers' interests were being protected by the authorities. After a failed attempt to conceal the evidence of seamstresses working late into the night by hiding them in a locked, adjoining room, Stéphanie promptly dismisses the unfortunate employee who dares to answer Donaldson's questions with any level of honesty. In the face of such ineffectiveness from the authorities, is it not, Lyttelton appears to ask her audience (many themselves likely to be customers of establishments such as Stéphanie's), down to wealthy patrons to demand to know more about how their clothes are made and take their custom elsewhere should conditions fall short?

In our age of increasing reliance on cheap imported goods from abroad, it's not difficult to identify the sagacious political comment that *Warp and Woof* continues to make. While our wardrobes are unlikely to be stuffed with gowns hand-stitched by women working in the back rooms of London, how many of us who shop on the high street can be confident that the clothes we wear aren't made in establishments similar to those Lyttelton was writing about more than a hundred years ago? That the modern equivalents to Madame Stéphanie's workrooms are geographically distant to the shop floors they now service makes little difference in the context of how the demands for up-to-date fashion are prioritised over the health, emotional well-being and opportunities of the poor. 'I don't believe you want us to work till we're ill and silly and dazed,' one of Stéphanie's employees blurts out in a moment of despair to a group of stunned customers, and largely, based on what we see of these characters, she's right. But neither do they check that they are *not*, albeit by proxy, oppressing the individuals who labour night and day to keep them in the latest fashions, and all for a pittance. It is this question of responsibility, and particularly on the part of the wealthy and the empowered in society, that means *Warp and Woof* continues to resonate sharply and forcefully down the years.

First performed: American Repertory Theater, Cambridge, MA, 1999

Cast breakdown: 3f

Publisher: Methuen, 2001

Anna and Claire are ladies of fashion and 'better than the best of friends'. Anna has acquired what she terms a 'protector', a gentleman whose annual stipend will comfortably keep her, plus Claire, in the manner to which they have become accustomed. All should be delightfully cosy for the women but the course of true love never did run smooth and Claire has, somewhat inconveniently, fallen head over heels for someone else: a girl she has just met. To make matters worse, the object of her affections is rather on the young side and constantly chaperoned by her ever-vigilant mother. Claire convinces Anna to let her use her house for a secret assignation and the stage is set for a grand seduction. But as soon as Claire's new friend claps eyes on Anna, the women's best-laid plans begin to go somewhat awry.

David Mamet's spiky, sexy and somewhat surreal two-act comedy delivers a delightfully unexpected evening of theatre. It's a mischievous and wickedly funny piece that derives much of its humour from confounding the audience's expectations. What we see (two nicely turned-out, polite Victorian ladies sipping tea) and what we hear (a stream of potty-mouthed obscenities and a plot to deflower an unsuspecting adolescent girl) sit playfully at odds, and Mamet never entirely allows his audience to lower their guard. The addition of Catherine, a maid whose role in the action, as well as in Anna's household, is unconventional to say the least, completes this trio of beguilingly weird characters colluding to create an off-kilter *ménage à trois*.

It's a piece that zips along and Mamet distils the action into just three scenes, all of which take place in Anna's chintz-festooned drawing room. Structurally, the play is simple but effective; Mamet gradually ratchets the tension up throughout the first half as the anticipated arrival of Claire's new friend gets ever closer, and then the first act concludes with a single-line reveal that precipitates the entire action of the second half.

Throughout, the audience is kept in a state of delicious agitation as Anna and Claire find themselves in a situation of increasingly perilous dimensions, their designs on Claire's young friend unexpectedly throwing the security offered by Anna's 'protector' into calamitous jeopardy. Constructed in the break-neck pace dialogue for which Mamet is renowned, Anna and Claire fire lines at one another like two players in an extended, endlessly engaging tennis volley. It's a linguistic battle being fought tooth and nail; each woman refusing to concede a single point and determined to employ every ounce of sarcasm, wit, obstinacy and charm she can muster in a bitter battle to come out on top. And when Catherine – at first a seeming bit-part player included in the action merely to serve as the butt of Anna and Claire's jokes – emerges as a third competitor, and an unexpectedly formidable opponent at that, the rules of the game shift again. Loaded with subtext (and no small amount of innuendo), the stakes are unrelentingly high, whether the women are discussing Anna's choice of decor, requesting more hot water for their tea, or engaging in an existential crisis.

To a certain extent, *Boston Marriage* is unusual among Mamet's work. A writer known for his depictions of machismo and his interest in the cut and thrust of contemporary life, a Sapphic comedy set in a nineteenth-century New England drawing room was not one audiences or critics were necessarily expecting when it premiered in a production directed by the author in 1999. While something of a leap away from Mamet's preferred territory, *Boston Marriage* shares the ferocity, bite and sophistication of his other work and the presence of corsets, teacups and chintz shouldn't fool an audience into thinking this world is any less savage, or crude, than that of *American Buffalo* or *Glengarry Glen Ross*. It's a jet-black comedy and one that takes a wryly comic view of sexual depravity (Anna finally agrees to let Claire seduce the girl under her roof on the condition she's allowed to watch through a hole in the wall), while revelling in the shock value of placing the filthiest language in the most delicate of mouths ('OH MIGHT YOU GET OFF MY TITS?' is one of Anna's ripostes to the much-abused and yet doggedly persistent Catherine). Deriving its title from a now largely forgotten nineteenth-century term used to describe two women living together, Mamet's depiction of one particularly explosive Boston marriage is diabolically funny, gorgeously frank and fantastically sharp.

First performed: Bristol Old Vic, Bristol, 1965

Cast breakdown: 4f

Publisher: Samuel French, 1966

June Buckridge has given six years' devoted service to *Applehurst*, the radio serial in which she plays district nurse, Sister George. She may be a senior member of the cast and the most-loved character in the show, but *Applehurst* is losing listeners and the dramatic death of one of its leads might be just the thing to stem the tide. Terrified of getting the axe, June descends into a state of paranoia and, badly behaved at the best of times (there was that rather unfortunate incident involving two nuns, a taxi, several pints of beer and an allegation of assault most recently), she becomes even more of a handful than usual. Between tantrums and tumblers of gin, June vents her outrage at anyone who has the misfortune to fall in her way.

'They are going to murder me,' June announces as she sweeps on stage at the start of Frank Marcus's offbeat and scintillatingly dark comedy. After six years on *Applehurst* and in the spotlight as one of the BBC's best-loved stars, where Sister George ends and June Buckridge begins is something that everyone appears to have lost track of. June herself is perhaps the most confused of all; as far as she is concerned she *is* Sister George, and her attachment to the character could be described as ill-advised at best and psychotic at worst. She ditched her real name long ago and now everyone simply refers to her as 'George', at work, in public, even in the privacy of her own home (a London flat with a conveniently clear view of Broadcasting House). Consequently, when the time comes for Sister George to be killed off, June finds herself plummeting into an identity crisis of the most bizarre proportions. Reduced to nights sat at the kitchen table drinking gin and wondering where it all went wrong, June is at a loss to understand why surviving *Applehurst* regulars were spared when she herself is being so cruelly dispatched. Of course, much of the humour derives from the marked difference between June and her alter-ego. Sister George is a mild-mannered, God-fearing, heart-of-gold district nurse, June a foulmouthed, alcoholic diva with a distinctly masochistic streak.

When the play appeared in the mid-1960s it was remarkable for its depiction of two women living together, written as it was at a time when homosexuality on stage was still a provocative and veiled subject. The play revolves around the relationship between June and Alice, or 'Childie', the girl-woman variously described as June's 'flatmate' or 'friend', but who is clearly her long-term partner. While a same-sex relationship is unlikely to arouse much response either way in an audience coming to the play today, the particular dynamic between June and Alice remains an admittedly odd one. Alice, we learn, is thirty-four years old and yet looks and behaves far more like a child. She owns a large collection of dolls, appears disturbed by even the slightest allusion to sex and yet spends sizeable chunks of the play running around the flat in her bra and knickers. Her relationship with June is one of antagonism and cruelty; early on in the action June demands Alice eats her cigarette butt when she feels the younger woman has spoken out of turn, a punishment to which Alice not-too-grudgingly submits. The sadistic games played out between June and Alice, and the seedier nature of their relationship, are what gives *The Killing of Sister George* its spiky edge and adds a steeliness to a comedy that could otherwise run the risk of descending into camp frippery. Although underemphasised compared to the 1968 film version of the play, the abuse meted out by June is something that, even at the play's funniest moments, cannot help but leave an audience feeling slightly uncomfortable.

Despite, or perhaps because of, its darker qualities, *The Killing of Sister George* is a piece that is almost unrelentingly hilarious. The idea of a BBC scriptwriting team running amok through the fictional 1960s village of Applehurst, doling out death and destruction in their desperation to spice up a flagging serial, is immensely enjoyable. In light of the sensational storylines of modern-day soap operas, the situation in *Applehurst* is possibly even funnier for audiences today, largely because the methods by which its characters are dispatched are so tame compared to current standards. What is happening in Applehurst appears to be paving the way for the sex, violence and drama that will in time fill the nation's airwaves and TV screens. 'She couldn't put a dressing on a salad!' is June's outraged response to the news that Nurse Lawrence, a young slip of a probationer, will be filling the gap left by the newly deceased, middle-aged and distinctly unsexy Sister George. Like it or not, soap operas are moving forward and it seems the mildly mannered, hymn-singing Sister George will not be going with them.

First performed: South Coast Repertory, Costa Mesa, 1996

Cast breakdown: 2f

Publisher: Theatre Communications Group, 1999

Lisa is a wannabe fiction writer who is getting to grips with her first term on a post-graduate creative-writing course. Ruth Steiner is her professor, a foremost American literary talent, veteran of the New York arts scene and Lisa's idol. When Ruth invites Lisa to attend a tutorial in her Greenwich Village apartment she has little idea of the collision between youth and experience she has unwittingly set in motion. A relationship that begins as mentor and protégée turns over the years into one of emotional ambiguity and mutual dependence. Lisa's writing career is flourishing, while Ruth is looking ahead to her own demise. But it is a dispute over whose stories are whose and, more importantly, who has the right to tell them, that puts the two writers' friendship and professional relationship to the test.

Margulies' immaculately structured two-act play depicts scenes in the birth, life and eventual death of the relationship between two writers, one at the beginning of her career and one at the end. Spanning six years, the play consists of a series of encounters between the two women, opening with their first meeting in which Lisa, a naive, nervy student, stands agog at being in the home of her heroine – a form of flattery to which Ruth is not entirely immune. By the final scene, Lisa is a published writer, hailed as the voice of her generation, a favourite with the critics and is being ordered out of that same apartment by the mentor who has so influenced her success. Picking up the action at critical moments along the increasingly messy trajectory of Ruth and Lisa's personal and professional entanglements, Margulies places his audience at a vantage point from which they can observe the increasingly diabolical dependence the two women have on one another with clarity unavailable to the characters themselves.

Through the central narrative event of the play, Margulies asks provocative questions about ownership of creative works and whether or not artists have the right to appropriate the stories of real-life individuals in their work. In the play's penultimate scene, Lisa reads from her new novel. As the audience gradually recognises the anecdotes Ruth has been telling about her personal life rehashed and retold by Lisa as though they are her own creations, the realisation that the younger woman has effectively plagiarised the events of the older woman's life is an electrifying, yet troubling theatrical moment. Having already exhausted her own history for tales of teenage bulimia, parental divorce and suburban angst to fill her first collection of short stories, Lisa has found herself with nothing left to say. She instead plunders Ruth's background for her difficult second book, using events from her friend's early life, including a dysfunctional yet defining love affair with a well-known poet that Ruth has for decades been at pains to keep private. When challenged, Lisa claims to be 'honouring' her friend. Ruth simply sees it as stealing.

Although a deftly drawn portrait of the shifting relationship between an old pro and a young pretender, *Collected Stories* is also a beguiling exploration of the rights and responsibilities of those who write fiction. The reasons for Lisa's apparent betrayal of Ruth are never made explicit by Margulies, and it's a play that is very much open to interpretation; one production could paint Lisa as an absolute villain and another as a well-intentioned if misguided devotee to her friend and literary idol. Likewise, Ruth could alternately be depicted as receiving her comeuppance for the six years of hero-worship she has accepted and even encouraged from her young and visibly fragile protégée, or alternatively as the innocent recipient of the most unwarranted of betrayals. It is perhaps these very ambiguities that make *Collected Stories* such a delight for actresses to play and for audiences to watch. Both roles are rich in complexity, pathos and humour, and, in grappling with big questions of artistic authorship in the context of an individual's right to privacy, the play explores the most profound of human fears, needs and insecurities.

First performed: Royal Court Theatre, London, 1988

Cast breakdown: 3f

Publisher: Nick Hern Books, 1994

Tackling sexual taboos head-on, *Low Level Panic* is a fascinating dissection of the debate surrounding the influence of pornography on ordinary lives. Body image, sexual expression and violence against women are explored by McIntyre through the interactions of three young housemates, Jo, Mary and Celia. As the girls go about the seemingly banal activities of any normal weekend – taking baths, sitting in the garden, attending parties and going on dates – the motivations beneath their actions take on an increasingly sinister resonance. Mary has recently been the victim of a violent assault and the ways in which the girls do or don't respond to this fact reveals much about them and the society in which they live.

'If I could grow six inches and be as fat as I am now I'd be really tall and thin,' Jo muses while soaking in the bathtub that sits centre-stage in *Low Level Panic*'s domestic bathroom set. Subsequently standing up to get out of the bath and drying herself during the action, the actress playing Jo will show the audience an entirely ordinary body, one unlike those generally found in pornographic material, or indeed, resembling the airbrushed depictions of female anatomy increasingly familiar to twenty-first-century audiences. With a directness that is sometimes shocking and sometimes extremely funny, Clare McIntyre addresses the chasm between the reality of female sexuality and its depiction in pornography, deftly prompting her audience to consider the many and complex ways in which the illusory nature of pornography creates false expectations. While the women in the play are not users of pornography (although the play begins with Mary reading aloud from a dirty magazine she has found deposited in the house's dustbin), it is an undeniable force in their lives, affecting them in ways that range from almost imperceptible to utterly devastating. Whether it's Jo's ardent belief that her life would be happier, better, more glamorous if only she were thinner, or Mary's near breakdown after her attack, McIntyre is undeniably critical of the role that unrealistic depictions of female physicality and sexuality plays in violence committed against women by themselves, and by others.

That's not to say that McIntyre's argument is purely didactic or simplistic. Far from it, and the play fearlessly enters into controversial territory, including women's own violent sexual fantasies (Jo is troubled by the fact she fantasises about being picked up and ravished by strangers whilst hitchhiking) and the lack of support offered by women to one another at times of crisis. Although markedly a play of the late 1980s, *Low Level Panic* is – perhaps troublingly – no less relevant today than when it was first performed. Indeed, the arrival of the internet has led to an explosion in pornography and made it accessible in ways that McIntyre couldn't have dreamt possible when writing the play. That said, like Sarah Daniels' 1983 *Masterpieces*, which also deals with the relationship between pornography and individuals, *Low Level Panic* is a play it would be hard to relocate from its original 1980s setting. Its specific depiction of contemporary opinions and social norms sets it rigidly in the time and context in which it was written: for instance, Mary repeatedly wonders whether she was attacked on the night she was because she was wearing a skirt and 'was more dressed-up than usual', an argument that was common currency among defence lawyers in the 1980s but which would receive far less credence in a modern courtroom. But crucially, while the nature of public opinion on pornography and the sexual objectification of women may have altered, the issues themselves haven't gone away; they have merely shifted, and McIntyre's play remains an intelligent, complex yet compassionate exploration of the debate.

The play was first staged at the Royal Court Theatre in association with the Women's Playhouse Trust. It won the Samuel Beckett Award. A television version of the play was screened in 1994. The play made a subsequent reappearance at the Royal Court in 2006 when it was selected as one of fifty 'hit' Royal Court plays to be revisited as part of the theatre's fiftieth anniversary celebration of John Osborne's *Look Back in Anger*, receiving a rehearsed reading.

First performed: by students at the University of Hull Drama
Department, 1980 (first professional production: Haymarket Theatre,
Leicester, 1981)

Cast breakdown: 10f (doubling possible)

Publisher: Methuen, in *Anthony Minghella Plays: 1*, 1992

Caroline is taking a year out from her degree. Pregnant, single, and not
entirely sure who the father is, she puts her life in Leeds and her studies
on hold. Heading home to the Isle of Wight, Caroline plans to sit out
the pregnancy and give the baby up for adoption once it arrives. It's low
season, and renting a cheap room in a house by the beach, she wants to
spend her days on long walks by the sea, thinking, throwing stones and
waiting calmly for the baby to come. But the romantic semi-hibernation
Caroline had envisaged for herself doesn't quite meet up to the reality.
The emotional detachment she'd felt towards the baby begins to shift
into something far more complicated, and with the conflicting advice,
opinions and feelings of her friends disrupting her quiet solitude, things
aren't quite as straightforward as Caroline had previously thought.

'She thinks she's Sylvia Plath' is the somewhat harsh analysis that Kate, Caroline's former English teacher, current housemate, and now would-be lover,
makes of the younger woman's decision to engage in a sombre self-imposed
exile by the sea. Everyone, it seems, has plenty to say about Caroline's
choices except, interestingly, Caroline herself. While baby-mad school friend
Fran, thoroughly modern landlady Stella and crushingly disappointed
mother Sheelagh all have their own take on what Caroline should or should-
n't be doing with the next nine months, or indeed, the rest of her life,
Caroline herself stays, outwardly at least, noncommittal. Like its protagonist, *Whale Music* is a quiet little piece and all the more arresting for it. By
refusing to be drawn to one side or the other of debates surrounding pregnancy, adoption and abortion, Minghella presents a richly complicated and
determinedly non-sentimental analysis of some of the most ethically complex and emotionally contentious of all aspects of human existence. Offering
no easy answers or fairytale endings, Minghella captures the fiercely difficult options open to women who find themselves unintentionally pregnant.

Working chronologically from the end of her first trimester through to the third week after her baby's birth, the play depicts episodes from Caroline's arrival on the island through to her eventual quiet departure back to Leeds. It's a resolutely low-key piece; there is no weeping, wailing or gnashing of teeth when Caroline parts with her baby, no agonised soul-searching in the months leading up to the birth, no explosive showdowns with her family members or the baby's potential fathers. Rather there's just a series of simply drawn, emotionally restrained moments of Caroline getting on with it and attempting to remain calm, sane and, most importantly, in control of her own future, as the inevitable day approaches. Even at the moment when the wheels of the adoption process spring into action, Minghella resists giving Caroline a lengthy monologue or impassioned speech by which to express how she feels. Instead he delivers the emotional crescendo of the play in one stage direction: 'we watch Caroline in bed for as long as the moment can be held whilst she faces the reality of losing her baby.' It is a harrowing conclusion to a play that has to that point felt deceptively easy viewing. Whether we view Caroline and her choices as woefully naive or eminently pragmatic, Minghella leaves us in little doubt that she departs the island with a troubling mixture of guilt, regret, relief and empowerment that will stay with her for the duration of her lifetime.

A particular favourite with university drama groups in the 1980s and 1990s due to its all-female, predominantly youthful cast of characters, *Whale Music* was a play that did, for a period, became undeniably dated. Now though, over thirty years after its premiere, and with Caroline's baby of an age to have children of his own, it's a play that seems ready to be taken back off the shelf, dusted down and given a revival. Certainly it's no longer a piece that reflects our times, but it is a fascinating document by which we can chart how much has changed in our society in just one generation. The expectations of a female undergraduate today in relation to the type of family, career and sex life she may want to have are markedly different to those of Caroline and her friends. On the other hand, if that same young woman were unexpectedly to find herself pregnant, would her choices be all that different? While progress has been made, for as long as women remain uncomfortable talking about unwanted pregnancies and the choices that have to be made, *Whale Music* will continue to be as relevant as ever.

First performed: Royal Court Theatre, London, 2003

Cast breakdown: 7f, 2m

Publisher: Nick Hern Books, 2003

Brenda Ford is not the woman she once was. As a teenager, her list of priorities read: 'Protestants, Ulster, the Queen, Britain and fuck everything else.' A proud and passionate member of the Women's Ulster Defence Association, the young Brenda took part in violent paramilitary activity and was a powerful presence in her local branch. Now in her mid-thirties with a teenaged daughter, Jenny, and a baby granddaughter to look after, Brenda's priorities have changed. She wants out of the UDA and certainly doesn't want Jenny to follow in her footsteps. But when a local girl is accused of encouraging suspected IRA members onto the estate, Brenda is called upon by the UDA to intervene. Her branch isn't ready to let one of its finest members go and, if anything, it wants Brenda to be even more involved than before. They're not going to release her without a fight, and Brenda's loyalties, and where they really lie, are tested to the extreme.

One of Northern Ireland's most performed contemporary playwrights, Gary Mitchell's work focuses almost exclusively on life in the shadow of the Troubles. Celebrated by critics as an authentic voice of working-class Protestant Belfast, Mitchell's work – and his tendency to depict paramilitary organisations as relying on a combination of violence, intimidation and corrupt collusion with the authorities to maintain their control of the streets – won him unfavourable attention from some of the very individuals upon whom he was basing his characters. Having grown up on the Rathcoole estate (on which *Loyal Women* is set), Mitchell and his family were forced to flee in November 2005 after a warning was issued that every 'Mitchell had to get out or be killed in four hours'. Men armed with baseball bats attacked his house, and petrol-bombed the family's car while Mitchell, his wife and seven-year-old son ran for safety. The house of Mitchell's uncle (also resident on the estate) was attacked and his elderly parents were forced to leave their home. Soon after the attack, Mitchell told the *Guardian*, 'We are in hiding now. I feel a mix of confusion, anger, frustration and despair. There is a feeling that certain people are jealous and feel that I am depicting them in a bad way. They have decided that they will do this no matter what anybody says... I haven't done anything other than write.'

In Brenda, Mitchell creates a woman pulled in every direction. There's her dysfunctional relationship with Jenny to navigate and the latter's evident desire to fill her otherwise empty youth with the thrill of signing up to the UDA. Rita, Brenda's troublesome and semi-bedbound mother-in-law, has taken up residence in the living room, while her son Terry, recently released after sixteen years in prison, is back in the house and very much making his presence felt. Mark is a 'friend' who evidently wants more, and on top of everything there's Jenny's neglected six-month-old baby to care for. Even without the local branch repeatedly commandeering her home for meetings, Brenda has more on her plate in the few days during which the action is set than most people have in a lifetime. As she negotiates one explosive situation after the next (generally with Jenny's fractious baby in her arms), the actions of her past and the hopes she has for her future come jarringly into conflict. Never letting the pace drop for a second, Mitchell keeps the action speeding along and the tension escalating. Reviewing the play's 2003 Royal Court premiere, Charles Spencer of the *Daily Telegraph* observed, 'Like Ibsen and Arthur Miller, Mitchell superbly shows the ways in which the past catches up with the present and infects it... the action builds, in [director] Josie Rourke's edge-of-your-seat production, into a series of shattering confrontations as Brenda faces up to her husband, her daughter, and her fellow UDA members in a desperate fight to the finish.'

The UDA's armed campaign was officially ended in 2007, four years after the play's premiere. Audiences coming to *Loyal Women* today will therefore automatically be seeing the play through a different lens to those for whom it was written. Regardless, it's a piece that remains powerfully arresting, offering a sobering glimpse of life lived under the cloud of political conflict. Full-blooded, pungent and stark, it is a play that is wryly funny but, above all, incredibly sad. 'Very angry women who have had nothing but disappointment in their lives' is the way Brenda describes the fellow members of her UDA branch. Mitchell shows with a chillingly dramatic precision how, in the midst of such lifelong disappointment, societies can all too easily turn in on themselves.

Splendour
by Abi Morgan (*b.* 1968, UK)

First performed: Traverse Theatre, Edinburgh, 2000

Cast breakdown: 4f

Publisher: Oberon Books, 2000

Katherine, a press photographer, arrives in a troubled Eastern European state to take a portrait of a General, the country's leader. Her visit coincides with an uprising that looks set to descend into civil war, and as the country teeters precariously, Katherine finds herself awaiting the increasingly delayed General in his luxurious home. Meanwhile, his wife and her best friend attempt small talk over vodka and the local girl employed as Katherine's translator surreptitiously pockets anything she can lay her hands on. As the light fades and the artillery fire gets closer, it is ever more clear that the General will not be coming home. While his regime tumbles and his wife awaits her fate, the picture Katherine decides to take is very different to the one she had planned.

Splendour is a fascinating play, and an outstanding achievement both in terms of its technicality and its emotional scope. Its non-linear structure takes the one encounter between four women and constantly re-explodes it in different directions. Time speeds up and slows down, events are shuffled into different orders, and the audience repeatedly finds itself reappraising what it has just seen and heard as the play's focus whirls around yet again and the same events are viewed from a different character's perspective. The experience of watching it could perhaps best be described as something akin to looking at an Escher drawing or a Cubist painting in which multiple viewpoints on the same subject are simultaneously presented. The result is both subtly unnerving and thrillingly complex. As it becomes increasingly evident that the General is not coming home, and the vodka bottle the women pass between them empties, the constantly shifting sands on which Morgan constructs her play create a nightmarishly disorientating sensation for audience and characters alike.

An additional layer of complexity sees the interior thought processes of the women being spoken aloud by the actresses, alongside their regular dialogue. In the published edition of the play, Morgan makes no distinction on the page as to what is interior thought and what is exterior dialogue, meaning *Splendour* is no easy read. While in its playing it is crystal clear, when reading it, several attempts may be required before it becomes discernible what is happening and at what point the characters are speaking to one another and at what point to the audience. Although tricky to get a handle of on the page (and likely to cause a certain amount of confusion in the early days of rehearsal), this constant switching in and out of direct address is one of the things that makes *Splendour* so emotionally affecting. It prevents the audience from sitting back detachedly from events and inevitably prompts us to question how we would behave in such circumstances. The window into what is happening inside the women's heads is also the main source of the play's dark humour, as the contradictions between what they think and what they say offers rich opportunity to explore their preconceptions and prejudices towards one another. It also permits one of the most touching aspects of the play – the divide between how the women present themselves and how they really are.

With great economy, Morgan vividly conjures a world outside the General's house, in which civil war is approaching and fast. Genevieve, the wife's best friend, listened earlier to the sound of her upstairs neighbours bumping a washing machine down the stairs, 'filling their cars with as much as they can carry'. Now the roads are jammed, the bridge is closed and, as the snow falls, desperate citizens are trying to get out 'knowing their Northern neighbours may no longer be their friends'. Morgan too captures how suddenly the touchpaper of revolution can be lit. Earlier that day, the General's wife had sat with friends enjoying a lunch at which her husband told jokes. Upon leaving, a vase she had given her hostess as a wedding present was kindly yet firmly returned to her; her first inkling that something was wrong. Now, increasingly fearful that her beloved husband has been done away with – in the way he has so ruthlessly done away with many others – she waits like a sitting duck. Refusing to let her fear show, she steadfastly declares she will 'take back nothing' and asks Katherine to photograph her 'before and after they come'. It is a fitting conclusion to a play that refuses to present us with just one perspective on lives on the cusp of civil war, but instead offers a multiplicity.

66 This Wide Night
by Chloë Moss (b. 1976, UK)

First performed: Clean Break at Soho Theatre, London, 2008

Cast breakdown: 2f

Publisher: Nick Hern Books, 2008

Marie and Lorraine were cellmates in prison. Released first, Marie has been doing her best on the outside and has managed to build a fragile but just-functioning existence for herself. All this is threatened when Lorraine turns up on her doorstep. Newly released from prison and keen to take up an offer Marie made long ago, Lorraine wants to stay. But life on the outside isn't as either woman had envisaged and neither is their friendship. Finding themselves operating within a different and in some ways even more difficult set of boundaries than when they were in prison, Marie and Lorraine must decide how – and if – they ought to be in one another's lives. Chloë Moss's bleakly beautiful portrait of friendship, freedom and surviving daily life won the 2009 Susan Smith Blackburn Prize, an annual international award recognising outstanding new plays by women in the English language.

Commissioned by Clean Break, a theatre company that stages new plays on the theme of women and the criminal justice system, *This Wide Night* was written in response to a playwriting residency Chloë Moss undertook in 2006 at HMP Cookham Wood. On completion of the residency, the challenge Moss felt 'was not what to write about, but what not to write about'. Spending time with the female inmates of the prison, Moss later said she came away from her three-month residency with 'enough material to write fifty different plays, each of which I could feel equally passionate about'. Despite this mass of possibilities, Moss settled on telling the story of Marie and Lorraine, whose close friendship in prison takes on a very different form once they are on the outside. Like two equally weak swimmers clinging to each other in choppy waters, the women are powerfully drawn together, but whether they are holding one another up or dragging each other under is never quite clear and, at times, weirdly, they almost seem to succeed in simultaneously doing both. It is this ambiguity and the fantastically complicated motives the two women appear to have in their behaviour towards one another that makes the play so fascinating, but also so heartbreakingly sad. Abandoned by or alienated from everyone who could have helped them make the transition from prison back into society, Marie and Lorraine, both incapable of taking care of themselves let alone anyone else, turn to one another. The consequences, as Moss shows, are morally complex, psychologically fraught, and ask bigger questions of society's relationship with, and responsibility towards, offenders and ex-offenders.

For Marie and Lorraine, life is difficult. That's not just the material difficulties they experience: the substandard accommodation, the lack of money, the poor employment prospects, or the inability to access even the most basic of opportunities. It is the emotional struggles they face. 'I am no good at getting through the day, Lorraine. Never mind getting through life,' Marie tells her friend. Having spent her childhood in care and now crushingly ill-equipped to deal with relationships or indeed a day-to-day adult existence, everything is a struggle for Marie – going to sleep at night scares her, waking up in the morning scares her, crowds scare her, empty rooms scare her, she has a 'fear of being away from home even though I haven't got one'. Now, subsisting on a cocktail of takeaway pizzas, lager, anti-depressants and daytime TV, Marie and Lorraine's life as free women doesn't look much more appealing than it did as prisoners. Moss said she wanted to write about 'resettlement – when "freedom" can actually feel like a very bleak and frightening prospect', and indeed, Marie and Lorraine do seem to be in a sad kind of hinterland, not imprisoned but, at the same time, far from being free. By setting the entirety of the action in Marie's cramped bedsit, Moss creates a claustrophobic atmosphere in which the tension between the two women who live, eat and sleep in one small room builds throughout. It's easy to feel the women have exchanged their prison cell for a bedsit, although their new home is perhaps all the harder to endure because what is keeping them prisoner there is harder to understand.

The respect, compassion and affection Moss feels for Marie and Lorraine (and presumably, those inmates of HMP Cookham Wood who inspired them) is evident in her writing of the characters. The dynamic between the two women is a complex one and they are roles that demand the greatest level of precision, curiosity and empathy from the actresses who play them, along with a healthy dose of humour. Neither of Moss's creations is an angel; they are damaged people who have hurt others deeply. They lie, they manipulate, they lash out, but they also care about each other with a passion that is ferocious. The intensity of feeling is difficult to understand for anyone who hasn't experienced life in prison, but one which Moss takes us some of the way towards appreciating in her taut, compact and deeply affecting drama.

First performed: New York International Fringe Festival, New York, 2004

Cast breakdown: 4f, 1m

Publisher: Samuel French, 2007

Three girls, seemingly unremarkable and yet with extraordinary stories to tell. Megan Mostyn-Brown's virtuosic three-part monologue play takes its audience deep into the vibrant interior worlds of fifteen-year-old Hannah, seventeen-year-old Lucy and twenty-three-year-old Lydia. All dealing with experiences and emotions far beyond their years, and doing so utterly alone, they forge a path forward in the face of a hostile world that is doing them unspeakable wrongs.

Megan Mostyn-Brown wrote *girl.* almost by accident. A professional actress since she was a child, she did an internship in her early twenties at Labyrinth, the renowned New York actors' ensemble. Asked on her first day in the office whether she wrote plays, she found herself lying 'yes' and then, asked to bring ten pages of her work in the next day, she went home and wrote the beginnings of a monologue. Over time, that monologue would become *girl.*, her first work as a writer – and a remarkable debut.

What makes *girl.* so refreshing is the seriousness with which it takes its young subjects. Mostyn-Brown gives voice to three girls the likes of whom are rarely seen or heard from on stage. These are those quiet, unassuming, uncomplaining girls who, however much they're dealing with, keep their heads down and get on with it. They aren't the desirable girls; they're not particularly pretty, or confident or popular, they don't resemble those in TV shows or movies, and they're certainly not prom-queen material. Neither do they conspicuously occupy the opposite end of the scale; they're not social catastrophes, kooky individuals or defiant loners. Each is just completely and utterly normal or, as Mostyn-Brown says, 'quiet, plain, the type of girl you probably wouldn't notice'. Their world is one of shopping malls, Seven Eleven stores, high-school classrooms and college dorms. They inhabit American cities that are nondescript and insignificant and yet, each girl becomes an engrossing and important dramatic subject. Allowing her audience to take a peep inside the heads of Hannah, Lucy and Lydia, Mostyn-Brown reveals the rich, colourful and complex depths that exist within. Fireworks are going off beneath their placid exteriors and with a steely poeticism, expert storytelling and self-deprecating humour, the girls allow us entry to their worlds. The result is a deeply compelling, achingly beautiful and incredibly powerful piece of theatre that gives a rare and bitingly honest insight into what life can mean for girls today.

Despite oblique references to Greek mythology, this is a bang-up-to-date piece of writing and these are twenty-first-century girls being battered every which way by the pressures of a modern Western world. There's the need to be physically attractive, conventionally feminine, sexually active (but not a 'slut', mind), to have a wide group of friends, to be capable but not demanding, liberated but not pushy. Like so many young women, Hannah, Lucy and Lydia struggle to meet these arguably unobtainable standards, not to mention coping with the undeniably raw deal that fate has given them. Each completely alone, they are mistreated by the family and friends who should be their closest allies, and are left to pick up the pieces of other people's selfishness, incapability and cowardice. These girls suffer in silence, their anger, hatred, love, fear and loneliness driven inside and finding expression there.

It is this internalising of emotion that makes *girl.* such an interesting dramatic proposition. Given that the 'meat and veg' of dramatic writing so often focuses on action, and how people externalise their emotions, how on earth can characters be written who, when put under pressure, don't outwardly *do* anything? Like so many girls, Hannah, Lucy and Lydia don't kick, punch, shout or scream as a result of their unhappiness. Even the few, small outward signs of their inner anguish – like the lattice of scars that adorn Hannah's limbs – are kept well hidden from prying eyes. Instead, Mostyn-Brown writes these girls by exploding the minutiae of their inner thoughts into a series of immaculately constructed extended monologues. Structured with meticulous precision on the page, these monologues capture the rhythms, cadences and innate humour of the girls' speech in a way that is somehow both deeply authentic and resoundingly poetic. *girl.* is a brave, dignified play that gives weight to the question of what it is to be a young woman. It exhibits a level of insight, compassion and imagination on the subject that is rarely achieved.

68 Iron
by Rona Munro (b. 1959, UK)

First performed: Traverse Theatre, Edinburgh, 2002

Cast breakdown: 3f, 1m

Publisher: Nick Hern Books, 2002

Josie can't remember a thing before her eleventh birthday. That was fifteen years ago and around the time her mother Fay was sentenced to life for murdering Josie's father. Wanting to fill in the blanks, Josie starts visiting the mother she hasn't seen since she was ten. The women gradually rebuild their relationship across the table of the prison's visitors' room and at first it seems good; Fay helps Josie recall her childhood memories and in return her daughter gives her a window to the outside world. But as Josie's past comes ever more sharply into focus, so too emerge disturbing recollections and frightening realisations. Nothing is quite what it seems, either in Josie's past or her present, and she must come to terms with the role Fay will, or won't, play in her future.

Rona Munro's taut psychological drama is both hard-hitting and deeply humane. Examining imprisonment in the broadest sense of the word, *Iron* takes a nuanced look at the many ways in which people can be made, or make themselves, into prisoners. Josie has been living an ostensibly successful life. She's travelled the world, has a great career, wears expensive clothes and is articulate, educated and capable. A somewhat incongruous presence in the prison's visitors' room, she stuns the guards with her sudden appearance and apparent determination to re-engage with a life, and a mother, she has done so well to leave behind. 'These walls swallow people,' one guard warns Josie, 'you might want to turn round and never come back.' It's advice she doesn't take. Despite the superficial glamour of her lifestyle, Josie is divorced, without any family or apparently even a single friend. In many ways she is as isolated as her mother and quickly becomes dependent on their weekly meetings. But the world Josie steps into when she enters the prison is a complex and increasingly confusing one. Prison life functions in a very different way to that on the outside and there are whole new codes of behaviour, ethics and communication for Josie to navigate. Most troubling of all, no one, not Fay, nor the guards who watch over her so closely, are entirely transparent and much of the play's steely tension comes from the twists and turns Munro skilfully weaves into each of the characters' dealings with Josie. Just when Josie – and the audience – think they've got a handle on one of the other characters, a new piece of evidence is brought to light, throwing doubt on who that person actually is, and what they really want.

After fifteen years without a single visitor, and practically no contact with the outside world, Fay is hit like a truck by Josie's appearance. Emotionally, she is totally unprepared for the surge of feeling that the unexpected entrance of her daughter unleashes into her life after so many years in the insulation of her prison cell. Josie arrives wanting to talk about the past, to explain why she's never visited before, to understand what Fay's life is like now. Fay just needs something easy. 'Give me a bit of small talk,' she begs her daughter. For Fay, having to feel things is a frightening prospect, particularly when it was the uncontrollable strength of her emotions that led to her imprisonment in the first place. Now, the best way to survive is by not allowing herself to experience any emotions, good or bad. Josie too has plenty to risk by abandoning the emotionally inert life she has selected for herself. Aware that reawakening her childhood memories will force her to reappraise not only where she has come from, but where she is going, she knows her meetings with Fay are about more than building bridges. The gradual and faltering steps both women take towards emotional engagement are depicted with sensitivity and dignity by Munro. For women like Fay and Josie, making the decision to feel is in itself a brave, bold and life-altering one.

Every aspect of Fay's waking life is dominated by her imprisonment. It is in the smells ('backing up toilets and boiled food'), the sounds (the 'sack of potatoes' thud of the woman next door trying to kill herself in the night by repeatedly diving headfirst off the radiator onto the stone floor), and the sights around her. It's in the eternal nearby presence of the guards, the ongoing curtailments to her personal liberty and the almost total lack of purpose. Although a free woman, as Josie's relationship with her mother develops, she too experiences the range of personal indignities and restrictions that come with attempting to conduct an intimate relationship with someone in prison. Her articulacy, self-possession and confidence don't exempt her from body searches, the bureaucracy of the prison system, nor allow her physical contact or a private conversation with her mother. Unyielding, sharp and provocative, *Iron* examines the physical and psychological brutalities inherent in prison life, both for prisoners and for those to whom they are close.

First performed: Gúna Nua Theatre and Civic Theatre Tallaght at the Dublin Fringe Festival, 2008

Cast breakdown: 3f

Publisher: Nick Hern Books, 2010

Amber is en route to her school-leavers' ball. Armed with enough hair-spray to withstand a hurricane, a killer fake tan and money for sambucas, it's going to be a great night. Paul's on her arm and adult life is looking good – what could possibly go wrong? Her mum Lorraine is struggling. There's always the cleaning to do, her job drives her mad and now HR are on at her about taking some time out to 'talk to someone'; apparently shouting at the customers for messing up the shop-floor displays isn't on. Kay, Lorraine's mum and Amber's gran, is nursing her husband Gem. He's had a stroke and now, months on, the love of her life is still a largely immobile thirteen-stone invalid. Sex is definitely off the agenda, although maybe a quick trip to Ann Summers will give Kay what she needs. Three generations of one family share their innermost thoughts, fears and hopes through intersecting monologues.

True to its name, Elaine Murphy's bittersweet comedy is indeed a little gem. It's an unassuming piece of work, which, with its undemanding technical requirements – it's really just three actresses, facing out front, talking to the audience – makes it straightforward to stage. The original production proved remarkably portable, transferring after its premiere at the Dublin Fringe Festival to the Edinburgh Fringe, and then popping over the Atlantic to New York's tiny Flea Theatre before coming back again, to London's Bush Theatre. While its compact nature no doubt helped this debut play have such an impressive initial run, the disarmingly honest manner in which Murphy dissects the themes of life, death, sex and love no doubt accounted for much of its universal draw. 'Its quiet ordinariness is part of its appeal,' Lyn Gardner commented in her *Guardian* review. Indeed, it is *Little Gem*'s depiction of the most extraordinary events – babies being born, loved ones dying, the flourishing of a new relationship – disrupting mundane day-to-day existences in an unremarkable Dublin suburb, that gives the play its emotional power.

Murphy's own background was in acting and, like so many actresses-turned-playwrights, her trigger to write came through the feeling that, for her and her contemporaries, 'decent parts are thin on the ground and I rarely recognised any of the women portrayed on the stages in front of me'. Having worked in a women's health organisation, Murphy wanted to write about the women she saw there and so created a 'mishmash' of them in Amber, Lorraine and Kay. They are, according to Murphy, women who are 'hardworking, not particularly rich or poor, ignored by the Celtic Tiger... you know, women like us, getting on with it'. It is this 'getting on with it' that sits at the heart of *Little Gem*. Whether proceeding with an unplanned pregnancy (particularly when it gives your ex-boyfriend the incentive he needs to do a flit to Australia), embarking on a new relationship when your heart is still broken from the last, or providing round-the-clock care for the man who was once your hero, Murphy highlights the extraordinary acts of courage and tenacity carried out by millions of women every day without asking for, or indeed expecting, any kind of recognition. Ask Amber, Lorraine or Kay if what they do is extraordinary and they'd probably tell you to stop being daft. Yet Murphy's play is in many ways a tribute to those women 'getting on with it'. For ninety minutes she turns the spotlight on the sacrifice, resilience and resourcefulness which, although generally unacknowledged, keeps the world ticking over and allows our societies to function as they do.

At the same time it's a play that never veers into sentimentality. Those looking for a nice, cosy, rose-tinted depiction of twee female solidarity in the face of adversity are not going to find it here. *Little Gem* is a play with plenty of bite and Amber, Lorraine and Kay are no-nonsense women, who refuse to tell it as anything other than what it is. Indeed, the candidness with which they share their thoughts is what makes the play so extremely entertaining and, at times, daringly funny. Whether it's Kay's description of her first experiment with a vibrator, Lorraine's misgivings over new boyfriend Niall's abundant body hair, or Amber's admission that there's a chance she might just have nodded off at the moment her son was being conceived, the play merrily dances through all sorts of taboo territory. The whole experience feels a bit like having three of your best friends confiding in you over a cuppa, although there's just as much chance you'll be weeping into your teacup as snorting with laughter. Presenting the highs of life as well as the lows, Murphy's *Little Gem* is a jewel of a play with a diamond-sharp edge.

First performed: South Coast Repertory and Centre Stage, Costa Mesa, 2003

Cast breakdown: 4f, 2m

Publisher: Dramatists Play Service, 2005

A talented seamstress and professional maker of ladies' lingerie, or 'intimate apparel', Esther is forever sewing wedding trousseaus for the girls who pass though the boarding house in which she lives. But, at the age of thirty-five, the chances of her ever celebrating her own wedding night look increasingly slim. An African-American woman living in 1905 Lower Manhattan, Esther's income is meagre, yet she has successfully squirreled away a small amount of savings every year, sewing the cash into the lining of her quilt and dreaming of the day she will use this money to open a beauty parlour in which black women will be treated as respectfully as their white employers. Her quietly independent lifestyle is shaken when she receives a letter from George, a Barbadian man working on the Panama Canal. Suddenly, romance and marriage seem tantalisingly close, but Esther is left to discover whether the dream reflects the reality.

Set in a series of bedrooms, *Intimate Apparel* is an intensely sensual play. Touch is key and the play deals heavily in the potency of physical contact, or rather, the lack of it. Esther, finding herself engaged to George, a man she has never seen, let alone had physical contact with, instead takes a tactile delight in her interaction with the gorgeous fabrics she purchases from Mr Marks, a Romanian Jewish immigrant (also engaged to a woman he has never seen) with whom she shares an obvious attraction. An African American woman and an Orthodox Jewish man unable to share physical contact connect instead over pieces of Japanese silk and richly brocaded satins. Likewise, Mrs Van Buren, Esther's wealthy white Fifth Avenue employer, who is trapped in a loveless marriage, becomes unhealthily dependent on her fitting sessions with Esther as her only physical contact with another human being. Subverting the rules of physical contact in a world so tightly governed by the boundaries of class, race, religion and gender is a beguiling prospect for the characters in *Intimate Apparel*, operating as they do within a system which is as simultaneously frustrating and seductive in its rigidity as one of Esther's corsets. The relationships in the play that threaten to challenge the social norms the most are those in which the need for touch often feels most urgent and also seemingly most natural. It is within marriage, the relationship officially sanctioned as the correct and proper environment for physical contact to occur, that intimacy is shown to be so alien.

The drabness of Manhattan's Lower East Side is offset by the astonishing array of gorgeous, vivid and ornate fabrics with which Esther works. Marks, himself perpetually wearing a worn black suit with a missing button, handles bolts of remarkable cloths, unfurling rolls of cobalt blue, magenta pink and muslins, taffetas and tulles for Esther's delectation. While most of this cloth will undoubtedly find its way into the homes of her white employers, a few offcuts are frugally retained by Esther and converted into rare objects of delight and beauty for the audience to glimpse briefly. A pale blue corset embossed with lavender flowers and blue glass beads for her prostitute friend Mayme, a red smoking jacket for her unemployed husband George, and a spectacular white wedding gown for herself, an uncertain bride; these small items of opulence and luxury shine out on stage amid the poverty and starkness of Esther's world.

Dealing not just with the colour of fabric, but the colour of skin, the play comments on the devastatingly oppressive effect that being born into the 'wrong' colour skin once had on an individual's life. At one point, Mayme and Mrs Van Buren stand side by side on stage dressed in identical corsets lovingly made for them by Esther. They are both women in their thirties, both live in New York and both hold a place of intimacy and friendship in Esther's life – yet they are worlds apart, simply because one of them is black and one white. Given the deeply ingrained racial iniquity that exists in Esther's world, it is perhaps no wonder that the other characters question her desire for a fairer way of living. Her plans for a black beauty parlour 'where you get pampered and treated real nice' is not something her friends or George can ever see becoming a reality for Esther, despite the entirely reasonable premise behind her idea (''cause no one does it for us, we just as soon wash our heads in a bucket and be treated like mules'). By the end of the play, after George has destroyed the quilt in which Esther keeps her savings, spent the money and disappeared, Esther's dream of opening the beauty parlour may be further away, but not necessarily gone. The play's closing image, in which Esther, having moved out of her marital home and returned to her old room in the boarding house, 'walks over to the old sewing machine and begins to sew together pieces of fabric, the beginnings of a new quilt', offers perhaps a small glimmer of hope.

First performed: National Theatre, London, 1982

Cast breakdown: 2f, 1m

Publisher: Faber and Faber, in *Harold Pinter: Plays 4*, 2012

A room with a bed. Inside that bed a woman – forties – has just woken, while a doctor looks on. There's nothing remarkable about the scene, except that the woman, Deborah, has been asleep not for a few hours, or even a few days, but for twenty-nine years. As a sixteen-year-old, Deborah just 'stopped'. In front of her family she froze one day, her arm outstretched in the act of placing a vase of flowers on a table, her eyes staring into space and her body rigid like a statue. A young doctor arrived. He took Deborah to a hospital, put her to bed and watched her while she slept. Now, years later, he has injected her with a miracle drug. Finally, Deborah is awake, but the world in which she finds herself is a bizarre and unfamiliar place.

Harold Pinter's short play, *A Kind of Alaska*, was inspired by Oliver Sacks' 1973 factual book *Awakenings*. In *Awakenings*, Sacks writes about his work with patients affected by a worldwide epidemic that began in Europe in the winter of 1916–17 and which claimed approximately five million victims of whom around a third died. Of the survivors, a significant proportion remained like statues, plunged into a deep sleep-like state, a condition subsequently identified as *encephalitis lethargica* and popularly known as 'sleeping sickness'. *Awakenings* focuses on a period in the late 1960s, when Sacks' experiments proved that sufferers of sleeping sickness could respond to L-DOPA, a drug commonly used to treat Parkinson's disease. Scores of patients were reawakened with the use of the drug and reunited with their surviving family members, but were faced too with the shock of having been asleep for so long, some by more than fifty years. Pinter takes such an extraordinary situation as the starting point for *A Kind of Alaska*, creating a fictional sixteen-year-old who awakens to discover she has lost nearly thirty years of her life.

'Something is happening,' Deborah whispers at the start of the play. Propped up in bed, having just been brought back to life by Hornby, the doctor who, some twenty-nine years ago removed a vase of flowers from her frozen grip, Deborah re-enters a world that is deeply unfamiliar and terrifyingly unreal. Lucid and yet unfocused, Deborah gabbles away as her adolescent self, unsure of exactly how old she is and yet adamant that her mother will be in shortly to get her out of bed. She has not been insensible for the past twenty-nine years – she is aware that people have been touching her, bending over her and trying to speak to her, but she refuses Hornby's explanation; that her mind has been suspended during that time in 'a kind of Alaska'. No, she tells him, she has been alert and alive, residing in 'a vast hall of glass', a calm and yet unsettling place where 'glass reflects glass. For ever and ever.' Now, sat in an unfamiliar bed in a room she knows is definitely not her own, the reality in which Deborah finds herself is no less strange than the glass-walled wonderland she has been locked into for so long.

Like much of Pinter's work, *A Kind of Alaska* exerts a curious, unsettling force on its audience. Deborah's predicament is a chilling one, the possibility of going to sleep and waking up thirty years later disturbing to say the least. But it is Pinter's depiction of the very different type of stasis endured by the other characters – Hornby and Pauline, Deborah's younger sister (who appears at the patient's bedside as soon as she awakes) – that is more troubling to observe. Pauline married Hornby, the omnipresent doctor in the family's life, and yet describes herself as a widow, her husband having always been more devoted to watching over her sleeping sister than being with her. In certain respects just as stuck as the inert woman in the bed, Pauline and Hornby's marriage exists in its own 'kind of Alaska', their predicament allowing Pinter to reference the frozen state in which so many relationships, desires and ambitions can exist, sometimes for the best part of a lifetime.

Very short, at just under twenty pages in length, *A Kind of Alaska* was originally performed by Judi Dench, Paul Rogers and Anna Massey as the final part of the Pinter triple bill *Other Places*, alongside *Family Voices* and *Victoria Station*. The play has frequently been staged in combination with any number of Pinter's other short plays or as a 'curtain raiser' to one of his full-length works.

72

The Beau Defeated
by Mary Pix (*b.* 1666, UK)

First performed: location unknown, 1700

Cast breakdown: 9f, 8m (doubling possible)

Publisher: Dodo Press, 2008

Mrs Rich has been left well provided for by her late husband, a successful if not entirely honest city banker. Not content with possession of a considerable fortune, Mrs Rich feels it's time to move up in the world and, with an eye to a second marriage, sets her sights on gaining a title. A ridiculous fop, Sir John Roverhead, seems her surest route into the aristocracy, but Mrs Rich isn't the only woman intent on obtaining his hand. Nor, as time will tell, is Sir John quite what he has claimed to be. Meanwhile, Clerimont, a younger brother left unintentionally disinherited after an argument between his older brother and recently deceased father, is finding it difficult to reconcile himself to his newly acquired penury. Salvation appears in the form of a masked lady who shares his box at the theatre. But who that lady is, and what she wants from him, are difficult to discern.

With a joyfully daft cast of snobs, social climbers, buffoons and ingénues (plus their particularly meddlesome array of servants), Mary Pix piles intrigue upon intrigue to construct a charmingly snappy comedy of manners. The plot of *The Beau Defeated* is one with a seemingly endless supply of twists and turns, demanding a sustained level of focus from its audience if they are to keep on top of who is currently attempting to mislead who, and why. The play revolves around multiple narrative strands, all of which are deftly balanced by Pix throughout until they build to a suitably rewarding conclusion. Beyond the Mrs Rich/Sir John storyline and the plot between Clerimont and the masked lady (actually the thoroughly respectable Lady Landsworth who disguises herself as a woman of dubious character in an effort to test Clerimont's virtue), there is young and silly Lucinda Rich's determined attempts to secure a husband, professional gamester Mrs Trickwell's efforts to win Mrs Rich's fortune from her, the estimable Mrs Clerimont's designs to achieve a happy ending for her cousins, and the ongoing machinations of the servants for their masters and mistresses to contend with. The large ensemble of colourful characters all have a hand in the mayhem, their dissembling and mischief-making building to a crescendo of nonsense which, of course, all ends happily. By the fall of the curtain every character has received his or her just desserts and we leave them either marching up the aisle towards a thoroughly suitable marriage, or limping away in disgrace.

As the increasingly contorted plot unfolds, Pix displays an irreverent humour that satirises human folly in its various forms. Vanity, social climbing and ignorance are all targets for her wit, and it's a piece that, more than three hundred years after its first performance, contains a suitably idiotic parade of characters to make audiences laugh out loud today. Mrs Rich is ridiculous in her affectations, as is her 'trifling coxcomb, all wig and no brains' would-be suitor Sir John and their circle of gossipy, boorish and charmless companions. Even the smaller characters are richly drawn and particular highlights among the 'supporting' cast include the blustering older Clerimont brother (never outside the company of his hounds either onstage or off, 'love me, love my dog', is his motto), the younger Clerimont brother's landlady Mrs Fidget (will do anything for a drink) and the sagacious chambermaid Betty (stoically bearing *de la Bette*, the new, grander title given to her by her ever-aspirational mistress Mrs Rich). Pix appears to possess a love of the ridiculous and positions her cavalcade of fools, hypocrites and dissemblers in the daftest of situations. The moment in which Lady La Bassett draws a pistol from her petticoats and challenges love rival Mrs Rich to a duel is just one of near-hysterical frenzy to which the action regularly builds.

At the heart of the play is a satirising of the battles between 'old money' and 'new money'. Prepared to marry Sir John though he is 'not worth a groat', Mrs Rich is wealthier than most of the aristocrats she dreams of being accepted by and yet is so fixated on becoming 'a Lady of quality', will marry any worthless fool that enables her to be presented at court. As the action progresses and the aristocratic characters are revealed to be unworthy of the exaltation they receive, Mrs Rich's efforts seem ever more redundant. Conversely, Clerimont and his Lady Landsworth, who test one another's scruples and discover they are each as morally spotless as the other, exit the play happily rewarded for their labours. Caught in the cross-fire between love and luck, each of Pix's characters take their turn against 'that damned jilt Fortune, or her left-handed daughter, as blind as she, Chance'.

73

The Prime of Miss Jean Brodie by Jay Presson Allen (*b*. 1922, USA), adapted from the novel by Muriel Spark (*b*. 1918, UK)

First performed: Helen Hayes Theatre, New York, 1966

Cast breakdown: 8f plus optional cast of non-speaking female roles, 4m (doubling possible)

Publisher: Samuel French, 2006

Miss Jean Brodie, teacher, advocate of culture, non-conformist, and a woman in her prime, cuts a remarkable shape in the otherwise conservative landscape of the Marcia Blaine Academy for Girls. Scourge of the headmistress, former flame of the art master, current lover of the music teacher, and a powerful force over her specially selected students (her 'crème de la crème'), Brodie resists every effort to make her conventional. But when her admiration for the activities of General Franco is expressed a little too keenly in class, her teaching career, and her relationship with her students, fall into jeopardy.

Initially published in the *New Yorker Magazine* and released as a book by Macmillan in 1961, Muriel Spark's slim novel, *The Prime of Miss Jean Brodie*, introduced to the world one of the most iconic figures of twentieth-century British literature. Jay Presson Allen, whose screenplays included *Marnie*, *Cabaret*, *Funny Lady* and *La Cage aux Folles*, adapted the novel in 1966, altering events, disposing of certain characters and combining others, yet remaining loyal to the spirit of Spark's original work. She captures the complexities, flamboyancy, determination and humour of Jean Brodie, the staunchly individual teacher who is ultimately destroyed by the depth of her own passion.

Spark claimed to have based Brodie in part on one of her own teachers, Miss Christina Kay, who taught her for a year in 1929 at James Gillespie's High School for Girls in Edinburgh. Kay, described by Spark in her autobiography *Curriculum Vitae* as 'that character in search of an author', would have been part of the generation of women who lost their lovers on the battlefields of the Great War, and in peacetime found they faced a scarcity of young, eligible men. By the time these women were reaching their 'prime' in the 1930s, many, like Kay, and the character she inspired, had remained unmarried, while younger generations had resumed courtship and marriage rituals as normal. Spinster Brodie's consequent dedication to her girls is complete. 'Give me a girl at an impressionable age,' she tells them, 'and she is mine for life. You girls are my vocation. If I were to receive a proposal of marriage tomorrow from the Lord Lyon King-of-Arms, I would decline it. I am dedicated to you in my prime.' The unsatisfactory love triangle that exists between Brodie, the married but dashing art teacher Mr Lloyd, and the single yet unprepossessing music master Mr Lowther is ostensibly humorous, yet subtly indicative of the unbalanced state of affairs that persisted for the generation whose lives were so unfortunately shaped by the Great War.

A dash of colour against the Calvinistic, monochrome backdrop of depressed 1930s Edinburgh, Brodie seeks to enliven her girls' outlook through tales of her exotic travels and an eclectic curriculum. She reports a private audience with the Pope during a trip to Rome ('I wore my long black gown with a lace mantilla and looked magnificent'), teaches them about the existence of Einstein, the basis of Eastern religions and the benefits of cleansing cream to the skin. Brodie's carefully selected girls receive this florid education away from the prying eyes of despairing headmistress, Mrs MacKay, who is forever looking for an opportunity to eject Brodie from the school. A renegade element at the Marcia Blaine Academy for Girls, Brodie fails to subscribe to that central tenet of contemporary girls' education, 'team spirit', dismissing it as a concept 'employed to cut across individualism'. 'Where,' she queries, 'would the team spirit have got Anna Pavlova?' Considering her girls to be the future generation of Pavlovas, Brodie dismisses the rest of the Marcia Blaine student body as mere corps de ballet, destined to play a supporting role to her 'crème de la crème' girls. Consequently, the Brodie set are reviled within the school. The fierce sense of loyalty Brodie inspires in this specially selected group of girls ironically proves her downfall.

Because of its setting in a 1930s girls' school, *The Prime of Miss Jean Brodie* is sometimes wrongly dismissed as a 'jolly hockey sticks' parody in the style of Denise Deegan's enjoyable but lightweight *Daisy Pulls It Off* (14f, 2m, 1983). This analysis is inaccurate, failing to recognise the thorny ideological questions the play asks about the role of education in moulding societies for either good or ill. Like its protagonist, *The Prime of Miss Jean Brodie* is not a play to be underestimated – beneath its show of eccentricity and verve lies a core of steel.

74

Dream Pill
by Rebecca Prichard (*b.* 1971, UK)

First performed: Clean Break at Soho Theatre, London, as part of *Charged*, 2010

Cast breakdown: 2f

Publisher: Nick Hern Books, in *Charged*, 2010

Just thirty minutes in length but packing a ferocious punch, *Dream Pill* looks at child trafficking through the eyes of two nine-year-old girls. Tunde and Bola have been flown into the UK from their native Nigeria and are now incarcerated in a basement, somewhere in London. Separated from their family and friends, 'Dedeh', the man who lurks upstairs, is their only protector. But he is also their pimp, their abuser and the dispenser of 'dream pills'. As the girls await the visit of a client, they chatter away to the audience with a gregarious charm that is as disconcerting as it is endearing. Rebecca Prichard's play is a sobering glimpse into one of the most shameful perversions of global trade.

Dream Pill was one of six short plays commissioned and premiered by Clean Break under the collective title *Charged*. First presented at Soho Theatre in London in 2010 and published in a collected anthology by Nick Hern Books, all the plays are written for entirely female casts. Alongside Prichard's *Dream Pill* are E V Crowe's *Doris Day* (2f), Sam Holcroft's *Dancing Bears* (7f), Rebecca Lenkiewicz's *That Almost Unnameable Lust* (4f), Chloë Moss' *Fatal Light* (5f) and Winsome Pinnock's *Taken* (3f). The *Independent* called *Charged* 'the most ambitious project to date in the thirty-year history of Clean Break', and noted that, while 'people unfamiliar with the company's output may flinch from the very idea of such a project, suspecting that it would constitute an orgy of narrowly issue-driven drama and tub-thumping political correctness, in fact, the plays take you in all kinds of unexpected directions.'

Performed in two cycles, *Charged* took over the entire Soho Theatre building with the plays being performed on three of its four floors, the audience promenading between them. *Dream Pill* was staged in the basement, the sounds of the theatre's bar above and the bustle of the busy Soho streets audible outside, an underscore to the actors' dialogue. Tunde and Bola live a clandestine existence in a basement, all but unseen and unheard. They sleep on mats and own just a handful of other people's broken and discarded possessions – and yet the wealth of London is a few metres away, directly above their heads. They are a part of the economic machinery of the city; commodities to be consumed and yet entirely dislocated from the affluence and opportunity which lies almost within touching distance. This proximity between freedom and bondage, public and private, privilege and oppression is what makes the play so chilling and also so incredibly affecting to watch.

There is a pervading sadness beneath the girls' playfulness, joking and childish desire to keep us, the audience, entertained with tales of their lives. Perhaps most disturbingly of all, they exhibit a disarming lack of understanding as to whether what is being done to them is wrong, or entirely normal. As their confidants, we are implicated and yet powerless to intervene. After thirty minutes of watching the girls prepare for their next appointment, of having them compliment us on our hair, chat about their journey from Nigeria, share some of their hopes, dreams, longings and fears, the eventual and inevitable arrival of the male client is a terrible moment. *Dream Pill* is not an easy play to watch.

Prichard rose to prominence in the late 1990s via the Royal Court's Young Writers' Programme. Her play *Essex Girls* (5f), a bittersweet comedy about young single-motherhood and girls growing up in Tory Britain, was staged as part of the 1994 Royal Court Young Writers' Festival and was published in the anthology *Coming On Strong* (Faber and Faber). *Fair Game*, her adaptation of Edna Mazya's *Games in the Backyard* was staged at the Royal Court in 1997, but it was her 1998 play *Yard Gal* (2f) for which she became best known. A co-production between Clean Break and the Royal Court, *Yard Gal* is an explosive and furiously energetic portrayal of loyalty and friendship between two teenage girls living in the gangland streets of Hackney, North London. The play gave a rare insight into the experience of girls in gangs and, like *Dream Pill*, plays with the audience/performer relationship to powerful effect, forcing us to reappraise our perceptions of its young protagonists. The play won Prichard a Critics' Circle Award for Most Promising Playwright.

75

Time and the Conways
by J.B. Priestley (*b.* 1894, UK)

First performed: Duchess Theatre, London, 1937

Cast breakdown: 6f, 4m

Publisher: Penguin, in *An Inspector Calls and Other Plays*, 2001

On an autumn night in 1919, in a prosperous suburb of an industrial town, Newlingham, notable local family the Conways are throwing a party. It is middle daughter Kay's twenty-first birthday and there is much to celebrate – the War is over, the men have been demobbed, an economic boom is around the corner and all the Conway children seem poised on the cusp of great things. But unknown to the family and their guests, that fated evening will set into motion a series of events that will revisit them cruelly in later life. Time is an unforgiving force and the seeds the Conways sow for themselves on that golden evening in 1919 will come to bear fruit in unexpected and terrible ways.

Time and the Conways is often grouped within the selection of J.B. Priestley's work widely described as his 'Time Plays'. In it, Priestley offers a theatrical response to the thesis proffered by J.W. Dunne in his 1927 book, *An Experiment with Time*, namely that all events happen on a concurrent basis and it is only the limitations of human consciousness that force us to see time as a linear structure, rather than experiencing past, present and future simultaneously and interchangeably. Regardless of whether an audience is au fait with the intricacies of Dunne's theories, Priestley's subversion of the usual order of a play's events gives *Time and the Conways* much of its poignancy.

While all three acts take place in the Conway's sitting room on Kay's birthday, the play jumps back and forth through time. In Act One we watch the first half of Kay's 1919 birthday party, in Act Two it is 1937 and we see her turn forty, while in Act Three it is 1919 once again and the last of the party guests are leaving. This jump of nearly twenty years at a time is a tremendous challenge for the play's actors, as they collectively age and then regress by two decades in the length of the time it takes for a scene change. The actress playing Kay, for instance, who in Act One is described by Priestley as 'an intelligent, sensitive girl', dreaming of becoming a novelist and on the threshold of adult life, must transform herself in the time it takes for the curtain to fall and rise again into someone who 'has a rather hard, efficient, well-groomed look, that of a woman of forty who has earned her living for years', before once again shifting back into the idealistic twenty-one-year-old with equal speed. It is not just the switches in physicality, voice and appearance the actors must master, but the very emotional landscape of their characters. Time does not treat the Conways kindly and the angry, scared and disappointed group we see in 1937 is entirely different to the family who gaze cheerfully and expectantly into their brilliant futures in 1919.

Although a chillingly stark depiction of how the sharpest and deepest wounds are often inflicted by our nearest and dearest, *Time and the Conways* is more than a domestic drama about a family destroying itself from within. In line with much of Priestley's work, it is a deeply political piece and a cautionary tale on the ills that can befall society if those with the greatest resources fail to look beyond their own narrow interests. Book-ending the brief period of peace between the First and Second World Wars, the play explores self-interest, short-termism and complacency in the middle classes via the spectacular fall from grace many families such as the Conways experienced in the inter-war period. By 1937, the boom the Conways so looked forward to in 1919 has come and gone without their taking advantage of it and now, after years of financial mismanagement, they face selling the family home in the midst of an economic slump. Shocked by how little the house is expected to fetch, one of the Conway daughters, Hazel, insists 'Mother was offered thousands and thousands for it after the War.' 'Yes, but this isn't just after the War,' her husband Ernest retorts dryly, 'it's just before the next War.'

Indeed, the cold presence of Ernest at the family's financial meeting in the 1937 section of the play encapsulates the changing face not just of the Conway's fortunes, but of the country's. It was in 1919 on the night of Kay's twenty-first birthday that Ernest, a lower-class would-be entrepreneur, first appears in the family's home. Brought to the party by a mutual friend because he is 'desperately anxious' to know the Conways, his presence at the party is barely tolerated by the family. Nearly twenty years later and with a wealth that now eclipses that of the family who once snubbed him, Ernest sees no reason why he should bail out the Conways. Pride comes before a fall, and as the family discovers they have not kept pace with the changes going on in the world around them, Priestley draws our attention to the perils awaiting those who fail to consider the future. Multilayered, theatrically inventive and likely to push the emotional buttons of anyone with a heart, a family, or a past, *Time and the Conways* is arguably one of Priestley's most humane and haunting pieces of work.

76

Phedra (Phèdre)
by Jean Racine (*b.* 1639, France)

First performed: Hôtel de Bourgogne, Paris, 1677

Cast breakdown: 5f, 3m (doubling possible)

Recommended version: by Julie Rose

Publisher: Nick Hern Books, 2001

No one knows what's wrong with Phedra. Afflicted by some undisclosed anguish, she can't sleep, won't eat and, in her distraction, is close to death. Only Oenon, her most trusted confidante, can elicit an explanation: Phedra is in love with Hippolytus, her husband Theseus's son. Horrified by the depth of her incestuous and adulterous desires, Phedra is resigned to ending her life, comforted only by the belief that her shameful secret will never be known. When a message arrives that Theseus is dead, everything changes. Encouraged by Oenon, Phedra reveals her feelings to Hippolytus, hoping that now, no longer married nor technically his stepmother, things between them can be different. But Theseus isn't dead and when he unexpectedly arrives home, Phedra's revelation sets in motion a calamitous sequence of events.

A knock-out role that runs the full gamut of emotion, Phedra is a character that has attracted generations of leading actresses. Racine originally wrote the role for his lover, La Champmeslé, one of France's foremost contemporary actresses, who in 1670s Paris commanded earnings comparable to those of today's Hollywood stars. Braving early performances in which Racine's opponents dominated the auditorium by buying up vast numbers of seats only to leave them empty, La Champmeslé stood her ground at the centre of a production which, in time, would come to be seen as the pinnacle of Racine's theatrical career. More recently, the 25th June 2009 marked a moment of theatre history when seventy-three cinemas across the UK and a further two hundred overseas filled with audiences eager to see Helen Mirren assume the role of the beleaguered queen as the National Theatre broadcast its inaugural NT Live performance from its London home.

Demanding exceptional energy, stamina and technical ability, playing Phedra is, in many ways, the acting equivalent of running a marathon. Across her epic speeches she rockets from the heights of one emotion, plunges to the depths of another, and all while giving the impression of being a woman at death's door. The role could be taken by an actress aged anywhere between her twenties and sixties, depending on whether a director wants to depict her as equivalent in age to her husband, or as a younger second wife, actually far closer in years to her stepson. The 2009 National Theatre production added an additional cross-generational frisson to the already loaded tale of illicit desire by matching the sixty-four-year-old Mirren against Dominic Cooper's twenty-something Hippolytus.

Although the title role is undoubtedly at the centre of attention, it's not the only excellent part for a woman in the play. Indeed, Oenon is arguably just as interesting a prospect, being as she is the real engine of the play, precipitating every one of the Queen's abysmal decisions. Whether she does so through blind love for the woman for whom she has sacrificed everything, abandoning even her home and own children in the process, or as a result of bare-faced manipulation, is open to debate. Racine's invention, Aricia, is a further tantalising role. The sole survivor of a royal dynasty destroyed by Theseus, and the woman that Hippolytus unexpectedly find himself in love with, Aricia enjoys less stage time than Phedra and Oenon but is just as much a linchpin in the unfolding action. The scenes she does have, in which the tremendous sway she holds over her enemy's son gradually dawns on her, are a masterful study in power and how the status of a character can transform in a matter of moments.

Countless English translations of the play exist, penned in differing styles and levels of elaborateness, and there will inevitably be one to suit the needs and interests of any director. Some are in free verse, whereas others stick religiously to Racine's careful alexandrines (twelve-beat lines). Others imitate the sensibilities of seventeenth-century language while some try their hardest to be intensely modern. Then there are those that at some point were up to date, but now seem hopelessly out of touch. For an understated poeticism and straightforward emotional honesty that allows the structure of Racine's original to breathe while offering the actors plenty of space in which to flex their muscles, Julie Rose's 2001 version is hard to beat.

First performed: St James's Theatre, London, 1954

Cast breakdown: 9f, 4m (doubling possible)

Publisher: Nick Hern Books, 1999

Separate Tables is two short plays: *Table by the Window* and *Table Number Seven*, both self-contained and performable in isolation from one another, but ideally viewed side by side. The action of both takes place in the public dining room and lounge of the Beauregard Hotel, Bournemouth, a guesthouse populated by a host of mainly elderly, mainly single 'regular residents', whose steady existence is occasionally broken up by the sporadic appearance of 'casuals'.

In *Table by the Window*, one such 'casual', an ageing model, finds herself locking eyes over her evening meal with her ex-husband, a former political star, now a middle-aged alcoholic living under a pseudonym at the Beauregard. After eight years apart and with the shadow of the scandal that caused their separation still hanging over them, the couple must confront the future, and whether they will step into it together, or apart. *Table Number Seven* revolves around the discovery among the permanent residents that one of them, Major Pollock, has been arrested for improper behaviour. Along with the revelation of his criminal activities, the residents discover that the Major is certainly not the person he has been claiming to be.

Within the walls of a seemingly unremarkable Bournemouth hotel, Rattigan neatly depicts a post-war Britain in the grip of extreme social, political and cultural change. The country's disintegrating class structure, changing attitudes towards sex, and the re-evaluation of social mores are laid bare for an audience, making *Separate Tables* a fascinating historical document of Britain in the 1950s, as well as a moving analysis of both the best and worst that humans can be. The play is populated by a cast of characters living in separate rooms and dining at separate tables, but forced nonetheless to form a weird kind of community as a result of their enforced proximity. In these environments (and the only two locations within which the play's action takes place), the characters' lives knock against one another, overlap and interweave in a way that is both subtly subversive and thrillingly dramatic. While quietly consuming their dinners and, in typically British fashion, conversing over the state of the weather, the residents of the Beauregard Hotel are actually grappling with some of the key social concerns of the post-war age and – either willingly or unwillingly – turning their eyes towards the new world awaiting them.

Like much of Rattigan's work, the play's supreme dramatic potency comes not from what his characters say, but from what remains unsaid. It is in the little moments in which the characters' emotions get the better of them – and their stiff upper lips momentarily relax – that the real dramatic punch of the piece is delivered. A snatched kiss in the public lounge, a hastily wiped-away tear and a pair of spectacles grasped so tightly that they shatter in the hand of the holder are moments in which the depth of their emotions are bought vividly and undeniably into view. These fleeting, and consequently all the more tantalising, indications of the characters' desires and despair are adeptly woven throughout the play, an elegant and understated portrait of private lives being conducted in public rooms.

Several years after Rattigan's death in 1977, his biographer Geoffrey Walsall came across an earlier version of a section of *Table Number Seven*. The extract, only a few lines long, is thought to be Rattigan's original version of the moment in which the hotel residents discover the Major's misdemeanour by stumbling across a report of his trial in a local newspaper. The extract revealed that, in Rattigan's initial version, the Major is arrested for propositioning men, not – as the later version had it – for molesting women in a cinema. Writing at a time when the Lord Chamberlain's office still censored plays and blocked anything it considered to be an affront to public decency, Rattigan most likely knew that writing a character into the play who was gay (and categorically so, rather than gay for those in the audience who wanted to see that, and straight for those who didn't) would render the play impossible to produce. While the winds of change were blowing through the rooms of the Beauregard Hotel, it seemed they were not in the Lord Chamberlain's office, and it would be another fourteen years until censorship of plays ended. With this original text in light, the Major becomes a far more sympathetic character. After all, who likes someone that spends his spare time molesting women in dark cinemas? Dreamt up by a gay playwright at a time when a gay character couldn't even be shown on stage for fear of 'offending public decency', the Major's adoption of a fake persona, albeit in a way that deceives even those closest to him, and his tendency to seek assignations in a somewhat shadowy manner, become all the more poignant and all the more understandable.

78

The Steamie
by Tony Roper (*b.* 1941, UK)

First performed: Crawford Theatre, Glasgow, 1987

Cast breakdown: 4f, 1m

Publisher: Nick Hern Books, in *Scot-Free: New Scottish Plays*, 1990

It's 7 p.m. on New Year's Eve and the Carnegie Street Steamie is as busy as ever. Mrs Culfeathers, Dolly, Doreen and Magrit race to get their washing done before the celebrations begin – although, having started early on their Hogmanay drinks, progress isn't quite as swift as usual. Word is that the days of the public washhouses (or 'steamies') are numbered and a new innovation – the launderette – is on its way. No longer obliging the women to do hours of back-breaking hand-washing, week in and week out, these shiny new launderettes and their automated machines will introduce an unknown concept to the women's lives: 'leisure time'. But as the hours tick away to the start of the new year, the women cannot help but look ahead with a mixture of apprehension and excitement.

Set in 1950s Glasgow, Tony Roper's mischievously funny *The Steamie* captures a moment of change for the city's working-class female population. It was Roper's first play and, defying its critics, turned out to be a runaway success. The original production ran for six months and was subsequently revived numerous times across Scotland and England (originally staged in London under the title *Talk of the Steamie*) and was adapted for television by Channel 4. Roper has always attributed the play's success to its foregrounding of the female experience, unusual in 1980s drama and even more so then for a play written by a man. Having himself been an actor who toured in plays to community centres, Roper had noticed that, of the small audiences who turned out, the majority were usually women. So when offered the chance to write a play he chose to focus on them. At the time, he recalls, 'most plays were all men with a token woman' and so he decided to buck the trend: 'This was all women with a token man.'

With a warmth that never descends into sentimentality, Roper explores the double-edged sword that post-war modernisation represented to working-class women such as those of the Carnegie Street Steamie. These women, Roper suggests, have always worked hard for their living and the concept of having time on their hands while an electric washing machine does their job for them is not necessarily a welcome one. Even more ominous is the loss of companionship that they fear the impending closure of the city's steamies will bring. As far as the women see it, their lives are an endless treadmill of cooking, cleaning, washing and childcare, and their husbands aren't up to much by way of conversation. At least at the steamie they get to have a good old natter and a bit of a laugh. It's a sense of community that, with the growing popularity of the new-fangled electric machines, seems doomed to be lost. 'In these launderettes they don't even speak tae wan another,' Dolly warns the others – a figure of authority on the matter since her sister-in-law bravely ventured into one. 'An' when the machines are in the hoose, we'll no need tae go oot at aw,' she ominously concludes.

Requiring a complex set, *The Steamie* is a play that's not impossible to stage on a small budget, but does require imagination to do so. The stage houses four laundry stalls, each of which contain washing tubs, boilers, sinks large enough to steep blankets in (and in which Dolly takes a quick bath when she thinks no one is looking), and taps that dispense hot running water. For its actresses it's a back-breaker of a show and Roper has them lugging piles of laundry, some of it sopping wet, from one part of the stage to the other, their constant scrubbing, rinsing, boiling, folding and stacking shaping the tempo and rhythm of the action. The wringers, mercifully, are offstage, but other than that, the women perform the entirety of a washing cycle by hand and in full view of the audience. As if that weren't enough, Roper includes six songs for his actresses to belt their way through (although their presence in the show feels somewhat indebted to the 1980s trend for plays accompanied by songs rather than a need to be there, and a modern production could easily dispense with these musical numbers if desired). Showcasing the sharpest of comedy writing, *The Steamie* is an absolute delight of a play. Certainly an actress reaching the end of a run may never want to look at a pile of laundry again, but for the joy of performing Roper's intelligent, refreshing and honest play, it's more than worth the work.

79

In the Next Room, or the vibrator play
by Sarah Ruhl (*b*. 1974, USA)

First performed: Berkeley Repertory Theatre, Berkeley, 2009

Cast breakdown: 4f, 3m

Publisher: Theatre Communications Group, 2012

Mrs Givings' husband is a doctor. Specialising in the treatment of women, and occasionally men, who suffer from hysteria, Dr Givings has recently acquired a marvellous new piece of medical equipment which he keeps carefully locked away. Powered by the latest innovation – electricity – it's at the cutting edge of technology and is proving astonishingly popular among his patients. So much so in fact that they can't seem to get enough of his 'electrical massage sessions' and Mrs Givings' living room seems to be forever full of patients eagerly awaiting their next appointment. But the machine in the next room makes an odd noise, and the moans that come from behind the door are both alarming and intriguing. Mrs Givings has never heard anything of the kind, and decides to investigate. What she finds is to have a dramatic effect on her and her husband, prompting revelations that will impact on their lives together in more ways than one.

'A play hovering at the dawn of electricity' is how Sarah Ruhl describes *In the Next Room, or the vibrator play*, her wonderfully sexy, funny, and slyly sensual tribute to the advent of the vibrator. Set in the 1880s but very much a play for our times, it sees its characters standing on the brink of a new technological epoch, looking ahead with a mixture of awe, bewilderment and trepidation. Electricity, a glorious new medium, is flooding their lives and as Edison's wonder-creation enters their homes, and their bedrooms, nothing will ever be the same again. It's a play that speaks strongly to contemporary audiences, capturing as it does the exquisite blend of wonder, fear and exhilaration that living in an age of exceptionally fast technological advancement inspires. Seeing themselves anew under the glare of the recently installed electric light bulbs, the inhabitants of the Givings' household – and their visitors – are reconsidering who they are; their entirely ordinary lives thrown into crisis and wonder amidst a whole new world of possibilities.

The play focuses on a little-known fact: that the vibrator was initially invented and used by nineteenth-century doctors to treat women considered to be suffering from 'hysteria', then a medically recognised condition. Although doctors had for some time been treating patients by manually inducing what was politely termed a 'paroxysm', it was a process many clinicians found frustratingly time-consuming and, for want of a better phrase, labour intensive. The vibrator was created as a handy time-saving device for doctors, offering a much speedier, and therefore cost-efficient way of treating patients. Initially a hefty piece of medical apparatus, plugged directly into the mains and operated only by trained staff, such equipment could, as Dr Givings proudly tells his new patient Mrs Daldry, produce the desired effect in 'three minutes, sometimes five at the outer limits'. Of course, all this might seem bizarre to a modern audience, but to a culture that considered female sexual arousal something of an anathema, the physical response a woman's body made to the touch of a vibrator was surely evidence of successful medical treatment. Whether a practice born out of an inability to see women as capable of sexual desire was laughably innocent or unspeakably barbaric is something Ruhl carefully leaves open to her audience to decide for themselves.

Much of the play's humour derives from the contrast between the knowingness of a modern audience and the lack of it in Ruhl's characters. An incredibly funny piece that's bound to elicit much laughter from an easy-going adult audience, it's a piece that is, at times, daringly risqué but always sensitive and dignified in its depiction of Dr Givings' (and subsequently Mrs Givings') 'medical' experiments. In her deft handling of the play's subject matter, Ruhl creates an incredibly moving depiction of human bewilderment in the face of change, and of emotions felt but not yet understood. Populated by complicated relationships, it's a piece that follows characters seeking desperately to understand newly awoken and previously unidentified feelings – whether that be new mother Mrs Givings' jealousy towards the wet nurse that her own insufficient milk supply has forced her to employ, or the confused tenderness Mrs Daldry feels towards Dr Giving's assistant Annie upon discovering she would far rather have her than him administer her 'treatments'. The potency of Ruhl's play lies not just in the way it illustrates a little-known but bizarre episode in medical history. It is in the way it leaves us to wonder what about our own sexuality we as individuals, and as a society, are yet to discover, or entirely understand.

First performed: Soho Theatre Company at the Cockpit Theatre, London, 1993

Cast breakdown: 5f, 1m

Publisher: Nick Hern Books, 2008

Eva Schlesinger has to leave Germany. Just nine years old and completely on her own, she must travel to England and wait there for her parents. The Nazis are in power and, for Jews like Eva, Germany is no longer a safe place to be. But having arrived in England and been placed in the care of a local family, Eva's links to her homeland begin to dim. As the chances of her parents joining her diminish, Eva's sense of identity undergoes a dramatic transformation. Forty years later, Eva now calls herself Evelyn. English through and through, and with a daughter of her own to deal with, Evelyn manages to think little about her history or who she was prior to the outbreak of war. But when her daughter goes rummaging through a box of old papers and discovers the truth, Evelyn must confront a past and a host of emotions long since buried.

The Movement for the Care of Children from Germany, which organised the transportation of individuals such as Eva out of Germany, is estimated to have saved the lives of around 10,000 unaccompanied children. Instigated after Kristallnacht, one of the most extreme coordinated acts of pre-war Nazi aggression towards Jews, the 'Kindertransport' was operational until the outbreak of the Second World War nine months later. It was an undoubted lifesaver, sparing thousands from the horrors of the camps and yet, for some of the children, as well as the families they left behind, it was also a life sentence. As Samuels explores in her powerfully moving and yet delicate play, the ramifications of being separated from parents, home and culture can be vast and continue to hold a powerful sway long past childhood. Although related to a very specific moment in history, *Kindertransport* speaks broadly, compassionately and unsentimentally about the plight of unaccompanied children everywhere.

Samuels wrote the play partly in response to watching a television documentary in which a middle-aged woman guiltily expressed her residual rage towards her dead parents for sending her away on the Kindertransport.

Even though she knew her parents' actions had probably saved her life, she was still burdened by ambivalence towards them. Through the fictional character of Eva/Evelyn, Samuels explores this muddle of guilt, grief, anger and abandonment, and asks provocative questions about what it is to be a survivor of trauma. Examining the ethical complexities of either actively remembering or actively forgetting, the play explores the fine line that exists between moving on and running away. In particular, it draws attention to the difficult choices faced by survivors of genocide and their descendants. Is dwelling on the event consigning those people forever to the status of victims? Or is it the only way to ensure such a tragedy never happens again?

An ensemble piece, *Kindertransport* provokes its audience to view this complex territory simultaneously from a range of perspectives; the child at the centre of the tragedy, the biological mother who cannot be with her, the adoptive mother who, however ill-equipped, looks after her, the struggling adult the child becomes, and the child she then produces and with whom she fails to connect emotionally. All of these characters are equally sympathetic and yet in their own way invite our criticism too, carrying out, as they do, acts of emotional violence towards one another that have profound effects. Whether they are victim or perpetrator, altruistic or self-interested is hard to say and it is these grey areas that Samuels animates with a rich theatricality.

Eight years in Eva's life play out simultaneously against just a few hours in Evelyn's, and 1930s Germany, 1940s England and late-twentieth-century London inhabit the same constantly shifting and yet static space. Eva and Evelyn coexist on the stage, the past and present of one person inextricably linked, forever overlapping, blurring and meeting. Through this landscape of fragmented memories, dreams and real-time action, the shadowy figure of the 'Ratcatcher' moves. Sprung from the pages of Eva's storybook, this Pied Piper figure with 'eyes as sharp as razors' lurks at the periphery of the action, a reminder of the sorrows suffered by a society imbued with death. Offering no easy answers, *Kindertransport* is a haunting, provocative and highly original piece of theatre that questions whether we can adequately remember the victims of an atrocity without robbing its survivors of a future.

First performed: Bacchanal women's bar, San Francisco, 1974

Cast breakdown: 7f

Publisher: Methuen, in *Ntozake Shange Plays: 1*, 1992

'orange butterflies and aqua sequins
ensconsed tween slight bosoms
silk roses darting from behind her ears
the passion flower of southwest los angeles
meandered down hoover street'

Ntozake Shange's verse play, *for colored girls who have considered suicide/ when the rainbow is enuf* is a piece of writing that is as beautiful as it is brutal and stirring as it is sobering. Seven women, each simply titled by the colour of the dress she wears, perform a collection of twenty-two dance poems. In turns haunting, funny, provocative and defiant, the poems consider what it is to be a woman of colour living in the USA.

'With as much space as a small studio on the Lower East Side, the five of us, five women, proceeded to dance, make poems, make music, make a woman's theatre for about twenty patrons.' So comments Ntozake Shange on the genesis of *for colored girls…*, her most celebrated work and a piece that, from its humble origins, achieved a remarkable trajectory. The play started life in 1974 as an informal performance staged on an ad hoc basis in San Francisco bars. Gathering momentum, it moved to New York where it again was performed in bars, before being given a workshop production in an Off-Broadway venue, and subsequently found a home at Joseph Papp's renowned Public Theater. By September 1976, *for colored girls…* had arrived on Broadway where, a world away from its low-key roots, it garnered a range of top awards. Throughout the entire period, Shange collaborated with an ever-shifting and eclectic range of artists in its ongoing development. Actresses, dancers, poets, directors, a horn trio and a reggae band were among those with whom she worked.

A play for anyone who loves language and the emotive power of words, it's a piece that has clearly been conceived by an accomplished poetic mind. Featuring Shange's powerfully unorthodox spelling and an almost total lack of conventional punctuation, *for colored girls…* is more concerned with the rhythmic and musical qualities of language than conforming to accepted ideals. These are words that are rich and potent, structured in a way that is highly sophisticated; a delight for any actress to speak and audience to hear. Shange's use of imagery is breathtaking and with exquisite detail she captures the various women who populate the play, weaving dreamlike fragments of stories in ways that are in turn delightful, wryly humorous and desperately dark.

At the same time, the words on the page give just a partial indication of the entirety of Shange's vision, given the importance of dance in her original rendering of the text. 'Seven women in brilliantly coloured dresses swirl through twenty-two dance-poems in an exposition of the "metaphysical dilemmas" of race, gender and environment' was the way that New York's *Time Out* described this 'downright extraordinary' performance to its readers. Indeed, Shange has often used the term 'choreopoem' to articulate what *for colored girls…* actually is. A creative polymath, Shange's range of artistic accomplishments was impressive (already a poet, essayist, performer, and lecturer in Humanities and Women's Studies by the time she began to compose *for colored girls…* at the age of twenty-six), but it was upon discovering dance that she uncovered a medium through which she could articulate in a whole new dimension her experiences. 'Knowing a woman's mind and spirit had been allowed me, with dance I discovered my body more intimately than I had imagined possible,' she recollects. 'With the acceptance of the ethnicity of my thighs & backside, came a clearer understanding of my voice as a woman & as a poet'. *for colored girls…* was the vehicle through which she would perfectly synthesise her expert grasp of the language of words and the language of dance.

A film based on the play was released in 2010 with a cast that includes Macy Gray, Whoopi Goldberg, Janet Jackson and Thandie Newton. Interestingly, the film's director Tyler Perry chose to update the piece to the modern day, rather than leaving it in its 1970s setting. While this is a salutary reminder of how, in certain respects, little has changed for the women Shange was writing about thirty-five years earlier, it points to the enduring quality and relevance of her words. An impassioned cry from the heart and an outstanding technical achievement, *for colored girls…* remains a dazzling, highly unusual and deeply moving theatrical event.

First performed: Manhattan Theatre Club, New York, 2004

Cast breakdown: 3f, 1m

Publisher: Theatre Communications Group, 2005

Sister Aloysius Beauvier is a nun of the order of the Sisters of Charity and is principal of Saint Nicholas, a Catholic school in the Bronx. Never one for sentimentalising over the children in her care, Sister Aloysius sees her role as one that ought to inspire fear in her pupils, rather than affection. It is 1964 and a new boy, Donald Muller, has joined the school. The first black student to be enrolled at Saint Nicholas, Donald's very presence makes him far from popular, and yet the bullying that Sister Aloysius had envisaged befalling him never materialises. Donald has a 'protector' in the form of Father Flynn, the popular, basketball-playing priest with whom the students share a far warmer relationship than Sister Aloysius would ever countenance. Suspicious that Father Flynn's attentions towards Donald might be of a more sinister nature than his benevolent exterior would suggest, Sister Aloysius feels duty-bound to act. Appointing herself both judge and jury, she privately and covertly sets about putting Father Flynn on trial.

'We are living in a courtroom culture,' Shanley announces in his introduction to *Doubt*. 'Discussion has given way to debate' and 'communication has become a contest of wills'. If so, what is the reason for all this argument, this energetic and forthright assertion of the superiority of one opinion over another? For Shanley the answer is nihilistic: 'Maybe it's because deep down under the chatter we have come to a place where we know that we don't know… anything.' Locating the action of his play in 1964, a time he remembers 'not just me, but the whole world seemed to be going through some kind of vast puberty', Shanley gives himself a platform from which he can speak in broad terms about doubt, not just as a niggle in the individual mind, but as an important part of the collective psyche. Writing a play set in the Catholic church, the dramatic stakes of which hinge around a taboo relationship and one triggered by the arrival of a black student in a formerly whites-only school, Shanley captures a moment in which doubt began to reconfigure how American society saw itself; doubt in the role of organised religion, doubt in the USA's treatment of its black citizens, doubt in the absolutes that had been taught about which relationships – sexual or otherwise – were right and which were wrong. This widespread uncertainty, ignited in the 1960s, was far from resolved by the time Shanley came to write *Doubt* at the dawn of the twenty-first century. Awarded the 2005 Pulitzer Prize, it's a play that powerfully taps into the condition of a society still reconsidering what it ought to be.

Doubt isn't a play about the discovery of paedophilic tendencies in a priest, nor is it about the vindication of the woman who suspects him. There is no moment of high drama in which Father Flynn is publically shamed (indeed, the moments in which Sister Aloysius voices her suspicions don't always receive the response she, or most probably the audience, were expecting), nor is there an emotional denouement in which he either announces his guilt or protests his innocence. Rather, it's a play that focuses on unpicking, stealthily and meticulously, the many layers of the human capacity for doubt and, as a result, is a far more provocative and affecting piece of work. Shanley's aim appears to be writing a play that sends the audience out from the theatre with more questions in their heads than when they came in, and it's likely to intensify an audience member's capacity for doubt, rather than reassure them with neat conclusions. Although the nature of Father Flynn's relationship with the twelve-year-old Donald remains ambiguous to the end, it's not the only puzzle which an audience member is likely to leave a performance of *Doubt* considering.

Intersected by Father Flynn delivering parables from the pulpit to an unseen congregation, Shanley's play is, of course, a parable in itself. *Doubt* (or to give it its full title, *Doubt, A Parable*) is constructed accordingly with storytelling that is lean, taut and unwaveringly direct. Nothing, not a single detail, is superfluous and every word, gesture, action and event serves to propel the narrative forward. As a consequence, the play has an extraordinary sense of momentum and, at around ninety minutes duration in performance, it whizzes by. Compact and immaculately structured, it's a play that, like the very best parables, contains whole worlds of insight and complexity within the simplest of structures.

First performed: Royal Court Theatre, London, 1985

Cast breakdown: 4f, 3m

Publisher: Theatre Communications Group, 2005

In the summer that Lemon is eleven, her parents' friend Danielle, or 'Aunt Dan', becomes a dazzling figure in the young girl's life. Night after night the two sit up alone while Aunt Dan spins wonderful tales of her extraordinary adventures. Filled with passion, promiscuity, circles of bohemian friends, and even a brief near-meeting with her beloved Henry Kissinger, Dan's life has been brilliant and bizarre. But, furnished with strong feelings about humankind's tendency to ill treat those weaker or less fortunate than themselves, Dan affects an unconventional stance and one that places her relationship with Lemon's parents under strain. As the chasm between them grows, Dan is drawn increasingly to the child and Lemon to her. Choosing Dan's perspectives over those of her parents, Lemon's fascination with the older woman's beliefs will play a fundamental role in how she goes on to encounter the world.

'Hello, dear audience, dear good people who have taken yourselves out for a special treat, a night at the theatre' is the direct and somewhat unsettling greeting with which the curious figure of Lemon welcomes the audience. A treat at the theatre they may have taken themselves out for, but, as the audience soon realises, this theatregoing experience will be anything other than straightforward. *Aunt Dan and Lemon* is a play that refuses to stick to the rules and which, with Shawn's trademark unpredictability, does anything but let the audience sit back and relax. Part of the way through writing the play, Shawn claims to have realised 'what I was doing was going to turn out to be my little contribution to the endless speculation on everyone's favourite topic, what people always with touching hopefulness insist on calling the "mystery" of man's inhuman treatment of his fellows (mass murder, etc.).' Upon achieving this realisation, his next thought was 'I'll be God damned if I'm going to allow the apparently built-in tendencies of theatre to force me to tell the audience what plays always tell the audience: Others are bad, you are good. (You are good because you can see so clearly that the ones on stage are bad, and you condemn them utterly.)'

Consequently, Shawn chose to write a play that 'would be *about* the audience, so that everything important that would happen would be in the audience and not on the stage.' *Aunt Dan and Lemon* therefore sets out to assault those comfortable beliefs an average educated and liberal-minded theatregoing audience might pride themselves in having. Set against the backdrop of the Vietnam War, the play questions the right of people entirely divorced and largely unaffected by conflict to criticise those in positions of responsibility who, at times, have to make difficult and unsanitary decisions. When Dan and Lemon's mother discuss the war over tea in the garden, Dan powerfully rallies to the defence of Kissinger: 'While we sit here in the sunshine and have our discussions about what we've read in the morning papers, there are these certain *other* people, like Kissinger, who happen to have the very bad luck to be society's leaders. And while we sit here chatting, they have to do what has to be done.' Dan's views are controversial, but are thought-provoking nonetheless. They challenge the moral supremacy assumed by the class which Shawn – himself a self-termed 'child of privilege' – was aware would form the majority of his theatre audiences. Five years later in his next play, *The Fever*, an extended monologue, Shawn took this point even further. Originally performed by Shawn himself in the homes of friends and acquaintances (although it has subsequently been performed by both male and female actors in more conventional theatrical settings), it asks probing and highly personal questions about the relationship between those of us in the wealthy developed nations, and our fellow human beings in the developing world.

Aunt Dan and Lemon is a play that won't be to everyone's taste. It's messy, chaotic and at times just downright weird. Characters come and go with little apparent logic, structurally it's all over the place, and it's never entirely clear what direction the play is taking. But even the play's harshest of critics will find it difficult to deny the unique bite that *Aunt Dan and Lemon* possesses. Despite its unconventional nature it succeeds in punching in the gut much more powerfully than so many plays of an openly political bent purport to do.

84 The Odd Couple (female version)
by Neil Simon (*b.* 1927, USA)

First performed: Broadhurst Theatre, New York, 1985

Cast breakdown: 6f, 2m

Publisher: Samuel French, 2007

Olive is the producer of a prime-time TV news show. Having split from her husband, she now lives happily alone in a state of chaos. Never one for housework, or indeed basic levels of cleanliness, Olive is perfectly content with her newly single existence, despite her apartment being a mess and her lifestyle far from healthy. But when her friend Florence is unexpectedly deserted by her husband, Olive takes pity and asks the other woman to move in. What Olive hasn't bargained for is Florence's many neuroses. A highly strung hypochondriac with a cleanliness obsession, Florence couldn't be more different to her friend. The resulting comedy is one in which these two most incompatible of roommates attempt to live together in some attempt at harmony.

Neil Simon's hit comedy *The Odd Couple* first opened on Broadway in 1965. A play about the disastrous efforts of two mismatched male friends living together, it was a huge commercial success and garnered a range of Tony Awards including Best Author (Play) for Simon and Best Actor for one of its stars, Walter Matthau. The play fostered a range of spin-offs including a 1968 film starring Jack Lemmon and, reprising his Broadway role, Walter Matthau, plus two ABC sitcoms and even a television cartoon about a dog and a cat living together. In 1985, Simon rewrote the play so that the warring roommates were women and *The Odd Couple* (female version) opened on Broadway, starring Oscar-winner Rita Moreno and sitcom star Sally Struthers. In this new version of the play, Oscar Madison has become Olive Madison and Felix Unger, Florence Unger. The poker games the men enjoy have been changed for a weekly evening of Trivial Pursuit, and Cecily and Gwendolyn Pigeon, the British sisters that the unlikely roommates attempt to seduce in the original, are exchanged for dashing Spanish brothers, Jesus and Manolo Costazuela.

The Odd Couple (female version) is a masterclass in comic writing for the stage and it's no exaggeration to say that almost every line delivers a laugh.

The plotting is exquisite; set-up lines threaded subtly into the dialogue during early scenes result in huge pay-offs in later ones, gags are timed like clockwork and the visual humour of the piece adds an additional, vibrant level. Sure, it's an admittedly light-hearted look at a marital break-up, and it's certainly not a play that could ever be accused of profundity, but for giving an audience a hugely enjoyable, laughter-packed evening at the theatre, you'd have to look hard to beat it. Perhaps with the benefit of having seen the original version run on stage for years, and able to analyse audience's responses to an almost scientific extent, Simon had perfected his understanding of how to elicit maximum laughter from the mismatched Olive and Florence. Yes, it's fair to say the scene in which the pair attempt a double date with the Costazuela brothers – despite the men's limited English and the women's even more limited Spanish – is somewhat groan-inducing ('I feel like Miss America,' Olive quips upon being presented with a bouquet of flowers. 'I miss Spain sometimes' is Jesus's sympathetic response). But by this point in the evening, the audience is so relaxed that Simon is able to get away with even the silliest of gags.

Alongside Olive and Florence, their four school friends, Sylvie, Micky, Vera and Renee, get their fair share of the comedy as they bicker, joke and gossip over their weekly Trivial Pursuit games in Olive's apartment. They are an excellent barometer against which to measure Florence's increasingly obsessive behaviour as the once laid-back Trivial Pursuit evenings become rigidly controlled events presided over by Florence with an almost maniacal energy. 'I get nervous she's going to sneak up behind us and shampoo our hair,' Sylvie moans, not entirely unfairly; Florence has even cleaned the Trivial Pursuit question cards. The six female roles, each working as an intrinsic part of the finely balanced ensemble Simon creates, partake fully in the play's gutsy, quick-paced and sharp humour. Any actress with a keen ear for timing and a love of the mechanics of comedy will delight in the roles, and Simon's female version of his classic comedy offers brilliant opportunities to actresses who enjoy nothing more than making audiences laugh.

First performed: Queens Theatre, London, 1938

Cast breakdown: 12f, 5m

Publisher: Samuel French, 1939

It is Charles and Dora Randolph's golden wedding anniversary and four generations of their family have assembled in the couple's capacious country house to celebrate. Within those walls that have been home to so many generations of Randolphs before them, Dora and Charles, their children, grandchildren, great-grandchildren and assorted in-laws come together for a weekend that brings with it all the squabbles, jealousy, jokes and reminiscences one would expect from a family reunion. Bonds are forged while others are broken, certain old rivalries are reignited and others laid to rest, memories are shared and vast quantities of food are consumed. Affectionate, warm and wily, Dodie Smith's gentle comedy celebrates family, 'that dear octopus from whose tentacles we never quite escape nor, in our inmost hearts, ever quite wish to'.

Regular theatregoers used to seeing plays in which families go from quietly dysfunctional at the rise of the curtain to totally eviscerated by its fall will find *Dear Octopus* either refreshingly upbeat or frustratingly mild. The Randolphs are that rare thing in drama – a family who end up happier by the end of the play than they are at the start. By the conclusion of *Dear Octopus*, any creases in the sunny contentedness of the Randolph family have been neatly and joyfully ironed out; the prodigal youngest daughter has returned home after a seven-year self-imposed exile, those people destined to fall in love have, and any rogue characters intent on spreading misery have well and truly been put in their place. At the head of the Randolph clan, Smith positions eminently cheerful couple Charles (a man so happy he is 'sometimes tempted to erect a statue to myself') and his utterly contented wife Dora. They form a serene and benevolent presence at the centre of their sometimes fractious family, the proverbial glue that binds this disparate group of personalities together.

Perhaps the most impressive of Smith's many achievements in *Dear Octopus* is the expertness with which she balances her cast of seventeen characters, masterfully orchestrating their individual trajectories to form one brilliant, energised and extremely entertaining whole. Indeed, anyone interested in learning how to write big-cast plays would do as well to study Smith in this respect as Chekhov. Every single character (even the fleetingly appearing servants) has a journey and a history that is detailed, rich and considered, and all contribute to the comedy and pathos of the play. Even the play's three children are exquisitely drawn, rich in genuine humour, and entirely lacking in mawkishness. 'I wish we didn't have dead people in the family. It sort of spoils the party' is ten-year-old Bill's pronouncement on his deceased aunt and uncle's absence from the family reunion, a prosaic comment that sets the tone for the children's mischievously comic and wholly unsentimental presence in the piece.

In a cast that ranges in years from infancy to mid-seventies, age is a constant preoccupation and *Dear Octopus* is a play that speaks touchingly, profoundly and humorously about the process of getting older. 'No one ever seems to like the age they are,' comments Dora, one of the few Randolph family members neither obsessed with her past nor fixated on her future, 'there are nice things about every age if people realise it in time instead of in retrospect.' It's a sage piece of advice and one that the remainder of the Randolphs would do well to heed. In a particularly effective move, Smith sets the central act of the play in that most emotive of all rooms of any grand house, the nursery. While the current Randolph youngsters play among the relics of their ancestors' childhoods, for the generations above them it is a room awash with memories and all the more poignant for it. For Charles and Dora's children, all in middle-age or fast approaching it, being back in the room of their childhoods is an experience that is bittersweet to say the least. 'This nursery's rather a harrowing place really' is the simple observation made by one.

For all its shrewd observations, *Dear Octopus* is a play that will send audiences out onto the street with a smile on their lips. It is a celebration of the family, a structure we love to bemoan but which doggedly survives despite the odds. It is, as Charles and Dora's son Nicholas declares as he toasts his parents' anniversary, 'like nearly every British institution, adaptable. It bends, it stretches – but it never breaks.'

First performed: Play Actors at the New Theatre, London, 1924

Cast breakdown: 6f, 5m (doubling possible)

Publisher: Women's Press, 2008

Confident that a substantial inheritance will put an end to his financial worries, Eustace Gaydon is stunned to discover that his recently deceased sister's entire fortune has been conferred not on him, but on Lois, her nineteen-year-old companion. A widower, Eustace decides his best chance of financial security is to marry the girl, and so claim possession of the funds. Over the following ten years, Lois builds up a successful dressmaking business and becomes an excellent 'mother' to Eustace's two daughters. But when she needs access to a large sum of cash, Lois discovers her own financial situation is not as secure as she had thought. Eustace has invested her inheritance in properties in his name and is draining money from her business. Despite her apparent autonomy, Lois is forced to question the extent of financial independence she (or any married woman) can ever have from her husband.

In 1912, a play called *Rutherford and Son* by an unknown writer, K.G. Sowerby played for four performances at the Royal Court. It was a hit and subsequently transferred to the Vaudeville Theatre in the West End, played in New York, and was translated into French, German, Italian, Russian and Czech. When the writer was revealed not to be a man, as had been widely assumed, but a young woman, the press and the public were amazed. Githa Sowerby became an overnight celebrity, her success almost as sudden and remarkable as the obscurity that followed. Although she wrote several further plays, only one of these – *Before Breakfast*, a one-act comedy – was ever published and the rest, including *The Stepmother*, were thought to have been lost. *The Stepmother* was never published and received just one performance at a private theatre club in January 1924.

After *Rutherford and Son* was brought back into the public eye by the National Theatre's 1994 revival, interest grew in discovering Sowerby's other works. However, attempts to trace copies of the lost plays were unsuccessful. It was only by a remarkable stroke of luck that in 2004,

Jonathan Bank, Artistic Director of Mint Theatre, a New York-based company that specialises in 'bringing worthy but neglected plays back to the stage', discovered the faded, typewritten manuscript of *The Stepmother* in a cardboard box in the basement of Samuel French's Theatre Bookshop. Bank handed the manuscript to Jackie Maxwell at the Shaw Festival, Ontario, who subsequently staged it. After eighty years languishing in a cardboard box, Sowerby's remarkable drama received what is thought to have been its first professional performance since its initial, fleeting appearance.

Sowerby opens *The Stepmother* with a prologue, the action of which takes place ten years prior to the remainder of the play. As the curtain rises on Act One, the changes that have occurred in the intervening decade are clear to the audience. The Gaydons' living room is now kitted out with electric lighting, a telephone has been installed and the hemlines of the ladies' skirts have risen dramatically. Offstage, World War One has come and gone, and women have won the vote, but the extent of their participation in society remains a matter for debate. The opening exchange between Eustace's elderly aunt, Charlotte, and his daughters, Betty and Monica, crystallises the varying responses to middle-class women working rather than staying at home. 'Dressmaker! They used to come in for three and sixpence a day and their dinner on a tray – and you talk as if it were a thing to be proud of' is Charlotte's unimpressed response to Lois's career. Betty's reply – 'Do you mean to say that a person who can earn money and make lovely things is to sit at home with her hands in front of her?' – is a question an increasing proportion of Sowerby's contemporaries may have been asking themselves.

The Stepmother is a play about a woman 'having it all'. Lois may be a successful career woman, but the hours she dedicates to running her business don't seem to be offset by the hours she is required to spend running the family home. As well as a financially disastrous husband to handle, Lois has stepdaughters to mother, elderly relatives to care for and the advances of an attractive neighbour to resist. When events come to a head, it's all that the chain-smoking, permanently fraught Lois can do to don her best evening dress and meet things head-on. Lois's predicament – arriving home from a hectic day at work to be plunged straight into the maelstrom of family life – is one that many of today's audience members will recognise. Eighty years in a cardboard box have made *The Stepmother* no less prescient.

87 Five Kinds of Silence
by Shelagh Stephenson (b. 1955, UK)

First performed: Lyric Hammersmith, London, 2000

Cast breakdown: 4f, 2m

Publisher: Methuen, in *Shelagh Stephenson Plays: 1*, 2003

Susan and Janet have shot their father dead. For years he has waged a war of physical, sexual and psychological violence against them and their mother Mary, and now, finally, they have had enough. But even with two bullets in his chest, Billy continues to exert a terrifying force over his family. A voice in their heads, and a marauding presence in their dreams, nothing, it seems, can free them from his malevolent grasp. As the wheels of the judicial system turn and the women go through the process of remand, bail and trial, they encounter a seemingly endless stream of psychiatrists, police and lawyers, all of whom want them to tell their story, their side of things and their feelings. But after so many years of silence, opening up to what has gone on is one of the most terrible challenges of all.

Often discussed along misleadingly simple terms, as a play about abuse, *Five Kinds of Silence* is a piece that, according to Shelagh Stephenson, has much broader themes: 'It's [a play] about madness and control, violence and despair, which happens to involve incestuous sex.' Stephenson has commented the word 'abuse' never entered her mind during the writing process, nor was it ever a topic of discussion in the rehearsal room. Indeed, *Five Kinds of Silence* is a complex, sophisticated and provocative exploration of the psychology of cruelty and one executed with a poeticism that somehow manages to capture through achingly beautiful language and imagery the ugliest of human behaviour. 'I think something – burst' is the disarmingly simple response Mary gives when a police inspector asks her why Janet and Susan might have killed their father.

The play was originally commissioned as a radio drama and, while Stephenson later redeveloped it into a stage play, this latter version retains the fantastically rich aural quality that the original – having been written to be listened to, rather than watched – possesses. Between sections of restrained dialogue, the action rotates from the interior thoughts of one family member to the next, each pouring forth in soliloquies of exquisite imagery and vividly expressed pain. 'I was born at six with teeth and a black, black heart,' the deceased Billy recollects of his childhood and, indeed, it is in these soliloquies that the audience receives a terribly vivid insight into how the hell of Mary and Billy's marital home took seed in their youths. He, the product of a violent home, fixated on getting revenge for the mother who beat him; she, the child of a dead mother and a drunkard father. Neglected throughout her early life, weak and easy prey, the adolescent Mary's fate was sealed as soon as the handsome young man with dark eyes said 'I love you'. Into this most unhealthy of matches, Susan and Janet had the misfortune to be born.

'Is this a cell?' Janet asks a police officer as he locks her up in one, 'it's beautiful.' After three-and-a-half decades under the obsessively controlling eye of their father, when the sisters are transferred to a remand centre, the experience is 'as close to Heaven' as they have ever encountered. The irony is not lost on them that their first taste of freedom comes from the inside of a prison. Having lived in a home in which the slightest 'misdemeanour' – producing a clicking sound when switching on a light or buttering Billy's toast in the wrong direction – attracted the most horrific of penalties, life in a remand centre is comparatively plain sailing. But while the physical threat of Billy has gone, the psychological damage remains. Both sisters and their mother remain terrified of him, and of his threat that he would kill them should they ever speak out. 'When he comes into my dreams I think my heart will stop,' Mary tells a psychiatrist, 'that's how he'll get me. I'll die of fright.' Confronted by constant requests to talk about what has happened, to relive the years of misery and pain, and to share their most embarrassing of memories, Susan, Janet and Mary endure a second torture. 'If you had to live inside our heads for five minutes you'd go mad and die,' Susan simply informs one of the psychiatrists. Humane, disturbing, but, in its depiction of survival, strangely beautiful, *Five Kinds of Silence* is a play that journeys bravely into some of the darkest aspects of the human soul.

88

Nine Till Six by Aimée Stuart (b. 1885, UK) and Philip Stuart (b. 1887, UK)

First performed: Arts Theatre, London, 1930

Cast breakdown: 16f (doubling possible)

Publisher: Manchester University Press in *Plays and Performance Texts by Women*, 2012

Mrs Pembroke is a self-made woman. Having dedicated her life to building up a successful millinery and dressmaking business, she now presides over a prestigious Regent Street shop and large staff. But times are changing and, as an economic slump seems ever more likely, keeping the books in the black is an increasing struggle. Largely on a whim, Mrs Pembroke takes on two new apprentices: Gracie Abbot and Bridget Penarth, teenagers whose backgrounds couldn't be more different. One, a working-class girl desperate for a wage; the other, the daughter of a lord, keen for a bit of pin money, the girls start work on the same day. Despite the gulf between them, they form an unlikely friendship, although it's one which many of the staff are far from happy about. As the collision between social classes threatens to destabilise the very core of Mrs Pembroke's business, she must use the extent of her wit, determination and compassion to maintain control.

Nine Till Six is a fascinating social document of British life at the beginning of the 1930s, capturing as it does the moment it first became apparent to the general public that the opulence of the 1920s would give way to severe economic depression. It's a play that will resonate with audiences living in any period of lean times, exploring, as it does, how individual lives are shaped by market forces. A detailed and insightful depiction of workplace politics, it will prove at times entertaining and at others uncomfortably recognisable viewing to anyone with experience of working in business at a time of crisis, whether on the shop floor or at boardroom level. As the economic uncertainty of the outside world begins to permeate the walls of Mrs Pembroke's establishment, sales diminish, insecurity among the staff grows, and so too do resentments, jealousies and the emergence of factions. Finding her finances stretched to breaking point, but at the helm of a staff convinced she's making steep profits at their expense while sharing none of the dividends, Mrs Pembroke's situation is far from enviable. At the same time, neither is that of her staff, many of them barely able to afford the most basic of essentials once rent and bills have been paid, but unable to see a way out.

This combustible situation ignites when heiress Bridget comes swanning onto the payroll. Her colleagues see her as someone who *chooses* to work rather than *needs* to work, and resent her taking up a job each of them knows countless relatives, friends and neighbours could sorely do with. Bridget isn't going to let their disapproval faze her. A pragmatist who can see that things are changing for Britain's upper classes and that marrying a rich man is no longer a safe bet ('the trouble is you can't be sure of anyone staying rich these days'), Bridget reasons she'll most likely have to earn her own living at some point so 'might as well get down to it'. It is the step towards independence that getting a job represents which precipitates Bridget's unexpected affinity with Gracie. Keen to escape home and the belligerent presence of her father, Gracie has had too much opportunity to observe the overworked, thankless existence of her mother to be convinced that marriage would offer her much, and has figured she'd rather take her chances in the world of business.

Within the walls of Mrs Pembroke's shop, husband-and-wife writing team Aimée and Philip Stuart present a sharply drawn microcosm of contemporary society. Particularly notable is the even-handedness with which they present each tier of the social strata. Writing at a time when the working classes were often represented on stage in only the most perfunctory of terms, the Stuarts give complexity, authenticity and, most importantly, dignity to the saleswomen, packers, apprentices and stock-keepers of Mrs Pembroke's establishment in a way that sets *Nine Till Six* apart from so much dramatic writing of the period. A play bursting with ideas, plotted immaculately, with an ensemble of intelligently wrought characters, it is a nuanced and timeless depiction of the world of work.

89

Brontë
by Polly Teale (*b*. 1962, UK)

First performed: Shared Experience at the Yvonne Arnaud Theatre, Guildford, 2005

Cast breakdown: 4f, 2m

Publisher: Nick Hern Books, 2011

Siblings Anne and Branwell Brontë have been away for months, working as governess and tutor to the children of a well-to-do family. Unexpectedly, the pair return home; Branwell has been dismissed for having an affair with the lady of the house and Anne has handed in her notice to ensure nothing untoward happens to her wayward brother on his return journey. Back in the company of their sisters Charlotte and Emily, and in the humdrum existence of rural life, the four Brontës focus on their artistic endeavours to provide entertainment, solace and release. As the sisters become increasingly successful in their writing, their achievements become all the starker in contrast to their brother's repeated artistic failures.

Teale's play sets out to question how 'three Victorian spinsters living in isolation on the Yorkshire moors' could write works of such passion, ferocity and scope. Although the play begins on the evening of Anne and Branwell's return to Haworth Parsonage, the action slips back and forward between past, present and future, as events from the sisters' childhood, adolescence and adulthood are played out. Throughout, Teale dramatises encounters, experiences and key relationships in the Brontës' lives, leaving her audience to draw the connections to themes found in the sisters' novels and poetry. Emily's obsession with wandering the moors, Charlotte's unrequited love for an older schoolteacher, Branwell's drunkenness and their mother's early death are among the formative experiences Teale presents as possible sources for the sisters' literary inspiration. In and out of these imagined snippets of the siblings' lives together, wander characters from the sisters' novels, an increasingly pervasive force in the action. Catherine Earnshaw, Mr Rochester and his first wife Bertha, Arthur Huntingdon and Heathcliff share the stage with their creators, serving as physical yet abstracted expressions of the sisters' desires, fears and aspirations.

Left alone with little company but one another and an endless supply of books, the Brontës are shown as children, reading vociferously and play-acting stories of their own making. In adult life, remaining unmarried allows Charlotte, Emily and Anne to focus almost entirely on writing, rather than on running households or raising children. Not being rich and not being beautiful means they do not find husbands, leave home or see the world, but it does mean they have the freedom and the time to create some of the best-loved works in English literature. Discussing their success and their fame, Charlotte wonders aloud to Anne 'maybe it is only com-pensation for having lived so very little'. Yet she also comments that, as women, 'nothing was expected of us. Nothing at all,' and, indeed, writing at a time when women were considered so intellectually and artistically inferior to men, the sisters find that, without the pressure of needing to prove themselves to the wider world, their creativity is free to flourish unfettered. Branwell, meanwhile, the only son of the family, buckles under the weight of the huge expectation placed on him by his father. As both poet and painter, he is stifled by the assumption that he will achieve great things, rather than emboldened by it.

Brontë is Teale's third play inspired by the life and work of Charlotte Brontë. Her 1997 adaptation of *Jane Eyre* (5f, 3m) toured the UK and was followed in 2003 by *After Mrs Rochester* (6f, 2m), which examines the life of Jean Rhys, author of *Wide Sargasso Sea*, the novel written as a prequel to *Jane Eyre* in which Bertha Rochester is the central figure. All three plays unpick the dichotomy between the two Mrs Rochesters; Jane as angelic, virginal and constricted and Bertha as sensual, exotic and untamed. Shared Experience, the company of which Teale is Artistic Director, produced each of the plays in the trilogy. Shared Experience has a strong tradition of offer-ing excellent roles for actresses and with their trademark combination of physical and text-based work matched by a rich visual style, the company has staged large-scale adaptations of novels including *Madame Bovary*, *The Mill on the Floss* and *Anna Karenina*, alongside new writing, classical texts and 'modern classics'.

90

Love Story of the Century from the poems by Märta Tikkanen (b. 1935, Finland), adapted for the stage by Clare Venables (b. 1943, UK), from a translation by Stina Katchadourian

First performed: Monstrous Regiment at the Strode Theatre, Street, 1990

Cast breakdown: 2f (but could be performed by a female cast of any number)

Publisher: Nick Hern Books, in *Monstrous Regiment*, 1991

'You who love
can't you some time
try to tell me what it is you mean
when you say
that you love me?'

Swedish-speaking Finnish writer Märta Tikkanen's interlinking poems published collectively in 1978 as *Love Story of the Century (Århundradets kärlekssaga)* were adapted for the stage by Clare Venables and first performed by theatre company Monstrous Regiment in 1990. In her autobiographical poems, Tikkanen unpacks the experience of being the wife of an alcoholic. She examines her anger, humiliation, pragmatism, forbearance and, above all, never-quite-extinguished hope that her husband will change. It is a work that deals with the emotional, psychological and physical fallout of alcohol abuse and associated domestic violence, and remains as potent, insightful, and – sadly – relevant today as when first written.

The poems that Tikkanen published as *Love Story of the Century* were part of an artistic dialogue that she and her husband, the artist and writer Henrik Tikkanen, conducted with one another over the course of several years. The couple unpicked their marriage in their novels, drawings and poetry, but while *Love Story of the Century* is part of this arc, Venables does not reference its bibliographical nature in her structuring of the stage version. Rather, the voice(s) speaking the text could belong to any woman, in any place, time, culture or class. Although in the published edition of Venables' version the text is divided up between two women, 'Gillian' and 'Mary', these are not characters as such, simply two figures named for the actresses, Gillian Hanna and Mary McCusker, who originally performed the piece. The poem could be allocated in myriad different ways and, in principle, could be performed by a cast of any size. While Tikkanen's depiction of what it is to live with an alcoholic is a depressingly universal and timeless one, it isn't unfair to say that the staging choices made in the Monstrous Regiment production as indicated through the stage directions are now somewhat dated. But Tikkanen's text is robust enough to support other theatrical interpretations and the published stage directions could either be followed faithfully, or viewed merely as a leaping-off point, by companies performing the play today.

In her poetry, Tikkanen takes us painstakingly through the phases of living in the intimate company of an alcoholic. There are the early days when the hope he'll change is all-consuming, then the rage when the effects on the children become clear. There are the days of dreadful anticipation as he builds towards his next binge and then the eye of the storm as she, ironically, can productively carry on with her life while he lies stupefied upstairs and out of the way. Then there is the dreadful desperation of his hangover to endure, the aggression, the mood swings, the self-loathing and the ever-decreasing determination to change. Tikkanen notes the minutiae of sharing a home and a bed with an alcoholic ('the smell of putrid hops / you breathe over me / when for the five thousandth time / you think beer enhances your sexual power'), as well as the particular agony of failing to communicate ('now mouths jabber without sound / arms gesticulate / feet stamp their emphasis / we throw up our arms / we still grasp nothing').

Formed in 1975, Monstrous Regiment was one of the most visible energies in the women's theatre movement for nearly two decades. Created by a group of female and male actors and musicians, it was part of a wave of politically focused touring theatre companies that rose to prominence across Britain in the 1970s. Originally a collective, although later moving to a more formalised management structure, the group was powered by the dual engines of feminism and socialism, and was committed to the creative act of telling female experiences on stage whilst practically improving employment opportunities for female theatre-makers. The group performed an eclectic range of work, a hint of which is given in the anthology, *Monstrous Regiment* (1991) in which *Love Story of the Century* is published. It appears alongside Claire Luckham and Chris Bond's *Scum: Death, Destruction and Dirty Washing* (subtitled 'a musical celebration of the events of the Paris Commune of 1871'; 5f, 2m, 1976), Wendy Kesselman's modern American classic *My Sister in This House* (4f, 1981), and Jenny McLeod's comedy set in an OAP home, *Island Life* (4f, 1988).

First performed: Théâtre du Rideau Vert, Montreal, 1968

Cast breakdown: 15f

Recommended version: *The Guid Sisters*, by Bill Findlay and Martin Bowman

Publisher: Nick Hern Books, 1991

Germaine has won a million Green Shield stamps in a competition. Her life-changing prize is contained in several enormous boxes that sit in the kitchen of her tenement flat and, needing to paste the stamps into collecting books before she can exchange them for goods, she has invited neighbours and family members to a 'stamp-stickin party' that night. But as her kitchen fills up and Germaine shows little hospitality and even less humility towards her not-so-fortunate guests, some of the books begin to disappear. Once the thieving begins, there is no stopping it, and by the end of the evening Germaine's precious stamps are nestling in the handbags and pockets of her nearest and dearest.

Written in 1965, as Quebec was undergoing its Quiet Revolution, *Les Belles Soeurs* would become one of the most important French-Canadian plays. It established Michel Tremblay as an artistic figurehead for a society finding its voice and turned the twenty-six-year-old linotypist from Montreal into a celebrity. The play foregrounds the experience of working-class Quebecoise women, a group who, if those who attend Germaine's party are anything to go by, have plenty to say for themselves, yet had seldom been represented on the stage. Controversially, Tremblay chose to write the play not in standard French, but in Joual, the patois of Quebec, and his decision to do so has generally been seen as a strong artistic and political statement. His use of Joual, considered by some as the true language of the people and by others as a crass corruption of French, provoked just as much condemnation from the critics as praise. More than twenty years after the play was first performed in Canada, Bill Findlay and Martin Bowman re-imagined *Les Belles Soeurs* as *The Guid Sisters*, in a production that opened at Glasgow's Tron Theatre in 1989. They translated Tremblay's dialogue into Scots, the popular spoken language of a country that shares not inconsiderable common ground with Quebec. *The Guid Sisters* therefore successfully retains the political overtones, as well as the original spirit, of *Les Belles Soeurs*.

André Brassard, a long-time collaborator of Tremblay's and the director of the original production of *Les Belles Soeurs*, has referred to Tremblay's plays as 'an artistic director's dream. The educated public can find layers of meaning, but he also offers an entertaining evening of theatre for people who want just that.' *Les Belles Soeurs* certainly adheres to this rule. The play makes shrewd observations on class, gender politics, religion and consumerism, but it is, above all, hugely enjoyable to watch. Brash, raucous and sometimes downright filthy, it's a piece that exhibits a sense of humour not for the easily offended. Some of its comedy is extremely dark (the interactions between Germaine's neighbour Thérèse and her ninety-three-year-old wheelchair-bound, senile mother-in-law sail particularly close to the boundaries of taste), there's a strong surreal element that runs throughout, and its characters are anything but predictable. 'An Ode to Bingo', an energetic choral celebration of the game (complete with rhythmic calling of bingo numbers and the refrain 'I'm daft on the bingo! I'm bingo-daft!'), that the characters spontaneously launch into is just one of many bizarre moments in this most surprising of plays.

Constantly playing with its audience's expectations as well as the conventions of theatrical form, *Les Belles Soeurs* achieves the unusual combination of being both quirky and weighty. Although, in narrative terms, very little happens – a group of women sit in a kitchen and paste stamps into booklets before pocketing them – theatrically and emotionally, a huge amount is going on. For all the characters' ostensibly banal chit-chat, this is a play with a supremely hard edge. The lives of Germaine and her guests are far from enjoyable and, by cutting in and out of various characters speaking their inner thoughts as spotlit monologues, Tremblay exposes the drudgery, emptiness and hopelessness that lies beneath their stoic exteriors and jam-packed schedules. His evident passion for presenting both the best and worst sides of the women makes for a sympathetic but not sentimental piece, and one to which Tremblay dedicates an idiosyncratic inventiveness. His writing jumps in and out of the women's heads, back and forth between realism and choral speaking and, by the end, stamps are raining from the ceiling. Bringing to the stage the experiences of an often silenced group, Tremblay captures the women of his homeland with an impressive blend of vibrancy, compassion, grittiness and verve.

First performed: New York Summer Plays Festival, New York, 2005

Cast breakdown: 3f

Publisher: Methuen, 2006

Laney and her mum Elise have just moved from Wisconsin to Mississippi. No one at her new school seems interested in talking to Laney except Maribel, the 'chubby and radiant' social outcast and evangelical Christian who seems just as devoted to saving Laney's soul as she is to becoming her friend. Stripped of the usual paths to teenage rebellion by her mother's liberal values, Laney throws her hand in with Maribel. She joins her new friend's church, welcomes Jesus into her heart and enjoys pitting Maribel's conservativism and religious views against Elise's atheism and feminist politics. When Laney and Maribel share a brief kiss, Laney decides her destiny is not just that of a Christian, but of a 'holiness lesbian'. Wholeheartedly she pledges herself to a relationship with Maribel – not that Maribel herself seems entirely aware that she's acquired a girlfriend. Meanwhile, Elise isn't so sure her daughter's newfound fervency for Jesus and for Maribel isn't symptomatic of something else.

'Catherine Trieschmann's *Crooked* may be a small-scale play,' *The New York Times* announced in its review of the 2008 Women's Project production, 'but it is the work of a big, accomplished writer's voice.' Indeed, Trieschmann's compact comedy-drama about a teenage girl attempting to decipher where she fits into the world, speaks to a much broader human impulse than a glance at the play's synopsis first suggests. Trieschmann adeptly transports her audience back to those fragile mid-teenage years, often as exciting as they are painful, when the need to work out who you are, and how you're going to make that known to those around you, can feel increasingly urgent. In Laney, Trieschmann pens a teenage protagonist dabbling in different possible identities until she works out what fits, an important although often fraught phase of growing up that audience members won't fail to recognise. That said, the impulse to define identity isn't restricted to Trieschmann's teenage creations. Even Elise, temporarily adrift after an unusually heartbreaking divorce and now living once again in her childhood home, finds herself having to redistinguish who she is. Having just abandoned a poorly paid career in social work because 'I'm in a place in life where I want to get paid', she's accepted a job with a personal-injury lawyer even though it goes against every impulse she has. After accepting the position, she tells Laney, 'I just sat there and cried, 'cause now I'm the kind of person who wants to get paid.'

Funny, charming and at times toe-curlingly uncomfortable, *Crooked*'s particular potency lies in the extreme recognisability of its characters. Trieschmann weaves together all the very worst bits of being an unpopular, unprepossessing teenage girl, creating a highly entertaining but poignant sixty minutes of drama. Maribel is all too familiar as *that* girl at school who is socially ostracised for being different and, in her perpetual attempts to remain jolly in the face of such adversity, unknowingly makes herself even more conspicuous. Enduring the worst kind of bullying, she clings steadfastly to her faith for strength ('Deedee Cummings pulled down my pants in gym class today – but I don't mind, because I know that the things of this earth, they're not lasting' is her opening salvo to Laney), and yet her belief that she is experiencing painful 'invisible stigmata' hints at an unarticulated unhappiness beneath her determinedly upbeat exterior. Laney is afflicted by dystonia, a condition that gives her the appearance of having a humped back because her muscles are in a constant state of tension. She is a compulsive liar, seems intent on coming to blows with Elise and channels her time into writing embarrassingly inept short stories. These gawky, not entirely likeable and at times frankly annoying girls are unconventional heroines and, in Trieschmann's hands, all the more captivating for it.

The play has an abrupt ending, one which some audience members will find frustratingly unresolved and others intriguingly open. Despite this, it's a notable piece of work, not least for the exquisite accuracy with which Trieschmannn captures the burgeoning relationship between two struggling misfits drawn together not so much by mutual attraction, but a shared rejection by everyone else around them. Perfect for an intimate studio space (the UK premiere was in the tiny room above a pub that the Bush Theatre previously occupied), *Crooked* is a play that will strike a chord with anyone who has ever had an awkward teenage moment or who has ever wished that they are someone they are not.

The Oldest Profession
by Paula Vogel (*b.* 1951, USA)

First performed: Theatre Network in Edmonton and 25th Street Theatre, Saskatoon, 1988

Cast breakdown: 5f

Publisher: Theatre Communications Group, in *The Baltimore Waltz and Other Plays*, 1996

If prostitution is the oldest profession, 'mother hen' Mae's 'girls' must be among the oldest professionals. Occupying a bench on the corner of Broadway and 72nd Street, Mae, Vera, Lillian, Ursula and Edna (average age seventy-five) may look to the uneducated eye like five retired ladies enjoying the sunshine, but actually they are some of New York City's most seasoned prostitutes. The working day is in full swing; there's their patch to defend, business matters to discuss, schedules to be arranged and appointments to attend. The girls still have the same zest for their work as they always did, but they need to face facts: business is grinding to a halt. The bulk of their elderly client base has kicked the bucket and those that remain are not exactly the most voracious of customers. What with rising rents and food costs to contend with, economies must be made and productivity increased. Professionals to the end, Mae and the girls devise a new business model. But in light of their own advancing years, the plan they decide on is not necessarily the most advisable.

Paula Vogel's outrageous and irreverent comedy *The Oldest Profession* is an absolute treat. Managing to somehow be both filthy and profoundly moving, the play takes an offbeat look at ageing, mature sex and death. It's a piece that will leave few audience members unruffled one way or the other, and Vogel appears to enjoy smashing her way through one taboo after another. The tone is set early on when septuagenarian Vera shares an anecdote about viewing the open casket of a much-loved client ('when his family wasn't looking, I slipped my hand down the side and behind his coat-tails and into his trousers, and then I tweaked the hell out of his marble behind for old times') and from hereon in the audience knows it is in for an evening of the very darkest humour.

Mae and her girls love sex. They enjoy their work and, despite their advancing years, show absolutely no loss of appetite for entertaining themselves, or their clients. It's a depiction of mature female sexuality (not to mention prostitution) the like of which is rarely seen on stage and one that, although far from being politically correct, is infectiously funny. Never shy about conflating sex and death into one punchline, nor discussing the realities of how older bodies behave in the bedroom, Vogel boldly heads into territory few writers are prepared to enter. The result is a laugh-out-loud piece and yet one that unwaveringly awards its characters absolute dignity and the highest respect. Whilst cracking jokes about arthritis, dementia and false teeth, at no point does it seem that Vogel is eliciting a single laugh at the expense of the women, nor their ageing gentlemen friends. Rather, the depiction of human desire and independence being gradually eroded by the frailties of the body and the mind is captured with infinite sensitivity. Life isn't kind the older one gets and, as the girls themselves begin to pass away, the sombre reality for those left behind emerges ever more sharply through the laughter. Surtitling the piece 'A Full-Length Play in Six Blackouts', Vogel picks off a different character in each of these blackouts, until one final employee remains on the bench alone, frail and frightened.

A provocative look at the relationship between economics, the State and individual health and happiness, *The Oldest Profession* is, despite its jokes, a play with something deadly serious to say. Vogel locates the action in 1980, 'on a sunny day shortly after the election of Ronald Reagan', and through the admittedly surreal story of five aged prostitutes literally working themselves to death in an effort to increase productivity, it explores the particular approach to the economy that the Reagan administration unleashed across the USA. 'President Reagan has called on all Americans to reduce the deficit, and to balance the budget,' Mae primly informs her staff, 'we can start here'. This 'here' is a programme of cost-cutting and increased labour that proves to be the ladies' undoing. Although, in the face of a government that advocates little support for those unable to pay their own way, do they necessarily have any choice? While the women chat about Keynesian economics in between reports of what they had for dinner the night before and tales of their sexual exploits, the sun shines on. But a new, more brutal age is dawning, and Vogel's depiction of five old women selling their bodies to keep a roof over their heads and their medical bills paid is subversive and, at times, unutterably bleak.

First performed: as *Don Juan Returns*, the Theatre of Courage, Vienna, 1952 (written 1936)

Cast breakdown: 22f, 1m (doubling possible)

Recommended version: by Duncan Macmillan

Publisher: Oberon Books, 2012

Berlin 1918, and Don Juan is back from the War. A survivor of the trenches, his heart weakened and his soul in shreds, the former soldier is, much like the city he returns to, clinging onto life and the semblance of a pre-1914 identity. Berlin is in disarray; people are hungry, riots rage on the streets, and hyperinflation has made money all but worthless. A generation of fathers, brothers, sons and husbands have been lost on the battlefields and now the women left behind dominate the city. Don Juan, who took delight in all the excesses of pre-war Berlin, now finds himself unmoved by the decadent pleasures that remain in the vanquished city. Middle-aged, bruised, battered and, for the first time, experiencing a previously unknown emotion – guilt – he wanders the streets, houses and brothels of Berlin, caught between who he once was and who, in the post-war landscape, he wants to be.

Duncan Macmillan's free adaptation of von Horváth's 1936 interpretation of the Don Juan legend is as bleak as it is powerful. The piece looks the horrors of The Great War – both for those on the battlefield and those left at home – squarely in the eye and doesn't shy away from depicting the seedier aspects of Don Juan's experiences on returning. From the opening scene in which a naked Don Juan takes a bath in the company of five women with whom he has just enjoyed a several-day-long orgy, to the penultimate scene in which, bloodied and near to death, he is forced to participate in a porn shoot by two business-minded prostitutes, Macmillan's version is uncompromising and unrelenting. It varies greatly from von Horváth's original text and those looking for a more faithful, and, arguably, brighter translation, might prefer Christopher Hampton's 1978 (35f, 1m) rendering. In Hampton's version, Don Juan drinks Cognac in cafés, socialises with fashion designers and turns his hand to art dealing. It is not as gritty as Macmillan's version, although shows perhaps less interest in understanding the experience of the women in the play. Its focus remains firmly on Don Juan throughout, in contrast to Macmillan's, which appears far more intent on presenting the complexities of the female characters' desires, motivations and predicaments. Tellingly, Macmillan doesn't preface his published version of the play, as Hampton does, with a translation of von Horváth's somewhat odd casting note on the play's thirty-five female characters ('These thirty-five women not only can but must be played by far fewer actresses... I make this observation not only with an eye to the practicability of this play, but prompted by something that has long been established: namely, that there are not thirty-five types of women, but significantly fewer'). He instead selects a quote made by Christopher Hitchens during a debate with Tony Blair: '[...] we know, ladies and gentlemen, as it happens, we're the first generation of people who do really know, what the cure for poverty really is. It eluded people for a long, long time. The cure for poverty has a name, in fact. It's called the "Empowerment of Women".'

Macmillan presents a nightmarish terrain as the discombobulated Don Juan moves unsteadily through his old stomping ground, now unfamiliar and almost unrecognisable in its drab post-war feel. Don Juan finds himself anaesthetised to the sights, sounds and sensations that once so enthralled him, a predicament that is tricky given he remains infamous for his old carousing. Wherever he goes, the man-starved female population of Berlin know who he is and are madder than ever to have him. In this female domain he becomes an object of fascination, almost freak-like, to be looked at, pawed at, and photographed. But however violent, ardent or downright desperate the women's attempts to seduce him become, Don Juan remains unmoved. Every encounter leaves him cold and none of the women can ignite in him those old feelings of lust, ardour or excitement. The play contains scenes of thwarted desire, unedifying fumbling, inappropriate advances, and simulated sex acts, but nothing in which a genuine emotional or physical connection between Don Juan and another character is made. Having finally got his greatest desire – to be the only living man in a world full of women – Don Juan finds he has lost his mojo.

Don Juan Comes Back From the War is a sensitive and sympathetic portrayal of what happens to a society when it no longer recognises itself. Von Horváth, who was killed in a freak accident just two years after completing the play, never saw it performed in his lifetime. Of Austrian nationality, his work was banned by the Nazis and, by the time the play premiered in Vienna in 1952, the part of Europe in which von Horváth was born would have undergone yet another huge transformation. *Don Juan Comes Back From the War* remains a stirring and unsettling record of how quickly and how indelibly a society can be altered by war.

95   The New Electric Ballroom
by Enda Walsh (b. 1967, Ireland)

First performed: Kammerspiel Theatre, Munich, 2004

Cast breakdown: 3f, 1m

Publisher: Nick Hern Books, 2008

Sisters Clara and Breda may be in their sixties, but they are still reliving the terrible evening when, as teenagers, they both had their hearts broken by the same man, the breathtaking Roller Royle. Now, together with their forty-year-old 'baby sister' Ada, they constantly re-enact that fated night at The New Electric Ballroom, complete with costumes, homemade sound effects, and the assistance of bit-part player, Patsy the fishmonger. It's the same story they've been telling for years, but something has changed and, tonight, it's time for a rewrite. Away from their familiar tract for the first time ever, some surprising twists await the sisters.

Enda Walsh's unconventional tale of thwarted love, sibling rivalry and fish explores the stories we tell ourselves to excuse or affirm why it is we live the way we do. 'By their nature people are talkers,' is the line with which the play opens and, indeed, Clara, Breda, Ada and Patsy are certainly that. They talk fervently, compulsively and constantly, as if afraid of silence, and recite again and again the same pre-rehearsed snippets of text, telling stories about themselves in an almost ritualistic process that appears to terrify them as much as it provides some perverse kind of comfort. It's a dramatic conceit that Walsh returns to in several of his plays and, indeed, *The New Electric Ballroom* has much in common with his 2006 hit *The Walworth Farce*, with the former being in many ways a female-led mirror image of the male-dominated latter. In particular, the same sinister feel pervades both plays ('the atmosphere immediately taut and aggressive' is the stage direction with which Walsh sets the scene for *The New Electric Ballroom*), sitting at odds with the naive, almost childlike approach to storytelling their characters employ. The playing of a cobbled-together Foley soundtrack on an old cassette player, a solo domestic lamp used in lieu of a spotlight and the constant application and reapplication of make-up appear to be important elements for Clara, Breda and Ada in their crude performance of that infamous night at The New Electric. It's a base version of theatricality that stands in sharp contrast to the sophistication of Walsh's own. Exquisitely structured and with a ceaseless momentum that propels its characters through the sharp-as-steel dialogue, *The New Electric Ballroom* is an exceptional piece of dramatic writing.

Clara and Breda appear frozen in time, reduced to dressing up in the outfits they wore the night the Roller Royle rejected them in favour of a fumble with a Doris Day lookalike in The New Electric's car park. Now in their sixties and still decked out as their 1950s teenage selves, their play-acting is a grotesque performance of the moment they abandoned any hope of ever being loved and entered instead a self-imposed emotional exile from the world. Ada, although over twenty years younger than her sisters, appears to have adopted their obsession with that revered and reviled night, and is a willing accomplice in their storytelling, if not the most committed player of all. But, although she can't quite put her finger on it, something has changed for Ada. There's a difference in the air and suddenly her accounting job at the cannery, 'turning fish into money' by day and play-acting with her sisters by night is no longer satisfying. When Patsy is allowed to take a bigger role than usual in the storytelling, what it is that Ada has been hankering after becomes all too clear. Though whether she will allow herself to be free of the eternal loop that is the legend of The New Electric Ballroom in order to get it, is another matter entirely.

Despite the fact the action never leaves the one room, Walsh adeptly conjures the small coastal town in which the women live, its cobbled streets, harbour, bingo hall and pub populated by little old ladies, their bellies full of Malibu. The lure of The New Electric Ballroom had seemed so great to the teenage Clara and Breda, well worth the ten-mile bicycle ride and so much more exciting than The Sunshine Ballroom of their own small town with 'its lonely fishermen'. But, horrified by what they found under the bright lights of the big town, the girls fled, peddling home as fast as their legs could carry them to the safety and security of their small town, and their small lives. They closed the door on love and adventure, but now Ada's focus has definitely turned towards what is on the outside. An incredibly dark, funny but moving piece about striving to get out, *The New Electric Ballroom* is an offbeat miniature rocket of a play.

First performed: The Women's Theatre Group at the ICA, London, 1981

Cast breakdown: 5f

Publisher: Faber and Faber, in *Timberlake Wertenbaker: Plays 1*, 1996

Isabelle Eberhardt (1877–1904) lived a short but remarkable life. As determined to be an explorer and writer as she was adamant her gender shouldn't stand in her way, she spent years successfully passing herself off as an Arab man, Si Mahmoud, and travelled widely across the deserts of North Africa. She was a convert to Islam, joined the secret Sufi brotherhood, the Qadria, survived an assassination attempt and then, in a characteristically improbable manner, drowned in a flood in the desert. Wertenbaker takes Eberhardt's extraordinary existence as the basis around which she constructs *New Anatomies*, a series of imagined encounters in Eberhardt's life. A fascinatingly layered deconstruction of gender and colonialism, it is a tribute to a figure that boldly reconsidered how a human body – and the personality caught inside it – could interact with the world.

New Anatomies is a play that, read on the page rather than seen in performance, is hard to appreciate fully. Designed for a cast of five women who between them play men, women, women pretending to be men, Europeans and Arabs, it contains multiple and complex dimensions that become visible when up on its feet, but are hard to envisage in their entirety when reading the play in one's head. The opening stage direction notes that 'except for the actress playing Isabelle, each actress plays a Western woman, an Arab man and a Western man. Changes should take place in such a way as to be visible to the audience and all five actresses should be on stage at all times.' It is this conscious 'visibility' of the play's inherent gender-bending and colour-blind approach to casting which makes it so rich theatrically. It's a play that opens up a world of possibilities for its actresses and director, and the scope of the piece to be reinterpreted by each new generation of theatre-makers in light of their particular political, social and artistic concerns is great. Although Isabelle Eberhardt remains a fixed constant in history, her story, and the way Wertenbaker tells it, has a timeless and universal relevance to any person, or any group wanting to re-evaluate how their identity has been constructed for them. As a *Scotsman* review of the original production observed, 'its metaphors extend beyond Isabelle to all women, and indeed to all people who are anywhere less than wholly free'.

Wertenbaker tackles the fertile territory of identity being an act of performance. Isabelle realises that by the simple action of donning a male costume, she is suddenly able to interact with the world on an entirely different basis. Under the alias and in the clothing of Si Mahmoud, she can access freedoms and accept opportunities previously denied to her. Conversely, identifying herself as an Arab, rather than a European, means she must face the indignities of life under colonial rule. In an encounter with an officious French army officer in the desert, she can only watch as her Arab friend, a moment ago discoursing intelligently on philosophy, transforms himself into a caricature of 'oriental servility' rather than risk a confrontation. Whatever identity Isabelle assumes, though, she remains in a strange in-between place, neither male nor female and yet somehow both, a European woman's body in an Arabic man's clothes. This sense of being trapped either within or outside of 'normality' is something she shares with some of the play's other identity-conflicted characters. In a scene set in a Parisian bar where crowds of women and women-dressed-as-men gather to watch a male impersonator perform, one of Isabelle's fellow drinkers muses over what she calls the 'golden cage' of normality, around which people such as her and Isabelle, 'poor banished species trail around, looking through the bars, wishing we were in there'. It's no good, though, she morosely concludes, 'We're destined for curiosity shops, labelled as the weird mistakes of nature, the moment of God's hesitation between Adam and Eve, anatomical convolutions, our souls inside out and alone, always alone, outside those bars.'

While the actions of Isabelle Eberhardt offended the social and religious mores of the day, Wertenbaker never gives the impression that her imagining of the character is assuming the identity of Si Mahmoud as a political statement or in an effort to defy the authorities conspicuously. Rather, it's a pragmatic act, the most expedient way for her to be able to get out into the desert, to explore and to achieve the freedom she so craves. Her actions are intended to hurt no one, to offend no one, but they are designed to permit her the opportunities that, had she been born into a different body, would have been her right. She remains baffled by the increasingly extreme attempts to curtail her decision to be Si Mahmoud, repeatedly but gently stating, 'I'm doing no harm… why won't they let me alone?' The play remains a powerful testament to a person deciding what they want their identity to be, and fixedly and calmly asserting it, in defiance of what has been decided for them.

First performed: Soho Theatre Company at the Pleasance Theatre, London, 1998

Cast breakdown: 6f

Publisher: Nick Hern Books, 2005

Mary is nineteen, pregnant, and about to be shunted off to St Saviours Home for Unmarried Mothers. It's 1964, The Ronettes are high in the charts, and girls from 'nice' families don't get into trouble – they disappear off on 'extended visits to distant relatives'. In the austere surroundings of St Saviours, with only the handful of other unmarried mothers and her Dansette record player for company, Mary waits out the final weeks of her pregnancy. But even her favourite singers cannot distract her from the dawning realisation that her baby won't be going home with her. As Mary comes to see that her future, and that of her unborn child, are in her hands of the faceless Welfare Services, she engages in a desperate fight to keep hold of her child.

When commissioned by Soho Theatre to write the play that would eventually become *Be My Baby* – and one of the most widely performed modern British plays – Whittington had originally planned to write about a mother being reunited with her adopted, adult child. But upon asking herself questions about the mother's past and what might have induced her to give her child up for adoption, Whittington became interested in whether the woman had been married when she became pregnant and, if not, whether she would have been sent to one of the church-run maternity homes still in operation in the 1960s. Amassing a wealth of personal accounts from women who had themselves been through such homes, and who were often forced against their will to sign their babies over to the Welfare Services, Whittington decided to relocate her play to the 1960s and to look at adoption through the eyes of nineteen-year-old Mary and her fellow St Saviours residents. The result is a tender account of an extraordinary episode in the lives of four young women as they face imminent childbirth and the inevitable subsequent loss of their children. *Be My Baby* gently draws the audience's attention to the many emotional and ethical complexities of adoption when carried out by force, and for largely ideological reasons.

At nineteen years old, Mary is no child. She has a secure job in a bank and is in a steady relationship with the father of her child, a trainee doctor who wants to marry her as soon as he completes his training. And yet, against her wishes and despite being an adult, her child is taken from her because the decision has been made that she will be incapable of caring for it. None of the girls in St Saviours is too young to competently look after children and, aged between seventeen and twenty, wouldn't have been unusually young first-time mothers in the 1960s. Yet the social stigma attached to having a child outside of wedlock is considered so great, it is thought to be in the best interest of everyone for the babies to be adopted and the mothers to return home as if nothing has happened. 'They don't look kindly on these girls where we come from,' Mary's mother tells the Matron of St Saviours as she confirms proceedings for the adoption, 'I've seen how they're treated, I know what they're called and while there's breath in my body they won't do that to Mary.' Apart for the mental trauma of sending a frightened teenager to live in an institution, isolated from family and friends, and treated not unlike a prisoner, Mary's physical health hasn't been spared in the desperate rush to hush up her pregnancy. She's not been to see her doctor ('he bowls with her father' is her mother's explanation to Matron), and even her medical notes can't be sent to St Saviours in case tongues start wagging. The culture of silence extends to childbirth itself. The scene in which the girls attempt to decode the jargon of a medical textbook in an effort to find out what's going to happen to them during labour is as bleak as it is funny, and reveals how hopelessly unprepared they have been for their impending births.

Woven throughout the play are hit pop songs by girl groups of the period such as The Ronettes, The Dixie Cups and The Shangri-Las, which the girls listen to avidly on Mary's record player. Like most young girls, they would rather be singing and dancing around to music than doing their chores and, miming to the records, they form their own quirky kind of girl group, characterised not by identical sequined outfits and fantastic hair-dos, but regulation pinafores and pregnancy bumps. Whittington says of her use of the songs that 'these three-minute pop dramas seemed to perfectly capture the passionate innocence of the play's characters – and gave an uplifting soundtrack to what becomes a pretty dark tale'. The play's all-female ensemble cast, along with this buoyant soundtrack, have helped make *Be My Baby* a runaway success with amateur dramatic groups, schools and youth theatres, and the play has received hundreds of amateur performances to date, in addition to several successful professional productions around the UK.

First performed: St James's Theatre, London, 1892

Cast breakdown: 9f, 7m (doubling possible)

Publisher: Penguin, 2011

Lady Windermere is deep in preparations for the party she is to host that night for her birthday. Satisfied that only the most select of London society will be in attendance, Lady Windermere has every reason to feel pleased with her life; she has wealth, social standing, a wide circle of respectable friends and a model husband. But when she learns that an unexpected guest is likely to be at the party, her birthday plans go increasingly awry. Mrs Erlynne, a lady of questionable character, has apparently struck up an inappropriately close friendship with Lady Windermere's husband and is intent on attending. As guests arrive and events unfurl, Lady Windermere finds that her life is entangled with Mrs Erlynne's in a far more surprising and irrevocable way than she could possibly have imagined.

Lady Windermere's Fan contains the characteristic blend of silliness and profundity that one would expect from an Oscar Wilde social comedy, complete with the usual barbed tittle-tattle, whispers in the ballroom, intercepted love letters, mistaken identity, and eavesdropping from adjacent rooms. While Mrs Erlynne and Lady Windermere are at the forefront of the action, a supporting cast of assorted lords, ladies, dukes, duchesses and other society players provide many of the additional laughs. The Duchess of Berwick ('I think a lady who doesn't part with a daughter every season has no real affection') and Lady Windermere's would-be lover, Lord Darlington ('I can resist everything except temptation') lead the play's sparkling ensemble of lesser characters and cameos who all in turn have their moment in the spotlight. Even the near-mute role of Lady Agatha, a debutante whose mother is attempting to marry her off with impressive zeal, is a fantastic comic opportunity for a young actress. Wilde lampoons members of polite society, skewering them with their own inane chit-chat and passive immorality. With his usual sophistication and wit, he lambasts the fickleness, inconsistency and buffoonery of the chattering classes.

Depicting twenty-four hours in the life of a woman who hovers over and then retreats from the precipice of ruin, the play is an exploration of the double standards meted out to husbands and wives. Most of the play's characters seem in agreement that for a man to be attracted to extra-marital affairs is natural and almost inevitable. 'It was only Berwick's brutal and incessant threats of suicide that made me accept him at all and before the year was out, he was running after all kinds of petticoats, every colour, every shape and every material,' the Duchess of Berwick tells Lady Windermere over afternoon tea. 'On several occasions after my marriage I had to pretend to be very ill and was obliged to drink the most unpleasant mineral waters, merely to get Berwick out of town.' Wives must take it upon themselves to do all they can to save their husbands from the inevitable lure of 'wicked women', and are permitted to use every tool of trickery and cunning in the book to do so. Conversely, for a wife to be involved in any kind of intrigue is outside the bounds of acceptability and sure guarantee of the termination of her marriage, separation from her children and exile from polite society. What is so interesting about Wilde's analysis of this state of affairs is not the fact that these double standards exist, but rather that it is often the women who are more intent on maintaining them than the men. Lady Windermere, in particular, is especially puritanical in her view on the polluting effects of 'vile' women such as Mrs Erlynne. Unbeknownst of how close she herself will come to being one of the women she so despises, Lady Windermere's righteous indignation towards Mrs Erlynne and all she represents is the rope with which she very nearly hangs herself.

Despite the inherent humour of *Lady Windermere's Fan*, there is an underlying sadness to the piece. Mrs Erlynne never reveals to Lady Windermere who she really is, and, resisting a traditional all-out denouement in this way, Wilde ends the play on a bittersweet rather than sensationalist note. Mrs Erlynne departs Lady Windermere's life asking to keep as a memento of her the birthday gift given by her husband – a fan which carries the inscription 'Margaret', the name both women share. The seemingly innocuous fan has been a key player in the drama between the two women and, although Lady Windermere will never know it, embodies the love-led sacrifices Mrs Erlynne has made for the younger woman. Although a witty and overwhelmingly critical analysis of the interplay between morality and respectability, *Lady Windermere's Fan* is ultimately a play about one individual's desire to save another from the mistakes she has made and, in the process, to return her own life to goodness and respectability. As one of the play's (and one of Wilde's) most quoted lines puts it, 'We are all in the gutter, but some of us are looking at the stars.'

First performed: alongside *Something Unspoken* under the collective title *Garden District*, York Theatre, New York City, 1958

Cast breakdown: 5f, 2m

Publisher: Penguin, 2009

'You can't tell such a story to civilized people in a civilized up-to-date country!' is the warning that George Holly gives his sister, Catherine. Ever since Catherine returned from a trip abroad, during which their cousin Sebastian was killed in bizarre circumstances, she has fixedly claimed that his death was down to a series of events which her family find too awful and too improbable to accept. In particular, Sebastian's unhealthily devoted mother, Mrs Venable, is determined to put a stop to her niece's damaging stories and, engaging the services of a young doctor with the promise of a substantial financial donation to his fledgling practice, seeks to get her lobotomised. As the doctor looks to establish Catherine's level of sanity, the terrible truth of what happened to Sebastian, and the facts of his gruesome death, are revealed to the family in all their horror.

A curious play, *Suddenly Last Summer* is among the darker and more implicitly violent of Tennessee Williams's works. Packed with imagery of death and destruction, it is a disturbing piece that focuses on the predicament of a young woman forced to prove her own sanity in the face of a family who clearly do not hold her best interests at heart. Catherine has been consigned to a lunatic asylum by her aunt where electric shock treatment and insulin injections have failed to stop her 'babbling' about the hideous nature of Sebastian's death or the trail of sexual indiscretions that led to it. Traumatised by the events she has witnessed, Catherine cannot help but talk compulsively about them and, as far as Mrs Venable is concerned, a lobotomy becomes the only option. It might not shut the girl up, 'but after the operation, who would *believe* her?' At the same time, it will nicely avenge Mrs Venable for the hurt she endured last summer when Sebastian suddenly transferred his affections from his previously adored mother to his young cousin. Catherine's own mother and brother, who stand to inherit handsomely if only Sebastian's estate were taken out of probate by Mrs Venable, seem all too eager to sacrifice Catherine in exchange for the cash.

'The set may be as unrealistic as the decor of a dramatic ballet' is the stage direction with which Williams opens the play. Set in the garden of a gothic Victorian mansion in New Orleans, Williams locates his tale of primal urges in a suitably evocative landscape. No neat lawns and rose bushes here, but a 'fantastic garden which is more like a tropical jungle, or forest, in the prehistoric age of giant fern-forests when living creatures had flippers turning to limbs and scales to skin'. This garden, which as Mrs Venable proudly tells the doctor at the opening of the action, was Sebastian's, is beautiful and sinister, threatening and alluring. 'There are massive tree-flowers that suggest organs of a body, torn out, still glistening with undried blood,' Williams notes, 'there are harsh cries and sibilant hissings and thrashing sounds in the garden as if it were inhabited by beasts, serpents, and birds, all of a savage nature.' Sebastian may never appear in person on stage, but his presence is very much felt, symbolically at least, through the imposing sights and sounds of the garden he left behind.

The play was originally performed under the title *Garden District* alongside *Something Unspoken* (2f), a largely inconsequential vignette about a wealthy Southern spinster attempting, and failing, to express her feelings to her private secretary. More often than not, nowadays, *Suddenly Last Summer* is performed without this curtain-raiser – which admittedly is not one of Williams's better works – or is instead paired with one of his many other short plays. Although made into a film in 1959 starring Katherine Hepburn, Elizabeth Taylor and Montgomery Clift, it failed to meet Williams's approval. He disliked it so much he walked out of a private screening held by its producer Sam Spiegel. Williams was affronted by the literal manner in which the film depicts Sebastian's death, saying the play is 'about how people devour each other in an allegorical sense'. Indeed it is his rich use of allegory combined with potent imagery and atmospheric detail that makes this hypnotic piece of theatre so affecting. It is by leaving much of the work up to his audience's imagination, that *Suddenly Last Summer* is so mesmeric, and so exceptionally unsettling.

First performed: National Theatre, London, 1988

Cast breakdown: 3f

Publisher: Nick Hern Books, 2009

Nicholas Wright's biographical drama presents a fictionalised account of one night in the life of renowned Viennese psychoanalyst Melanie Klein (1882–1960). As the action begins, Klein is preparing to leave her London home and travel to Budapest where she will attend the funeral of her son Hans, who has recently died, supposedly in a climbing accident. In her absence, Klein is entrusting the care of her household and the running of her professional affairs to Paula Heimann, a German Jewish refugee and fellow analyst. Given that the two women barely know each other, it's an odd choice on Klein's part, one that proves stranger still when her analyst daughter Melitta – who has clearly not been asked to look after her mother's affairs – arrives. Melitta is convinced that her mother has played a direct role in Hans's death and, over the course of the night, there are revelations, recriminations and a charged battle for power between these three most complex of women.

Melanie Klein was a hugely influential figure in the field of psychoanalysis who sought to develop Freud's theories in new directions and particularly through her analysis of young children. Restricted by the need to be at home caring for her family, much of her professional attention was focused on her own two children, Melitta and Hans, who, controversially, she psychoanalysed intensively over several years. Publishing papers in which she gave her children pseudonyms, she meticulously recorded the content of their sessions, an activity which profoundly advanced psychoanalytic theory but raised considerable ethical questions regarding the impact on her children. Having become a psychoanalyst herself, but finding her approach more and more at variance with her mother's, Melitta Schmideberg-Klein's (1904–1983) adult relationship with Klein became even more complicated than her childhood one. Colleagues at the British Psychoanalytical Society, the pair were not only parent and child, analyst and patient; they also became professional opponents. Nicholas Wright unpicks this extraordinarily multilayered relationship, locating the action at a pivotal moment just after Hans's death, and when Paula Heimann (1899–1982), had just entered Klein's life. Paula, a friend and contemporary of Melitta's, wrote to Klein to express her sympathy over Hans's death and instantly found herself consumed into the older woman's personal and professional life. Over time Paula would replace Melitta, symbolically as Klein's 'daughter' and literally as her professional collaborator.

Early in the action, Klein shows Paula a sealed letter from a Dr Schmideberg, a 'professional enemy', who she describes as 'a vampire' and someone who 'needs help'. It is only later that it dawns on the audience that Klein is in fact referring to her own daughter. While Klein protests she has no problem with her daughter Melitta, her professional adversary Dr Schmideberg she dislikes intensely. It is this confused, almost schizophrenic relationship between the two women that forms the dramatic thrust of the action. For someone whose theories had such an important effect on how we understand children, Klein's relationship with her own offspring, or at least as depicted by Wright, is highly dysfunctional. Melitta recalls how her mother was absent for long periods of her childhood, only to reappear later, seemingly intent on being her analyst, a role that automatically demanded an almost complete emotional detachment. Now, her daughter grown-up, Klein's feelings towards Melitta seem no less cool, and yet, with Paula, her transparency and instant dependency are extreme. Paula, a highly educated refugee who is forced to live in an East London slum, unable to practise and separated from her own young daughter, is only too pleased to receive Klein's attention. The final image of the play, in which Klein and Paula engage in a psychoanalysis session and fixedly ignore Melitta's repeated ringing on the doorbell, is both chilling and symbolic of what is to come.

'Psychoanalysis as its enemies often point out, is a closed system: objections are treated as though they came from within, which makes them easier to absorb and neutralise,' Wright comments in his introduction to the play. Consequently, he chose to construct *Mrs Klein* following 'theatre's own closed system': Aristotle's principle of unity of time, place and action. Compressing the events of one night into a playing time of a couple of hours and set entirely in a single room in Klein's house, the play has a stealthily gathering tension. A stunningly evocative dramatisation of a pivotal moment in the lives of three women who dedicated themselves to understanding the human psyche, *Mrs Klein* is an intelligent, precise and utterly engrossing piece of theatre.

10 Great Plays for One Woman

Here's a selection of ten outstanding plays for performance by a solo female.

Bed Among the Lentils by Alan Bennett (b. 1934, UK)

First performed: Minerva Theatre, Chichester, 1996 (originally screened as a television play by the BBC in 1987)

Publisher: BBC Books, in *Talking Heads*, 2007

'Geoffrey's bad enough but I'm glad I wasn't married to Jesus.'

Susan is a vicar's wife. She's dreadful at flower arranging, can't make a decent Victoria sponge to save her life, and isn't entirely sure she actually believes in God. If the sherry runs dry or the communion wine mysteriously disappears, all eyes turn to Susan. Not that that deters Mr Ramesh, the alluring shopkeeper who is all too keen to make a bed for Susan and himself among the lentils in his stockroom. One of a range of outstanding monologues written for women by Alan Bennett as part of his BBC *Talking Heads* series, *Bed Among the Lentils* was first performed by Maggie Smith.

Grounded by George Brant (b. 1969, USA)

First performed: National New Play Network Rolling World Premiere with the San Francisco Playhouse, San Francisco; Borderlands Theatre, Tucson; and Unicorn Theatre, Kansas City, 2013

Publisher: Oberon Books, 2013

'It would be a very different book
The Odyssey
If Odysseus came home every day
Every single day
A very different book'

Returning to work after maternity leave, a US fighter pilot finds herself out of her plane and transferred instead to the 'Chair Force'; stationed in a trailer in the Nevada desert, controlling a drone that hovers over enemy territory thousands of miles away. Her Commander tells her it's the ideal situation – this way she'll be on active service, but close enough to home to be back for dinner every night. But commuting to war on a daily basis is a bizarre and disorientating experience. As the bodies begin to pile up abroad and the casualties are felt at home, the combustible combination of work, family, war and duty push this hardened fighter into the darkest of places.

My Name is Rachel Corrie taken from the writings of Rachel Corrie (b. 1979, USA), edited by Alan Rickman and Katherine Viner, produced with the kind permission of Rachel Corrie's family

First performed: Royal Court Theatre, London, 2005

Publisher: Nick Hern Books, 2005

'I'm sorry I scare you. But I want to write and I want to see. And what would I write about if I only stayed within the doll's house, the flower-world I grew up in?'

Rachel Corrie (1979–2003) was twenty-three when she left her home in Washington, USA, to work for the International Solidarity Movement in Gaza. She was killed two months into her stay, crushed under a bulldozer while trying to protect Palestinian homes. *My Name is Rachel Corrie* combines entries from Rachel's journals, emails and other personal writings to reveal the hopes, fears and aspirations of a young woman determined to act in the face of wrongs being done to others. The result is a poetic, surprising and deeply affecting insight into a brief but extraordinary young life.

The Year of Magical Thinking by Joan Didion (b. 1934, USA), based on her memoir

First performed: Booth Theatre, New York, 2007

Publisher: Fourth Estate, 2008

'You don't want to think it could happen to you.
That's why I'm here.'

30th December 2003, and writer Joan Didion was chatting to her husband John whilst preparing dinner. John suddenly slumped in his chair, fell silent and, having been sped to hospital in an ambulance, was pronounced dead on arrival. Taking the moment everyone dreads and looking it squarely in the face, Didion's play traverses the events and emotions of the months following her sudden bereavement. Capturing the fragility and transitory nature of life, *The Year of Magical Thinking* candidly explores how, in just one second, everything can change. It was premiered on Broadway and later transferred to the National Theatre, performed by Vanessa Redgrave.

Spoonface Steinberg by Lee Hall (b. 1966, UK)

First performed: Crucible Theatre, Sheffield, 1999

Publisher: Methuen, in *Lee Hall Plays: 1*, 2002

'I thought, if I wasn't scared of when I wasn't born why would I be scared of when I wasn't existed at the other end.'

Little Spoonface Steinberg has autism, a phenomenal talent for numbers, a deep love of opera, and terminal cancer. Even the doctors at the hospital and their 'zapper' machine can't seem to save her, and as Spoonface watches her parents disintegrate, and everyone around her give up hope, she discovers her own sense of acceptance in the face of approaching death. Lee Hall's beautiful, restrained and funny depiction of one little girl's philosophical appraisal of the end of her life was originally voiced in radio and television versions by child actor Becky Simpson, before being adapted for the stage and performed by Kathryn Hunter.

Man to Man (Jacke wie Hose) by Manfred Karge (b. 1938, Germany)

First performed: Bochum Theatre, Bochum, 1982

Recommended version: by Tinch Minter and Anthony Vivis

Publisher: Methuen, 1988

> 'I, my own widow, my late lamented husband, had to be
> Man enough to wear the fucking trousers.'

People are starving in the Weimar Republic, so when Ella's husband dies she needs to find a way to survive. Appropriating his identity and his job, Ella becomes 'Max' and so begins a new life constructed around her closely kept secret. But as the decades pass, relinquishing Max and resuming life as Ella becomes a less and less viable option. Dry and darkly poetic, East German writer Manfred Karge's verse play was inspired by a true story. Through the eyes of his fictional creation, the charismatic and endlessly fascinating Max Gericke, Karge flies through the extraordinary events of fifty years of German history. Tilda Swinton played the troubled and troubling Max in the 1987 English-language premiere, a role she returned to for a 1992 television-film reworking.

Request Programme (Wunschkonzert) by Franz Xaver Kroetz (b. 1946, Germany)

First performed: Württembergisches Staatstheater, Stuttgart, 1973

Recommended version: by Katharina Hehn

Publisher: Methuen, in *Franz Xaver Kroetz Plays: 1*, 2004

'In many instances suicide takes place with incredible tidiness. The preparations proceed as one part of a daily, and therefore normal, routine, and the act is undertaken with the same love of order, as cleanly, stolidly and dumbly despairingly as the life which led to it.'

With these words Kroetz introduces *Request Programme*, his silent play composed entirely of stage directions. Miss Rasch, a lone, early-forties bedsit dweller returns home from work. We watch her methodically go through the banal activities of her evening's activities: making dinner, washing her underwear, going to the toilet, manicuring her nails. All the while, a radio request show plays in the background, Rasch's final contact with the outside world before she ends the evening in a startling manner. Kroetz's challenging but compelling play is an unsettling and at times mortifyingly sharp study of loneliness and mortality.

Jordan by Anna Reynolds (*b.* 1968, UK) with Moira Buffini (*b.* 1965, UK)

First performed: Lilian Baylis Theatre, London, 1992

Publisher: Nick Hern Books, in *Singular Female Voices*, 2006

'I dig and I dig and I rip my memory into shreds and then try to piece it all together like a torn photograph, hoping somehow you'll understand. I'll understand.'

Shirley is in her early twenties. She doesn't have much that's good in her life; an abusive boyfriend, a dysfunctional family background and a stinking, filthy flat. But she does have Jordan, her baby son, her pride and joy. Shirley would do anything to protect Jordan. But when everything seems to be working against their fragile little family unit, is it the ferocity of her love for him that will prove to be the greatest risk of all? *Jordan* is published by Nick Hern Books in an anthology of short one-woman plays, alongside Catherine Johnson's *The Lost Art of Keeping a Secret* and Stewart Permutt's *Unsuspecting Susan*.

Shirley Valentine by Willy Russell (b. 1947, UK)

First performed: Everyman Theatre, Liverpool, 1986

Publisher: Methuen, 1988

'I always said I'd leave him when the kids grew up – but by the time they'd grown up there was nowhere to go. Well you don't start again at forty-two do y'?'

Shirley Valentine, Willy Russell's eponymous housewife, who heads from her Merseyside home to Greece in search of sun, sand and herself, is the subject of one of the best-known of all one-woman plays. Bored of talking to the kitchen wall and a husband who hardly notices her existence, Shirley decides there must be more out there, and heads off on a two-week holiday that will change her world for ever. Simply drawn and supremely touching, Russell's depiction of one woman falling in love with life is a disarmingly funny and profoundly moving play.

Bunny by Jack Thorne (b. 1978, UK)

First performed: nabokov at Underbelly Cowgate, Edinburgh Festival Fringe, 2010

Publisher: Nick Hern Books, 2010

'I think most of my problems can be put down to three facts: (i) I was a late developer, (ii) I think too much about what my problems are, (iii) I think too much full stop.'

Katie is eighteen. She's bound for Essex University, lives in Luton and has a boyfriend who's twenty-four. She's white, he's black, and usually they wouldn't have much to do with the Asians who live on the other side of town. But when a petty act of aggression spirals into something much bigger, Katie finds herself in the back of a stranger's car and on a journey. It is one that will leave her looking at her home town – and herself – in a way she never has before. Jack Thorne's darkly funny depiction of one girl's voyage through the mean streets of Luton sees Katie navigate her way through the choppy waters of race, class, sex and suburban identity.

Finally...

So there you go: 100 great plays for women (110 if you count the one-woman plays). We know they exist, so now let's put them on.

The ubiquitous but woefully inaccurate phrase 'There just aren't any good plays for women' only exists because not enough plays like these are performed enough of the time. But shining a spotlight on their existence and what makes them so good is just one part of the puzzle. Now all of us who care about theatre being the very best it can be – theatre-makers, audience members and students of theatre alike – need to ask big questions, questions about why, in our apparently world-leading theatre industry, these plays – plays that foreground the stories, experiences and voices of half the population – aren't being performed more often. And once we've asked those questions, we need to change that.

Creating a shift in the stories we see on our stages is a shared responsibility. It's the responsibility of drama schools to ensure they don't settle for giving their female students (who are, after all, paying the same fees as their male counterparts) a raw deal, of educators to make sure a more balanced range of plays is presented to their students, of exam boards to consider more carefully the selection of plays they detail on their syllabuses. And it is down to the 'gatekeepers' of resources and opportunities in the theatre industry, who, even in the face of their almost impossibly huge workloads and pressure to make every penny stretch further, to ensure that they, even they, and especially they, recognise it is their responsibility to find the best work and the best theatre-makers to create productions for audiences. Not just those who are most visible, immediately to hand, or who happen to resemble what has always conventionally been considered 'great'.

I wrote this book because I wanted to see more work on stage that examines the world through the eyes of women, *as well* as through the eyes of men. I know this is a desire that is shared by countless people around me. So let's get these 100 great plays for women on stage and then start looking for more. Here's to the next 100...

Plays by Title

* One-woman plays

Chronology of Plays
by first performance

TONIC THEATRE

Tonic Theatre was created in 2011 as a way of supporting the theatre industry to achieve greater gender equality in its workforces and repertoires. Today, Tonic partners with leading theatre companies around the UK on a range of projects, schemes and creative works. Current projects include *Advance*, a six-month programme with artistic directors from across England, exploring how their organisations work with female artists, and the launch of *Platform*, a range of new plays commissioned to increase opportunity and aspiration among girls and young women who take part in youth drama.

Tonic's approach involves getting to grips with the principles that lie beneath how our industry functions – our working methods, decision-making processes, and organisational structures – and identifying how, in their current form, these can create barriers. Once we have done that, we devise practical yet imaginative alternative approaches and work with our partners to trial and deliver them. Essentially, our goal is to equip our colleagues in UK theatre with the tools they need to ensure a greater level of female talent is able to rise to the top.

Tonic was created with support from the National Theatre and Royal Opera House's Step Change scheme and was a Company on Attachment at the National Theatre Studio in 2012. Tonic is currently an Associate of Company of Angels.

www.tonictheatre.co.uk